Fodor's EXPLORING
HAWAII

FODOR'S TRAVEL PUBLICATIONS

NEW YORK • TORONTO • LONDON • SYDNEY • AUCKLAND

WWW.FODORS.COM

Published in the United States by Fodor's Travel Publications.
Published in the United Kingdom by AA Publishing.

Fodor's is a registered trademark of Random House, Inc.

ISBN 0-679-00682-6
ISSN 1524-6787
Third Edition

Fodor's Exploring Hawaii

Author: **Emma Stanford**
Updated by: **Rick Gaffney**
Joint Series Editor: **Josephine Perry**
Original Copy Editor: **Susan Whimster**
Original Photography: **Kirk Lee Aeder**
Cartography: **The Automobile Association**
Cover Design: **Tigist Getachew, Fabrizio La Rocca**
Cover photograph: **Jack Hollingsworth**

Special Sales
Fodor's Travel Publications are available at special discounts for bulk purchases (100 copies or more) for sales promotions or premiums. Special editions, including personalized covers, excerpts of existing guides, and corporate imprints, can be created in large quantities for special needs. For more information, contact your local bookseller or write to Special Marketing, Fodor's Travel Publications, 280 Park Avenue, New York, NY 10017. Inquiries from Canada should be directed to your local Canadian bookseller or sent to Random House of Canada Ltd., Marketing Department, 2775 Matheson Blvd., Mississauga, Ontario L4W 4P7.

Printed and bound in Italy by Printer Trento srl

How to use this book

ORGANIZATION

Hawaii Is, Hawaii Was
Discusses aspects of life and culture in contemporary Hawaii and explores significant periods in its history.

A–Z
An alphabetical listing of places to visit. The book begins with a section on Honolulu and Waikiki, and is subsequently arranged by island. Places of interest are listed alphabetically within each section. Suggested walks, drives and Focus On articles, which provide an insight into aspects of life in Hawaii, are included in each section.

Travel Facts
Contains the strictly practical information that is vital for a successful trip.

Accommodations & Restaurants
An alphabetical listing of places to stay and places to eat. Entries are graded budget, moderate or expensive.

ABOUT THE RATINGS
Most places described in this book have been given a separate rating. These are as follows:

- ►►► **Do not miss**
- ►► **Highly recommended**
- ► **Worth seeing**

MAP REFERENCES
To make the location of a particular place easier to find, every main entry in this book is given a map reference, such as 176B3. The first number (176) indicates the page on which the map can be found, the letter (B) and the second number (3) pinpoint the square in which the main entry is located. The maps on the inside front cover and inside back cover are referred to as IFC and IBC respectively.

Contents

WAIKIKI
HONOLULU
8

Emma Stanford has written books on California, Florida, the Caribbean, France, and Spain, as well as Mediterranean port guides for the U.S. Navy. In *Exploring Hawaii* Emma reveals the history of the *hula*, the lush flora and unusual fauna, the Polynesian legacy and the impact of the Europeans.

My Hawaii

The headlights bore into the darkness and an enormous halogen-bright moon rose over the massive, sleeping shoulder of Mauna Loa. Despite the illuminations, the landscape remained featureless, an enigma all but forgotten in the comfort of a luxurious oceanfront hotel complete with golden beach and emerald green gardens. The next morning I drove back to Kailua-Kona, and the full drama of blackened and barren lava fields was revealed.

Hawaii is full of surprises and abrupt contrasts. These extraordinary islands far out in the mid-Pacific are as idiosyncratic as they are beautiful. A few hours after a freezing, yet spectacular, dawn on the lip of Maui's Haleakala crater, I found myself alone and deep in rainforest jungle positively reeling from the exertion of clambering up a rocky streambed in the heat of the day and the scent of crushed, fermenting mangoes and guavas on the path. Sodden and mud-splattered from a hike in Kauai's Kokee State Park, I soaked in the claw-foot bath of an old plantation cottage at Waimea, and then found an obliging gardener to lop the top off a coconut that had landed on my car (a small dent there) so I could slurp the juice on the *lanai*, watching the sunset over the Forbidden Island of Niihau.

If you come here looking for a straightforward beach holiday served up with a round of golf and several rounds of *mai-tais*, Hawaii is happy to oblige. But look beyond your beachfront *lanai* (and I urge you to do so), and you'll find even more staggeringly beautiful vistas and, of course, the Hawaiian people, who remain the embodiment of *aloha*. The endless patience of the Molokai Visitors Bureau and Mike, the golf buggy rally driver; the laconic *paniolo* cowboy riding out one crisp, upcountry morning; Mr. Kamaka, the ukulele-maker; and Debbie, the wedding specialist, all spring to mind. So does the charming waitress who dressed me up with napkins when a mix-up left me luggage-less and sartorially challenged for a dinner date at the exclusive Lodge at Koele on Lanai. At 1,200 feet on a cool May evening, open fires notwithstanding, shorts and a T-shirt did little to conceal the goose bumps...

Emma Stanford

Hawaii Is

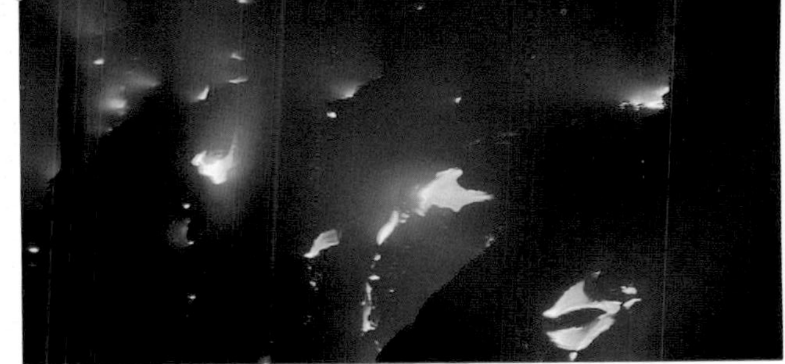

Ask the man in the street to describe Hawaii, and his response will probably include coconut palms and idyllic beaches, beautiful grass-skirted girls garlanded with fragrant flowers, the lazy notes of the slack-key guitar, and maybe even Elvis crooning away in front of a lurid technicolor sunset.

ALOHA Replace Elvis with a trio of talented local musicians, and every word of it is true. Hawaii really is Everyman's tropical paradise. All the necessary ingredients are in place, plus one vital addition: the spirit of *aloha*, the warmth and generosity of the islands and the welcome of their people that make the Hawaiian experience so memorable.

SETTING THE SCENE The Hawaiian archipelago numbers 132 islands, shoals, and reefs spread across 1,523 miles of the mid-Pacific. You will not hit a mainland city for almost 2,400 miles to the east, or 3,800 miles to the west. Just eight main islands—Oahu, Kauai, Maui, Molokai, Lanai, Hawaii, Niihau, and Kahoolawe—account for 99 percent of the total 6,450-square-mile Hawaiian landmass. Of these, Kahoolawe was once used for bombing practice, and family-owned Niihau is accessible only by private invitation or by authorized helicopter tours.

Kapiolani Park's Kodak Hula Show

ISLAND ROUNDUP Thus the visitor is left with a choice of six Hawaiian islands. There is, however, no need to feel short-changed. Each island has its own individual style, and almost all can boast an astonishing range of physical beauties, from lush rain forest to blistering beaches, and from misty volcanic peaks to rolling upcountry pasture, most within a short drive of the main resort areas.

Oahu, home to the state capital, Honolulu, is usually the first stop for visitors to Hawaii. Nicknamed the "Gathering Place," it is the most developed island, but still preserves quiet corners where life proceeds at a leisurely pace that is far removed from the frenetic action of Honolulu and Waikiki.

To the north, beautiful **Kauai** is known as the "Garden Isle." Mount Waialeale, one of the wettest spots on earth, ensures that Kauai's streams and waterfalls rarely run dry, and it is a haven for nature lovers, offering dozens of hiking trails, gardens, horseback riding, canoeing, diving, snorkeling, and other outdoor pursuits.

South of Oahu, across the Kaiwi Channel, rural **Molokai** hides behind a wall of vertiginous sea cliffs, among the tallest in the world. However, this natural barrier belies the easygoing nature of the "Friendly Isle," where native Hawaiians comprise over 50 percent of the population, and farming and fishing still take precedence over tourism. Molokai has only a few low-key resorts and is just the place for some quiet fishing, mountain biking, kayaking, golf, or to unwind.

Hanauma Bay, east of Honolulu

It is a 9-mile hop across the Pailolo Channel from Molokai to **Maui**, number two in the visitor stakes after Oahu. The "Valley Island" combines sophisticated resorts with cowboy country, and white-sand beaches with spectacular Haleakala, the 10,023-foot dormant volcano that dominates the southern half of the island. A jet-set destination with a difference, Maui is more than big enough to cope with the crowds of vacationers who flock here.

A football team would constitute a crowd on **Lanai**. The "Private Island" was once famous for its pineapples, but now has two exclusive resort hotels, a small inn, and a campsite. Snorkeling, golf, hiking, and off-road jeep trails are the order of the day; great cuisine and utter quiet prevail at night.

And so to **Hawaii**, the "Big Island" at the southern end of the main island group, by far the largest and most diverse of the islands. Its sunny beaches, calm waters, snow-capped volcanoes, and rain forests provide a wealth of natural beauties and activities for visitors.

Hawaii and its people have been described as both "the meeting place of East and West" and a "melting pot"—and more. Interracial marriages account for some 50 percent of all Hawaiian weddings, and the children of these unions may combine half a dozen ancestral nationalities.

MIX Of a total population of 1.2 million, the three main groups are the Hawaiians or part-Hawaiians (20.6 percent), *haole*—whites—(22 percent), and the Japanese (18.2 percent). Minority groups include Filipinos (12.7 percent), Chinese (4 percent), and other Asian and Pacific peoples such as Koreans, Vietnamese, and Samoans. Hawaiian people of all backgrounds tend to identify with one or another of the various ethnic groups.

Much is made of Hawaii's "golden" (mixed-race) children and a relative lack of racism is experienced in the islands, but that is not to say tension does not exist. Resentments do arise, particularly if one ethnic group is seen to have prospered to the detriment of another.

THE HAWAIIANS The fastest-growing ethnic group is the Hawaiians or, more accurately, people of Hawaiian blood. (Less than 4 percent of Hawaiians can claim to be pure-blooded descendants of the first Polynesian settlers.) A drop of Hawaiian blood guarantees entry into the Hawaiian community with its extended families, but the Hawaiians are also the most disenfranchised sector of society. Proportionately, they receive a higher level of welfare and are convicted of more crimes than any other group.

The resurgence of Hawaiian culture since the 1970s has spawned a number of successful rallying points for the community, from Hawaiian-language and traditional craft programs to schools teaching hula, and chants. A sense of empowerment has in turn fueled political activism, notably the Hawaiian sovereignty movement. The movement's many factions have no single, united agenda, but between them they address valid political points such as the need for official recognition of the Hawaiian race, in addition to several issues viewed with concern by non-Hawaiians. Examples are the suggestion of recompense to full- and part-blood Hawaiians for U.S. annexation of the islands in 1898, and the demand that the U.S. withdraw, to be replaced by a Hawaiian kingdom. These issues hamper the movement's credibility in the view of outsiders, and betray resentment of other ethnic groups. However, the Hawaiians have found an identity and a voice that they are now not afraid to use.

***HAOLE* HEAVEN** After the Hawaiians came the *haole*, a catchall term used to embrace the original white-skinned New England missionaries and whalers, European and British traders, and plantation managers. The ruling-class *kamaaina haole*

Modern replicas of ancient idols

(old-timers) have been joined by a stream of immigrants of all social backgrounds from the U.S. mainland. The ties between the various *haole* classes are loose, and many of them have intermarried with the islands' other ethnic groups.

EASTERN PROMISE The close-knit Japanese community makes the fewest interracial marriages and has maintained strong peer-group and family bonds. Americans of Japanese Ancestry (AJAs) hold roughly 50 percent of government positions at all levels and represent Hawaii's most powerful political lobby. Japanese success in business is matched only by that of the long-standing Chinese community, which

Shells markets are becoming less common because they cause environmental problems

can count among its numbers some of Hawaii's top merchants, financiers, and philanthropists, as well as the first Asian-American member of Congress, former Senator Hiram Fong.

Meanwhile, the Filipinos and Portuguese add their Catholic heritage and colorful fiestas to the Hawaiian scene—Filipino women are particularly noticeable on special holidays because of their elaborate formal dress—and the presence of Pacific Islanders coming to live in Hawaii continues to grow.

"Hula is the language of the heart, and therefore the heartbeat of the Hawaiian people," wrote King David Kalakaua. But when the "Merrie Monarch," as Kalakaua was affectionately known, ascended to the Hawaiian throne in 1874, the hula was a dying art.

ORIGINS OF THE *HULA* Before the written word existed in Hawaii, the time-honored traditions of the *mele oli* (poetic chants) and *mele hula* (chants with movements) were the chief means of passing information from one generation to the next. Legend traces the origins of *hula* to the goddess Laka, and *hula halau* (*hula* schools) were established near *heiau* (temples) constructed in her honor. Here, students were taught the sacred music and dance forms of the *kahiko*, or classical *hula*. The training was rigorous and the stylized delivery of the chants and dances had to be strictly observed. Far from being the "exhibitions of unrivaled licentiousness" that the missionaries claimed, the *mele hula* was performed at religious and ceremonial occasions, and recorded historical events, ancestor genealogies, customs, and legends.

Hula *is performed regularly*

The Hawaiians believed that by evoking physical events through words and gestures they could control them. A broad repertoire of chants was created to extol every aspect of Hawaiian life and legend. Dozens of individual movements were added to accompany the *mele hula*, each telling a story in itself. A flutter of the hand, a particular sway of the hips or a footstep can be used to signify a bird, blossom, rainstorm, or canoe ride. However, by the time Kalakaua ascended the throne, many of these movements, and the ancient *mele* (chants) themselves, had been lost and forgotten. In less than half a century, zealous missionaries had virtually expunged the mainstay of Hawaiian history and culture by suppressing the native dance form and replacing the traditional *mele* with Christian hymns.

***HULA* REVIVED** In keeping with his dual passions for entertainment

and things Hawaiian, Kalakaua set up a royal *hula* troupe to revive old dances and introduce new ones. He wrote much-admired *mele*, including the state anthem *Hawaii Ponoi*, and had them set to music by the Prussian bandmaster Henri Berger, director of the Royal Hawaiian Band.

During the 19th century, Hawaiian music underwent a sea change. Traditionally, the *hula* had been accompanied by rhythmic chants and rudimentary native instruments such as drums, simple flutes, wooden sticks, and rattles. Then the hymn-singing missionaries and the whalers with their sea shanties introduced harmonies that the musical Hawaiians embraced with gusto. They also adopted a four-stringed guitar, known as the *braguinha* to the Portuguese immigrants who brought it from Madeira in 1879, which they renamed the ukulele, or "jumping flea." From this fusion of styles and influences a definitive Hawaiian sound began to emerge.

***HULA* HITS HOLLYWOOD** A Hawaiian *hula* troupe brought the house down at the 1915 Panama–Pacific Exposition in San Francisco. Before long every reputable music hall and vaudeville theater worth its salt fielded a "Hawaiian revue," though most of the latter bore little relation to the

The next generation continues the tradition with Keiki hula

real thing. English lyrics and phony Hawaiian words were thrown together, and the good-humored Hawaiians adapted the *hula* in a way that confirmed all the missionaries' worst fears. Popular demand became so great that Hollywood initiated a series of Hawaiian films with such stars as Bing Crosby and Elvis Presley.

Today, *hula* is back on course. The revival of interest in Hawaiian culture over the last 20 years has turned it from a picaresque tourist sideshow into a respected cultural art form. For a glimpse of superb *hula*, look in the newspapers for details of competitions. The most prestigious is the annual springtime Merrie Monarch Festival held on the Big Island (see page 26).

Chanting a mele hula

*First, take a fertile volcanic island or six and place in a bountiful ocean. Add balmy temperatures, sunshine and rain, and leave to set. Then sprinkle liberally with the food-stuffs of dozens of ethnic groups, top with exotic fruits and spices—*et voilà*! Here is a recipe for culinary brilliance.*

CULINARY MIX From the staples introduced by the early Polynesian settlers, the Hawaiian larder has burgeoned. Captain Cook donated onions, pumpkins, and melons. Citrus fruits, mangoes, guavas, papayas, and pineapples followed, and Chinese immigrants brought rice, spices, Chinese vegetables, lychees, and persimmons.

Hawaii's range of cuisines provides some of the most diverse culinary experiences imaginable. Filipino chicken *adobo*, Chinese *dim sum*, Japanese *sushi*, and Korean *kim chee* are familiar favorites, alongside Uncle Sam's hamburgers and pizza parlors. Meanwhile, the talented chefs of Hawaii's top restaurants are going back to their multicultural roots to develop an innovative new style they call Hawaiian regional cuisine, which features fresh local produce and ingredients prepared with a distinctive Euro-Asian flair.

LONG LIVE THE *LUAU* We can only guess what the substantial Hawaiians of old would make of the delicious but dainty dishes of modern-day Hawaiian regional cuisine. It is said that the Hawaiian does not stop eating when he is full but will carry on until he is tired, and there is no better place to experience the generosity of Hawaiian portion control than at that most traditional of local culinary and social events, the *luau*.

In ancient times, the Hawaiians would arrange feasts to thank the gods for a good harvest or victory in battle. Today, holidays and festivities from the birth of a child to a wedding are all good excuses for a *luau*. Preparations begin with the *imu*, a cooking-pit dug into the earth and lined with lava stones. A fire is

Opening the imu, *the traditional ceremony that launches every* luau

Taro root is a traditional staple, without which no luau *is complete*

lit to heat the stones, then the ashes are swept away and the food is added, wrapped in a protective layer of banana or *ti*-leaves. The centerpiece is generally a whole pig, and there are plenty of *laulau*, little packages of other meats, vegetables, or fish wrapped in taro leaves. The pit is then covered with more leaves, layers of earth, and damp burlap sacks. For the next four or five hours the *imu* bakes and steams away until the coverings are ready to be stripped off amid clouds of steam.

Few visitors are lucky enough to attend a real Hawaiian *luau*, and most of the commercial *luau* ventures are a pale imitation of the real thing. However, one of the best is the Kona Village Luau on the Big Island (see page 171), where the groaning buffet provides all the usual *kalua* (cooked in an *imu*) favorites, plus other traditional foods such as mauve *poi* paste and *lomi* salmon (a salad of salted salmon with onions and tomatoes).

***POI*-FECTION?** Beloved of the Hawaiians, *poi* is definitely an acquired taste. This highly nutritious food is usually made from the root of the taro plant, *poi* is served up in several consistencies measured by how many fingers are needed to eat it: "one-finger" *poi* is thick, "three-finger" runny.

FIRST-CLASS FISH Hawaiian restaurant menus are long on excellent, locally caught seafood. Lovers of fish should look for *ono* (wahoo, a relative of the tuna family), *opakapuka* (pink snapper), *onaga* (red snapper), *uku* (gray snapper), *ulua* (jack fish), and the ever-popular *mahimahi* (dolphin fish—a fish, not a mammal). Other local favorites include *ahi* (yellowfin or big-eye tuna), as well as *moi* (threadfin), *opihi* (limpets), and *ula* (lobsters).

Ground-baked Kalua *pig*

Mark Twain described Hawaii as "the loveliest fleet of islands anchored in any ocean." Like the galleons of the past, this Hawaiian fleet is laden with treasures, including some of the world's most spectacular scenery. Hawaii's extraordinary diversity of landscapes and outstanding natural habitats are some of its most arresting features.

THE SEEDS OF CHANGE The early Polynesian settlers changed the face of Hawaii forever by introducing non-native food plants and clearing land for farming. Later, vast tracts of forest and native vegetation were destroyed by logging, clearance for sugar-cane and pineapple plantations during the 19th century, and by 20th-century development.

However, all has not been lost. Hawaii's rugged topography has confounded the most tenacious developers, and an impressive number of national, state, and county parks ensures that many of Hawaii's most precious landscapes will be preserved for future generations.

Waterfalls in the pali *on the island of Kauai*

THE COAST The six main islands of Oahu, Kauai, Molokai, Maui, Lanai, and Hawaii boast almost 1,000 miles of tidal shoreline among them. The palm-fringed strands of golden sand, such as Maui's Kapalua, are just one variation in a range of coastal scenery that includes the undulating dunes of Polihale State Park on Kauai, and the jewel-like bays of Hanauma on Oahu and Kealakekua on the Big Island, which shelter two of Hawaii's underwater parks.

For towering cliffs, head for Kauai's beautiful Na Pali coast, or dramatic Palaau State Park on Molokai. Maui's Waianapanapa State Park has windswept headlands of black volcanic rock battered and carved into bizarre shapes by wave action. Meanwhile, jet-black beaches of volcanic sand are being continually created on Big Island's southern shore by the eruptions of Kilauea. Punaluu (see page 162) is the best accessible example.

VOLCANO WATCH Sulfurous Hawaii Volcanoes National Park is a must for any visitor to the Big Island. The 229,000-acre park covers parts of Kilauea and Mauna Loa, two of the five volcanoes comprising the Big Island. Both are still active and offer more than a dozen special ecological areas. The dormant Haleakala crater on Maui is another tourist favorite, and although volcanic activity is a thing of the past on Oahu, the cinder cones of Diamond Head, and the Koko and Punchbowl craters are still very impressive.

IN A CLASS OF ITS OWN Carved by the Waimea River and dozens of

Rainbows add to the spectacle

lesser streams and waterfalls, Kauai's Waimea Canyon is arguably the single most spectacular natural feature in the state. The red- and purple-faced gorge,10 miles long and over 3,000 feet deep, is more than a match for its nickname, the "Grand Canyon of the Pacific."

WATER, WATER EVERYWHERE Hawaii offers waterfalls aplenty, often surrounded by luxuriant rain-forest. The 420-foot-high Akaka Falls on the Big Island are an example, as are the waterfalls cascading past giant breadfruit, mango, *kukui* (candlenut), and *hau* trees on the winding road to Hana on Maui's windward coast. Helicopter rides along Kauai's Na Pali coast reveal dozens of waterfalls coursing down from Mount Waialeale, which also feeds the Opaekaa and Wailua Falls, popular beauty spots on the island's windward coast. Oahu has the Manoa Falls above Honolulu, and Nuuanu valley sports an array of waterfalls when the *pali* catches passing rain clouds

FORESTS AND SWAMPS Hawaii's lush native forests are an endangered ecosystem. The precious Kamakou Preserve on Molokai boasts 219 uniquely Hawaiian plants among its towering woodlands, densely massed ferns, and the eerie Pepeopae Bog on the mountain top. Both Kamakou and the upland forest and Alakai Swamp areas of Kauai's Kokee State Park are important havens for Hawaiian birdlife, as are the rain-forested windward coasts of Maui and the Big Island.

Maui moonscape: Haleakala crater

Hawaii's flora is as diverse and eclectic as its people. Thousands of plants from all over the globe have flourished in the islands' friendly environment, but their very success has threatened, or even vanquished entirely, some of the world's rarest plants, indigenous species that occur only on these isolated islands.

A CLOSED WORLD The first plant seeds to be washed up on Hawaiian shores found an inhospitable world of barren lava. Only the adaptable survived, but with no competitors and only a few birds and insects representing the animal kingdom, these plants rarely developed the ability to compete with vigorous nonnative species when they were introduced.

Nowhere is the adaptability of the islands' endemic plants better shown than in the *ohia*. A member of the myrtle family, the *ohia* is one of the first plants to colonize new lava flows; there is a miniaturized variety that grows in swamps and bogs, and it can grow to heights of 80 feet or more in forest areas. The size, color, and texture of the *ohia* leaves change from tree to tree, and its distinctive red pompom blooms, *lehua*, are said to be the property of the volcano goddess, Pele.

❑ Indigenous Hawaiian plants are those that exist nowhere else in the world. These are distinct from native plants whose sea-, wind-, or animal-borne seeds arrived without human intervention. Nonnative plants are those that have been introduced deliberately by humans. ❑

Red torch ginger

COCONUTS AND CANDLENUTS The Polynesians came well prepared to colonize new lands. They brought the coconut palms that shade the beaches, breadfruit, bananas, yams, and taro. The light green-leaved *kukui*, or candlenut tree, was also an import, named for its nuts, which could be burned for light. The timber of the magnificent endemic *koa* tree was highly prized for canoe-building and surfboards.

CULTURE CLASH Since Captain George Vancouver presented several hundred orange tree saplings to the Big Island chieftains in 1792, almost 2,000 nonnative plant species have been introduced to the islands. Exotic foreign fruits such as mangoes, papayas, guavas, and Java plums now grow in the wild. Ornamental bamboos, orchids, gingers, and heliconias have joined them. Ironwood trees and weeds such as lantana and

Fragrant plumeria blossoms

the parasitic strangler fig have taken a firm grip on the environment, ousting less robust native species. But even though the botanical mixture may alarm the conservationists, Hawaii's wealth of native and introduced flowers and trees is a real treat for visitors.

Many of Hawaii's indigenous plants survive only in high and inaccessible areas, so the majority of the plants and trees enjoyed by the visitor are nonnatives. The *lei*-makers' favorite fragrant plumeria, scarlet-bloomed poincianas from Madagascar, monkeypod trees from South America, banyans and the aptly named yellow-flowering "golden shower" from India are common-place, as are the spreading thorny branches of nonnative *kiawe* (mesquite) in dry areas.

Native plants that have survived in coastal regions include the distinctive *hala* (screw pine, *Pandanus*), balanced on a tepee of aerial roots, and creeping plants such as *pohinahina* (vitex), *ilima*, *Pau-o-Hiaka* (convolvulus, or morning glory), and beach *naupaka* with its half-formed white flowers (see panel, page 165). Nonnative seagrape trees, Indian almonds, and the heliotrope have also colonized Hawaiian shores. The *noni*, or Indian mulberry, was used both as a dye and as a medicine.

GLORIOUS GARDENS To come to grips with the best of Hawaii's indigenous, native, and nonnative flora, buy one of the specialist plant guides on sale in good bookshops. Plant lovers will find that the islands' botanical gardens can also provide a colorful on-site introduction to what to look for. The Foster Botanical Garden and Lyon Arboretum in Honolulu are two of Oahu's finest gardens. On the other islands, try Kauai's National Tropical Botanical Garden (see page 104); Kula Botanical Gardens, Maui (see page 141); and the Hawaii Tropical Botanical Garden, north of Hilo, Hawaii (see page 176).

Deep in the jungle: Hawaii Tropical Botanical Garden, Hilo

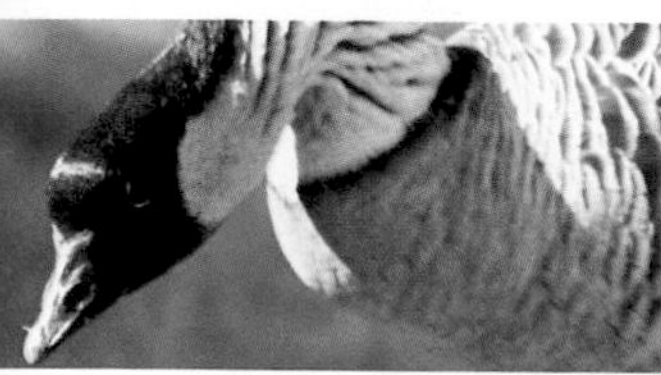

Just 15 or so species of land birds found their way to the Hawaiian Islands before the arrival of the early Polynesians. Left to their own devices, these birds performed a small miracle, evolving into more than 70 different varieties indigenous to the islands.

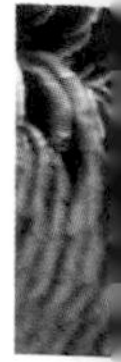

HONEYCREEPERS By far the most intriguing family of Hawaiian birds, the honeycreeper finches (*Drepanidadae*) diversified into at least 40 different types. The most common today is the crimson *apapane* with its black beak and tail feathers. It lives high up in the forest treetops and feeds off red *lehua* flowers, which makes it difficult to spot. One of the rarest is the crested honeycreeper (*akohekohe*), found only on the windward slopes of Haleakala on the island of Maui. It can be distinguished by the splash of orange plumage at the neck of its otherwise black and gray coloring.

FASHION ACCESSORIES Two native Hawaiian birds were particularly prized for their plumage. The *iiwi*, with its brilliantly colored orange-red body feathers and matching curved beak, escaped from extinction when the bottom dropped out of the royal feathered-cape market. The "king of Hawaiian plumage birds," the *ooaa*, which supplied the all-important yellow feathers (80,000 of them for a full-length cape), may still survive in Kauai's Alakai Swamp, but has not been seen for years.

Hawaii has a native owl, the *pueo*, that hunts by day. Recognized as a benign ancestor spirit by some Hawaiians, the brown and white owl grows to between 15 and 18 inches high, and has huge yellow eyes. Another hunter, the Hawaiian hawk (*io*), is similarly revered, and soars above the forests of the Big Island on the lookout for its prey.

❑ Since the arrival of humans, more than half of Hawaii's indigenous birds have gone, hunted to extinction, preyed upon by introduced species, or deprived of their natural habitats. Most of the survivors are confined to upland areas of native forest and swamp, where they delight ornithologists and scientists, providing an unrivaled opportunity for the study of evolution. ❑

Top: the nene goose
Below: the tiny iiwi *honeycreeper*

GOOSEY, GOOSEY GANDER Hawaii's state bird, the *nene*, rescued from extinction by captive breeding programs, is a conservation success story. Gaggles of these brown and white geese (their name means "to chirp or to croak") can be seen waddling about the Hawaii

Volcanoes National Park and at Haleakala on Maui, and they have recently been introduced to Kauai's Na Pali coast.

HERE TO STAY Many of the most common birds seen around the islands have been introduced. Cardinals, bulbuls, finches, and mynah birds have all been released over the years. Sparrows and pigeons have made their home here, too, though they are outnumbered by flocks of zebra doves imported from Asia.

In upland regions, gamebirds include several types of pheasant, francolin, and quail. There are chukar (a red-legged partridge), grouse, and wild turkey, too, and in the Kokee State Park on Kauai, jungle fowl (*moa*), descended from domestic birds imported by the Polynesians, forage around in the undergrowth.

COMMON NATIVES The yellow-green *amakihi*, a small honeycreeper, is the most widely seen native bird, and the plumage of the Pacific golden plover makes it an easy bird to identify. Ponds and marshy regions make valuable nesting and feeding places for a variety of waterfowl, from gallinules and ducks to the increasingly rare Hawaiian coot (*alae keokeo*) and the Hawaiian stilt (*aeo*) with its long pink legs. At cliff sites such as Kilauea

Red-crested cardinals are residents of the islands

Point on Kauai, brown boobies, Newell's shear-waters (*ao*), and great frigate birds roost and rear their young on the rocky headlands. Other species nest here, including red-footed boobies with their unmistakable red galoshes, blue beaks, and black-tipped, 40-inch wings.

A well-balanced red-footed booby

Scattered over the six main islands, more than seven dozen challenging and attractive courses cater to golfers of every ability. Several times a year top golfers flock to the Hawaiian Islands for championship tournaments, and there is a busy calendar of local professional and amateur events.

BETTER THAN SCOTLAND? There are few places where golfers can enjoy themselves as much as they do in Hawaii. Golf can be played 365 days of the year, and the game has boomed on the islands in the last decade with the addition of more than two dozen new courses carved out of ancient lava flows, laid out on magnificent clifftop sites, and tucked into rain-forested mountain valleys.

A COURSE A DAY It is possible to play a different course each day for five weeks on Oahu without a repeat. In addition to municipal and public courses, such as the spectacular mountainside Koolau Golf Course, Oahu has superb resort courses. The Links at Kuilima is an Arnold Palmer and Ed Seay creation at the Turtle Bay Hilton and Country Club; the same duo was responsible for the Hawaii Prince Golf Club at Ewa. The Ko Olina Golf Club in the southwest is a Ted Robinson design, and the Sheraton Makaha Resort and Country Club, on the west coast, offers great sea views as well as challenging golf.

Oahu
Hawaii Prince Golf Club
(tel: 808/944-4567)
Koolau Golf Course
(tel: 808/236-4653)
Ko Olina Golf Club
(tel: 808/676-5300)
Links at Kuilima
(tel: 808/293-8574)
Sheraton Makaha Resort & Country Club
(tel: 808/695-9544)
Kauai
Kauai Lagoons Resort
(tel: 808/241-6000 or 800/634-6400)
Poipu Bay Resort Golf Course
(tel: 808/742-8711 or 808/742-9489)
Prince Course
(tel: 808/826-5000)
Molokai
Kaluakoi Resort & Country Club
(tel: 808/552-2739)
Lanai
Challenge at Manele
(tel: 808/565-2222)
Experience at Koele
(tel: 808/565-4653)

THE NEIGHBOR ISLANDS Kauai is a favorite with the professional tour circuit and amateurs alike. Robert Trent Jones Jr.'s Prince Course at Princeville is considered one of the hardest 18 holes of golf in the islands. Also well known are his Princeville Makai Course, the Poipu Bay Resort Golf Course, and the Kiele Course, one of two Jack Nicklaus-designed courses at Kauai Lagoons.

Molokai's Kaluakoi Resort and Country Club, designed by Ted Robinson, occupies a stunning oceanfront site where axis deer and wild turkeys strut about the greens. Whale-watching is an additional attraction at the Challenge at Manele, Jack Nicklaus's renowned tour de force on Lanai.

Each of Maui's three top resort areas offers a choice of fine golf courses. Around the Kapalua Bay resort are the oceanfront Bay Course, Ben Crenshaw and Bill Coore's Plantation Course, and Arnold Palmer's Village Course. Just down the road are another two 18-hole layouts at Kaanapali.

The Challenge at Manele Bay, Lanai

On East Maui's leeward coast, Wailea's Blue, Gold, and Emerald courses and the two neighboring Makena courses each provide an entirely different golfing experience in the lee of Mount Haleakala.

Maui
Kaanapali Golf Courses (tel: 808/661-3691)
Kapalua Bay Course (tel: 808/669-8820)
Kapalua Plantation Course (tel: 808/669-8877)
Kapalua Village Course (tel: 808/669-8835)
Makena Golf Club (tel: 808/879-3344)
Wailea Golf Club (tel: 808/875-7450)

Hawaii
Hapuna Golf Course (tel: 808/880-3000)
Makalei Hawaii Country Club (tel: 808/325-6625)
Mauna Kea Beach Golf Club (tel: 808/882-5400)
Mauna Lani Resort (tel: 808/885-6655)
Waikoloa Beach Course (tel: 808/886-6060)
Waikoloa Kings' Course (tel: 808/885-4647)
Waikoloa Village Golf Club (tel: 808/883-9621)
Note: www.gvhawaii.com provides additional details on Hawaiian golf courses

On Hawaii are the emerald-green Mauna Lani Resort courses etched against the black lava fields, Robert Trent Jones Sr.'s much-acclaimed Mauna Kea Golf Course, and the Palmer/Seay Hapuna Course. There are three very individual courses at the Waikoloa Resort, and the nearby Makalei Hawaii Country Club is a fine upcountry course between 2,100 and 2,800 feet above sea level.

Teeing off at Poipu, Kauai

The Hawaiian calendar is packed full with festivals and events: international surfing competitions, children's hula *contests, ukulele festivals, long-distance outrigger races. Some are statewide celebrations, while others are low-key local or island activities. There is something for everyone—the events listed below are just a sample of what's offered.*

JANUARY
Molokai Makahiki, Molokai. New Year's celebrations with Hawaiian games, sports, ceremonies, and popular local entertainers.
Hawaiian Open PGA Golf Tournament, Oahu.

FEBRUARY
Hilo Mardi Gras, Hawaii. Costumed revels in the Big Island's capital.
Narcissus Festival, Oahu. Chinese New Year is celebrated in Honolulu's Chinatown.
Cherry Blossom Festival, Oahu. Japanese cultural celebrations with music, dancing, and food in Kapiolani Park, Waikiki. (Also in March.)
Buffalo's Big Board Classic, Oahu. Spectacular surfing plus cultural events on the Waianae Coast.

MARCH
Molokai Hawaiian *Paniolo* Heritage Rodeo, Molokai. Celebration of Hawaii's *paniolo* heritage.
Prince Kuhio Festival, Kauai. Music, *hula*, canoe races, pageants, and a royal ball feature in the week's festivities.

APRIL
Merrie Monarch Festival, Hawaii. Advance reservations are a must for this festival, the most prestigious *hula* competition in the islands (tel: 808/935-9168).
Maui County Agricultural Trade Show & Sampling, Maui. Upcountry celebration of Maui's agricultural bounty.

MAY
***Lei* Day**, statewide flower festival and *lei*-making competitions on May 1. Concerts in Oahu's Kapiolani Park.

On parade in Kailua-Kona

Many traditional Hawaiian festivals have been revived

Molokai Ka Hula Piko, Molokai. *Hula* demonstrations, music, crafts, cultural lectures, and "talking story."

JUNE

King Kamehameha Day, statewide celebrations on June 11. Parades, bands, and *hula* competitions in Honolulu.

JULY

Fourth of July, statewide events and celebrations. Rodeos at Parker Ranch, Hawaii, and Makawao, Maui.

Hawaiian International Billfish Tournament, Hawaii (into August).

Hoolaulea O Ke Kai—Molokai Sea Fest, Molokai. Celebration of Molokai's marine heritage.

Prince Lot *Hula* Festival, Oahu. Ancient and modern *hula*, arts and crafts in Moanalua Gardens, Honolulu (third Saturday).

Ukulele Festival, Kapiolani Park, Waikiki, Oahu (last Sunday).

AUGUST

Kihoalu Gabby-Style Slack-Key Guitar Festival, Oahu.

Queen Liliuokalani Keiki *Hula* Competition, Oahu. Children's *hula* festival featuring *halau* (groups) from all islands.

SEPTEMBER

Mokihana Festival, Kauai. Ten days of *hula*, concert, and arts and crafts exhibitions.

***Aloha* festivals**, statewide cultural events and entertainment lasting through October.

OCTOBER

Bankoh Molokai Hoe outrigger canoe championships, Molokai to Oahu.

Ironman Triathlon World Championship, Hawaii. The world's first and best-known triathlon.

***Aloha* Classic World Wavesailing Championship**, Maui. World's top windsurfers compete in an exciting world final.

NOVEMBER

Kona Coffee Cultural Festival, Hawaii. A week-long party of coffee tastings, pageants, craft fairs, and beauty contests.

Triple Crown of Surfing, North Shore, Oahu.

DECEMBER

***Aloha* Bowl**, Maui. Nationally televised collegiate football classic.

Honolulu Marathon, Oahu. Attracts top runners from all around the world.

First Night, Maui and Kona. Street entertainment leads up to fireworks at midnight for the New Year.

A display of haku*-style* lei

The language of the first Polynesians to reach Hawaii (see page 32) has become Hawaiian but is closely related to that of other Polynesian peoples. It is a melodic language with many vowels and repeated syllables. Several Hawaiian words are now common among the island's English speakers: mahalo *(thank you),* kapu *(forbidden), and* aloha, *used as both a greeting and farewell.*

HAWAIIAN The missionaries were the first people to write Hawaiian and they kept it simple, giving the alphabet just 12 letters. In Hawaiian, a consonant (h, k, l, m, n, p, w) is always followed by a vowel (a, e, i, o, u), forming two-letter syllables. Vowels also come in pairs, and sometimes threes, but a glottal stop (a silent consonant, represented here by a single quote mark) will break them up, as in Ka'a'awa. A *w* in the middle of a word is often sounded as *v*, hence Ka'a'awa is pronounced "ka-ah-ah-vah."

PIDGIN While Hawaiian is an official state language alongside English, Pidgin is the language of the streets and derives from the plantation days when the *haole* (white owners) and Portuguese *luna* (overseers) needed to communicate with their mainly Asian labor force. Pidgin is an organic patois of words and phrases drawn from half a dozen languages and is constantly changing. Although it is the preferred tongue of many islanders, they may not appreciate tourists and *malihini* (newcomers) attempting to use it.

Hawaiian is often used on signs

❑ **Common Hawaiian words**

alii	ancient Hawaiian royalty
hale	house or building
haole	originally any foreigner; now, white people
heiau	place of worship, temple
hula	Hawaiian dance form accompanied by chants
kahili	royal standard made of feathers
kahuna	priest, minister, or expert
kamaaina	native-born Hawaiian, longtime resident
kane	man
keiki	child
lanai	veranda, porch
lei	garland of flowers
luau	Hawaiian feast
makai	toward the sea (directions)
mauka	toward the mountains
mele	song or chant
muumuu	loose-fitting gown
ono	delicious, tasty
pali	cliff
pupu	hors-d'oeuvres
shaka	hand signal made with closed fist, raised thumb and little finger used as greeting or to mean "hang loose"
wahine	woman ❑

Hawaii Was

Fire and brimstone

Hawaii is a geological infant formed by volcanic activity in the middle of the Pacific Ocean over 2,000 miles from the nearest continent. When other corners of the planet were already inhabited by a wide variety of plants and animals and the dinosaurs had come and gone, Hawaii was just a bubble of magma on the ocean floor.

HOT SPOTS AND VOLCANOES The 1,500-mile chain of Hawaiian islands did not appear all at once. The partly submerged mountain range arrived peak by peak, starting in the north with the Kure Atoll and Midway Islands. These northernmost Hawaiian islands once occupied a position near the modern location of Hawaii, the most southerly island in the chain. Here, a fixed hot spot some 18,000 feet beneath the ocean's surface pumps molten lava up through a group of vents at a weak spot in the earth's crust.

Countless eruptions over millions of years formed shield volcanoes (see box) that eventually rose from the sea and were carried gradually north by the movement of the Pacific Plate. As each volcano and its vent was carried inexorably northward away from the hot spot, there was a decreasing likelihood of eruption and it became extinct. The hot spot would then begin all over again, creating a new volcano.

Nowadays, there are two active volcanoes in the islands: Mauna Loa and Kilauea, both on Hawaii. There

❑ Shield volcanoes are named for their gently sloping shape, which resembles a warrior's long, convex shield. The comparatively young volcanoes of the Big Island, Mauna Loa and Kilauea, still retain this appearance. However, the extinct volcanoes of the more senior Hawaiian Islands have been dramatically eroded by wind, rain, and waves. As a result, the oldest in the island chain have been reduced to little more than shoals and reefs, though beneath the waves there are still substantial mountains rising from the sea bed. ❑

Steam rises from a cinder cone

are also three dormant volcanoes: Mauna Kea and Hualalai on Hawaii, and Haleakala on Maui. Some 21 miles southeast of the Big Island, the Loihi Sea Mount has another 3,000 feet, and perhaps several thousand years, to go before it breaks the surface to become the latest link in the chain.

Hawaii's active volcanoes produce two different types of lava with the same chemical composition. Fast-flowing, smooth *pahoehoe* ("pa-ho-eh-ho-eh") courses down the mountainside at a considerable rate. As the lava's surface cools and sets into a crust, it insulates the molten lava beneath, which can travel on for miles. Slow-moving *aa* ("ah-ah") lava is partially solidified and laced with jagged chunks of rock.

WATER, WINDS, AND EROSION The towering peaks of these volcanoes snag moisture-laden clouds carried on the northeastern trade winds, releasing hundreds of inches of rain every year. Rainwater and winds have eroded deep clefts and gullies into the mountainsides and created the fluted knife-edge ridges and folds of the *pali* (cliffs). The effects of erosion are most visible on the islands' windward coasts, such as the north face of Molokai, where forbidding cliffs slashed by plunging valleys rise 3,300 feet sheer out of the ocean. Kauai's serrated Na Pali coast and magnificent Waimea Canyon were carved with the help of torrents of rain gushing down Mount Waialeale, "the wettest spot on earth," which receives an average of 37 feet (444 inches) of rain a year.

Molten lava flows beneath the old crust

SIGNS OF LIFE In whatever manner the first living organisms arrived in Hawaii, it is fairly safe to assume it was by chance. Seeds, spores, and insects were washed up by the ocean, blown in on the wind, or came attached to lost birds. The volcanic islands offered fresh rainwater and fertile soil, and with no competitors the estimated 250 original plant varieties and an equal number of insect species, plus approximately 15 species of land birds, flourished. They gradually evolved into thousands of new species found nowhere else in the world.

Streams of lava hit the ocean, creating a new coastline

Around AD 500, a small group of Polynesians reached Hawaii. Probably fewer than 100 people disembarked from their double-hulled voyaging canoes onto the beach. They had brought provisions that would allow them to settle the land, but exactly why they had sailed across 2,000 miles of uncharted ocean remains a mystery.

FIRST INHABITANTS The first settlers are thought to have journeyed from the Marquesas Islands, a group of islands in French Polynesia. They were warlike people, and perhaps the early emigrations were a result of internecine fighting. Alternatively, overpopulation might have caused emigration, or perhaps the Polynesians just decided to put to use the navigational skills they had honed over several thousand years. Legends spoke of a "heavenly homeland" in the north, and navigating by the stars and prevailing winds, the sailors ended up in Hawaii. Here they stayed, undisturbed for more than five centuries.

Hawaiians built koa-*wood canoes*

These early Hawaiians introduced pigs, chickens, dogs, and perhaps two dozen species of plants for food, medicine, and fiber. Unintentional additions probably included rats, mice, lice, fleas, small lizards, and weeds. The Hawaiians cleared forests with fire, built terraces in the hills, and irrigated them by diverting mountain streams and waterfalls. Taro fields, coconut, *kukui* (candlenut), banana, and breadfruit groves were planted. Fishermen harvested the ocean with nets, spears, hooks, and traps, and stone-walled fishponds were constructed along the shore.

PARADISE LOST This peaceable lifestyle was brought to an end by the arrival of Tahitian immigrants in

the 12th or 13th century. The Tahitians were led by the powerful figure of Paao, and they initiated a century of two-way traffic between Tahiti and Hawaii that resulted in eight of the Hawaiian islands being inhabited. Unimpressed by the laid-back lifestyle of the early Hawaiians, Paao launched a rigorous shakeup of religious and social practices. He introduced warlike gods, human sacrifice, and a rigid social hierarchy, which he enforced with the *kapu* (taboo) system that ruled every aspect of daily life.

KAPU Under *kapu*, society was broken down into four main classes. The *alii* were chiefs and royalty, one step removed from the gods, and were invested with considerable spiritual powers, or *mana*. Priests, professionals, and craftsmen were *kahuna*; ordinary citizens were *makaainana*; and there was an under-class known as the *kauwa*. Commoners were forbidden to eat certain foods reserved for the *alii*, and had to prostrate themselves on the ground in the presence of these superior beings. Women could not eat with men, or touch foods such as pork, bananas, or coconut. Certain fish were *kapu* during certain seasons, while others, along with many of the best fishing and

Terraces were cut into the hillsides and irrigated to grow taro

hunting areas, were reserved exclusively for the *alii*.

To break *kapu* was to insult the gods, who could retaliate by arranging natural disasters—from tempests and tidal waves to fire and famine. The punishment for breaking *kapu* was death; there were no mitigating circumstances. The only hope for a *kapu*-breaker was to reach sanctuary in a sacred *puuhonua* refuge, where the priests could perform a purification ceremony. Only one of these refuges remains, Puuhonua O Honaunau, on the Big Island of Hawaii.

To appease the gods and ask their assistance with new ventures, huge open-air temples, or *heiau*, were constructed from black volcanic boulders arranged in a series of stone terraces. More demanding gods, such as Ku, the god of war, were worshiped at *luakini*, sacrificial temples. Religious ceremonies played a large part in Hawaiian life, and with them developed the *hula* (dance form) and *mele* (song or chant), which described important events, traced the *alii* genealogies back to the gods, and told the *Kumulipo*, the Hawaiian version of the Creation (see pages 34–35).

In the beginning, there was darkness, po, *until the gods descended to earth and created light,* ao. *Kane, the life-giving god of sunlight and fresh water, fashioned Man (who takes his name) from sand or clay, and made Woman from his shadow. He breathed life into them, and all Mankind is descended from him.*

POLYNESIAN PANTHEON The Polynesians brought their gods and animist beliefs with them to Hawaii. There were four main gods: Kane; Kanaloa, the god of the sea, trade winds, and healing; Ku, the god of war, also responsible for rain, fishing, and sorcery; and peaceable Lono, whose jurisdiction included clouds, agriculture, and fertility. Beneath these major figures were numerous lesser deities, and protective spirits known as *aumakua*, which guarded individuals and families. Many natural things were also believed to be invested with some degree of *mana*, or spiritual power, from trees and waterfalls to rocks and mountains.

SKY FATHER, EARTH MOTHER The gods and the earth were given life by Wakea, the Sky Father, and Papa, the Earth Mother. Wakea and Papa's first Hawaiian island children were Hawaii, Maui, and Kahoolawe. Needing a rest, Papa went home to Tahiti, but while she was away Wakea decided to continue without her, producing Lanai with his second wife, and Molokai with his third. Papa, in a fury, ran off with a dashing young god called Lua, and gave birth to Oahu. Reconciled, Wakea and Papa produced Kauai, Niihau, Kaula, and Nihoa.

The only island named for a god is Maui, a favorite subject for the Hawaiian storytellers. Maui was a son of the goddess Hina, and shortly after his birth he was cast into the ocean to die, but survived and grew into a strapping young demigod with a knack for mischief and useful feats of strength. He stole, he tricked, he womanized, but all in a good cause as he lifted the sky so Man could walk erect, fished up new islands

The ancient Hawaiians built heiau *(temples) throughout the islands*

with a magic hook, and discovered the secret of fire. Maui's most useful and celebrated good deed was to trap the sun in a lasso made from his sister's hair and force it to slow down its passage through the sky, thereby giving more daylight hours for fishing and farming.

MADAME PELE Today, long after many more important deities have been forgotten, the legendary powers of Madame Pele, the goddess of fire and volcanoes, still command respect. As a young and beautiful goddess, Pele fell in love with a handsome *alii* chief from Kauai, but fought over him with her sister Namakaokahai, the sea goddess. After Namakaokahai dashed Pele into fragments on the rocky coast of Maui, she pieced herself together and took up residence in the firepit of the Kilauea volcano on the Big Island. Here Madame Pele lives today, able to manifest herself in numerous disguises and giving vent to explosive bursts of temper. The red *lehua* is Pele's flower, and she is partial to *ohelo* berries, which are often left as offerings.

MISTAKEN IDENTITY When the god Lono left Hawaii on a voyage, he promised to return on a floating island. During his absence, the

Traditional ceremonies are still performed on the volcanoes to appease Madame Pele

Hawaiian people continued to honor him in the winter Makahiki season, when they celebrated the end of harvest. The absentee god's image, perched on top of a long pole draped with white *tapa* cloth, was carried around by representatives of the *alii* as they collected tithes.

On January 18, 1778, near the end of the Makahiki season, a floating island moved by white sails came into view off the islands. When Captain James Cook dropped anchor in Waimea Bay on Kauai, some Hawaiians may have believed Lono had returned.

Ferocious carved Kii *idols protected sacred sites*

Captain James Cook, one of the world's greatest explorers, first sighted the Hawaiian Islands in January 1778. Although Ferdinand Magellan had made the first circumnavigation of the globe in 1519, and Spanish galleons had sailed from Mexico to the Philippines for over 200 years, the isolated Hawaiian archipelago had thus far remained little known territory.

THE SANDWICH ISLANDS Captain James Cook had visited the South Pacific twice before in search of the mythical Great Southern Continent. On this voyage, his goal was to discover the equally elusive (and of course nonexistent) Northwest Passage linking the Pacific and the Atlantic across the top of the North American continent. He set sail from England in 1776, and came around Africa to Polynesia, then struck north from the Society Islands for the west coast of America and Alaska.

On January 18, 1778, his two ships, HMS *Resolution* and HMS *Discovery*, sighted Oahu. They landed at Waimea on Kauai two days later during the Makahiki festival when the god Lono (see pages 34–35) is fêted with feasts, sports, and entertainment. Cook's expedition spent two weeks reprovisioning, cleaning their ships, and being royally entertained by their Hawaiian hosts.

Captain James Cook (1728–1779)

Cook named his finds the Sandwich Islands for his patron, the Earl of Sandwich, First Lord of the Admiralty. The captain was pleased to note similarities in the language and culture of the Hawaiians with the already familiar Polynesian people of Tahiti. He was impressed by the Hawaiians' friendliness, generosity, and swimming and surfing skills, and made presents of goats, pigs, and vegetables, as well as iron, which was highly prized by the Hawaiians. Then, after a brief stop in Niihau, the expedition sailed north.

LONO RETURNS The news of Cook's visit to Kauai probably reached Hawaii during the 10 months that he spent in a fruitless search for the Northwest Passage. The expedition abandoned the task in the fall, and returned to winter in the Hawaiian Islands, sighting Maui on November 25-26. The ships then spent almost two months sailing around the archipelago before putting in to Kealakekua Bay on the Kona Coast of Hawaii on January 17, 1779. In a rerun of the previous year, Cook and his men arrived during the Makahiki festival. His auspicious arrival during the Makahiki season was further augmented by his chosen landing place: *kealakekua* means "path of the gods."

Cook entertained the Hawaiian chieftain, Kalaniopuu, and his retinue on board and introduced them to all manner of Western gadgets and weapons. Yet despite the cordial atmosphere, several small incidents occurred over the following weeks that may have had a bearing on what was to come.

The crews of Cook's ships were welcomed at first

The curious Hawaiians were attracted like magnets to anything made of iron and freely took for their own use any object they needed. Personal property was not a Polynesian concept. Cook's men chased them off in a most inhospitable and, to the offended Hawaiians, ungodlike manner. A ship's boat was taken, and a member of the *alii* (royal or chieftain class) was treated roughly as it was recovered.

TROUBLE IN PARADISE Reprovisioned, Cook's ships upped anchor and sailed northward once more on February 4, but were forced to return a week later after a storm damaged a mast of HMS *Resolution*. This time there was no welcome as Cook set about repairs. Another boat was taken, and Cook went ashore with a party of marines to take Kalaniopuu hostage until the craft was returned. A scuffle broke out, and Cook and four of his men were hacked to death, close to the point where a white obelisk now stands overlooking Kealakekua Bay.

Death of Cook at Kealakekua Bay

After Cook's ships sailed away from Kealakekua Bay, the Hawaiians saw no more visitors until 1786. Chief Kalaniopuu fought with his great rival, Kahekili of Maui, and his nephew Kamehameha acquitted himself well on the battlefield. When Kalaniopuu died, he bequeathed his lands to his son Kiwalao, but the guardianship of the family war god, Kukailimoku, he left to Kamehameha.

KUKAILIMOKU, THE LAND SNATCHER Following Kalaniopuu's death in 1782, a power struggle developed between Kiwalao, his brother Keoua, and Kamehameha. After Kiwalao was killed in battle, Keoua controlled the Puna area of Hawaii in the south, while Kamehameha held sway in the north. In 1790, Kamehameha launched an offensive against Kahekili on Maui, and began the construction of a vast *luakini heiau* (sacrificial temple) to Kukailimoku on the northwest coast of Hawaii at Kawaihae (Puukohala *heiau* National Historic Site). It was prophesied that Kamehameha would conquer all the islands if he honored the war god in this fashion.

As the building work was under way, Kamehameha successfully repelled a combined warring party of warriors from the other islands. It was a good omen. The gods also appeared to be on his side when Madame Pele's firepit dispatched a contingent of Keoua's troops as they crossed the Kilauea crater. The Puukohala *heiau* was completed in 1791, and Keoua was summoned to the dedication ceremony. Bravely he appeared, resplendent in his finest robes, and was slaughtered on the beach. His body was the inaugural human sacrifice to Kukailimoku, the Land Snatcher.

Kamehameha I (c.1758–1819)

THE RED-MOUTHED WEAPON Cook was a man ahead of his time in his concern that contact with the West would change the Hawaiian way of life forever. Captain George Vancouver, who had sailed with Cook and who became a trusted adviser to Kamehameha, refused to trade guns with the Hawaiians, but other visitors were less high-minded. After 1785, ships en route to China from the American northwest found the islands a convenient stopping point for provisions. Kamehameha acquired guns and small cannons, and used them to great effect as he conquered first Maui, then Molokai, Lanai and, finally, Oahu.

In 1794, Kamehameha sailed for Maui with 16,000 warriors and easily defeated the opposition. Faced with a flotilla of war canoes 4 miles long, Molokai, too, was subdued in short order. Kahekili died the same year and, in February 1795, Kamehameha landed with his army at Waikiki, and cornered and conquered the defenders in the Nuuanu Valley.

Kamehameha was now the power in the land, though Kauai still eluded him. Two attempts to lead a seaborne invasion were defeated by the weather, but the island was finally

brought under his control in 1810 when the Kauai chief, Kaumualii, agreed to act as the governor of his own island under the ultimate rule of King Kamehameha.

Kamehameha the Great, Hawaii's warrior king

KAMEHAMEHA THE GREAT

Kamehameha consolidated his position by adhering strictly to the old religion and enacting laws that forbade Hawaiians from trading directly with Western ships. Visiting captains had to seek the king's assent to trade. The safe anchorage of Honolulu harbor was the center of the action, and Kamehameha moved his court here in 1804. He appointed loyal counselors to oversee the other islands, including the Englishman John Young in Hawaii, who also acted as the king's business agent.

In 1812 Kamehameha returned to Hawaii and died there in 1819. The succession was secured by the sons borne for him by Keopuolani, his "Sacred Wife," whom he had married in 1795. Though the king had perhaps 20 other wives, Keopuolani was *naiupio*, the highest possible caste, the daughter of a Molokai chieftainess and her brother in a prescribed marriage ordained to produce just such a *naiupio* child.

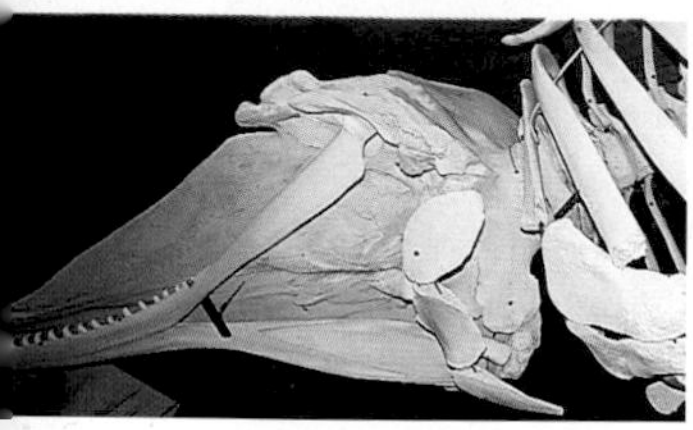

The first whale was killed in the north central Pacific in 1819, and by 1823 up to 60 ships were operating out of the islands. At the height of the "Golden Age" of whaling, 20 years later, 395 ships called at Maui alone, whose whaling port of Lahaina was the busiest in the Pacific, a boom town teeming with foreign sailors.

PRESS-GANGED INTO SERVICE It has been estimated that over 100,000 men sailed from New England aboard ships for the rich whaling grounds of the Pacific. However, unlike their contemporaries, the strait-laced, well-intentioned, and zealous missionaries, morality was not the whalers' strong suit and a good many were not volunteers. To fill their crew lists, captains frequently relied on the services of ruthless press gangs, so careless drunks and down-and-outs were in very real danger of waking up one morning to an unplanned life sailing the seven seas.

LIFE ON THE OCEAN WAVE Life on board a whaling ship was surely one of the most unpleasant experiences imaginable. It was dirty, dangerous, lonely, and badly paid. Men were signed up for three- or four-year voyages that took them to the Arctic whaling grounds in summer, and the waters off Japan in winter. Wages were a mere pittance, and after deductions for food and grog many men ended up in debt to the ship. They lived in cramped, filthy quarters, spent months on end at sea, and risked their lives to provide the whale oils that greased the cogs of America's industrial age, provided the fuel to light homes and streets, and were transformed into soap, candles, and cosmetics.

CATCHING THE WHALES Boredom and danger were two constants in the life of a whaler. The initial journey from New England around Cape Horn could be a terrifying experience, but it paled into insignificance alongside the realities of 19th-century

Lahaina was home to a huge whaling fleet

whale hunting. When a whale was spotted, the whaling ship drew near to it and cast off her boats. These six-man vessels were about half the size of the whale and only a fraction of its weight. Hand-launched harpoons were plunged into the whale, which could then tow the puny craft for miles before tiring enough to allow the crew to come alongside and pierce the giant beast through its lungs to kill it.

Harvesting the whale oil was almost as dangerous as capturing its source. As the oil-rich blubber was cut away, the ship's decks turned into a treacherous slick of blood and oil. Most of the carcass and flesh was then thrown overboard, except for the baleen found in the mouths of toothless whales. Known quite erroneously as "whalebone," these hair plates are used by the whale to filter its food, and are made of keratin, as are human nails and hair. "Whalebone" baleen, which was both strong and flexible, was the forerunner of modern plastics and was widely used for making buggy

Harpooning whales in the Pacific

whips, fishing rods, corset stays, and hoops for crinolines.

SHORE EXCESSES At the end of the season, the whalers sailed for Lahaina and Honolulu to off-load their cargoes and set about an orgy of drinking and whoring. Missionaries tried to curb the whalers' wild behavior by imposing curfews and forbidding native women on the ships. The sailors for their part took potshots at the missionary house in Lahaina, and continued to bestow their legacy of venereal diseases, influenza, and smallpox on a native population with no natural defenses.

By the late 1860s the whaling boom was over. The introduction of petroleum reduced the market for whale oil, and the sheer hardship of the whaling lifestyle took its toll. Equally, between 1835 and 1872 the American whaling fleet slaughtered 292,714 whales; they were no longer abundant in the central Pacific, and the whaling fleets moved on.

Within six months of the death of Kamehameha in May 1819, the ancient kapu *(taboo) system, which underpinned both Hawaiian society and religion, had been destroyed. Chiefly responsible were Kamehameha's queens, Keopuolani and Kaahumanu, who persuaded the young king Kamehameha II to break* kapu *by dining with them at a public feast.*

***KAPU* COLLAPSES** After the arrival of Captain Cook, some Hawaiians began to question the alleged power of the gods as Westerners appeared to be able to break *kapu* without any retribution. Kamehameha I had managed to keep the old religion afloat, but Kamehameha II was no match for the royal womenfolk who were determined to dispense with the restrictive *kapu* regime. When the public flouting of the *kapu* against men eating with women, and women eating taboo foods such as pork, bananas, and coconut provoked no response from the gods, *heiau* (temples) were desecrated, idols smashed, and the Hawaiians were left in a spiritual vacuum.

CUE THE BRIG *THADDEUS* In October 1819, 14 Protestant missionaries bound for Hawaii sailed from Boston, Massachusetts, aboard the brig *Thaddeus*. They arrived in Kailua, on the Big Island, in April 1820, and then went on to Honolulu on Oahu, where on April 25 the Reverend Hiram Bingham offered his first service on Hawaiian soil. Several of the mission brothers and their wives were reported to have been moved to tears at the sight of the Hawaiian "naked savages," but they soon pulled themselves together and got down to their work.

Missionary church in Halawa Valley

❑ The original mission buildings in Honolulu now contain the fascinating Mission Houses Museum (see page 64). Other fine mission house museums include the Waioli Mission at Hanalei, Kauai (see page 100); the Baldwin House at Lahaina, Maui (see page 127); and Lyman House in Hilo, Hawaii (see page 157). ❑

The headquarters of the Sandwich Islands Mission was founded in Honolulu, and by the 1840s there were 17 mission outposts spread throughout the islands. The missionaries built churches, schools, and printing houses, and in their first few years achieved several important conversions. Both Keopuolani and Kaahumanu were converts, as was the powerful chieftainess of Hawaii, Kapiolani, who made a dramatic declaration of faith at the Kilauea crater, home of Madame Pele. There she ate sacred *ohelo* berries, flung stones into the firepit, and declared the Christian God, not Pele, responsible for the volcano's actions.

The missionaries provided the Hawaiians with an alphabet, the means of written communication for their native tongue, but they were also responsible for all but expunging the ancient oral and visual traditions of the *hula* (dance form). Deemed licentious and depraved, the *hula* was swiftly banned. Its female practitioners were covered up in sacklike *muumuu* (loose-fitting gowns), and taught more socially acceptable pastimes such as hymn singing and quilting. Games and entertainments were forbidden on the Sabbath, and considerable energy was expended in preaching against alcohol, adultery, and gambling, to the initial bemusement of the easygoing Hawaiians.

MERCHANTS AND MINISTERS Never had a contingent of missionaries turned up at a more propitious moment in a host country's history. With Hawaiian society in disarray and organized religion conveniently dismantled by the Hawaiian people themselves, the missionaries were extraordinarily successful in their efforts. By the 1850s, around a third of the population had been converted and the New Englanders were able to entrust the continuance of their work to the Hawaiians. Catholic missions followed the Protestants, and after them came the Mormons.

Missionary influence extended far beyond the introduction and spread of Christianity in the Hawaiian islands. They started commercial and trading ventures and were increasingly drawn into the political arena. By the time Kamehameha III had ascended the throne in 1827, Hawaii was in political turmoil; foreign newcomers tried to achieve a political toehold, challenging the legitimacy of Hawaiian rule by claiming the islands for their European countries (see page 44). Kamehameha III turned to the missionaries for advice, and William Richards was released from his religious duties to help the king.

Other prominent missionaries were Gerrit Judd, who served as chief government minister, and Samuel Alexander and Henry Baldwin, who met as mission children in Lahaina and went on to found together one of Hawaii's most important trading companies. Wilcoxes, Thurstons, and Cookes also flourished, their influence playing a vital part in securing close ties between Hawaii and the U.S.

A legendary figure, missionary Father Damien tended people with Hansen's disease, once known as leprosy, at their refuge on Molokai

When Kamehameha II died in 1824, and was succeeded by his nine-year-old brother, Kamehameha III, control of the kingdom passed to the dowager queen, Kaahumanu, and, later, to the king's sister, Kinau. Following advice from the missionaries, the basic framework of government and legal systems began to take shape.

LIBERTINE TURNED LAWMAKER
Even after he had achieved his majority, Kamehameha III showed very little interest in the workings of state. The funloving king declared "war" on missionary morality; he drank, gambled, danced the forbidden *hula*, surfed, and conducted a passionate love affair with his younger sister Nahienaena, to the horror of the Christian brothers. But after Nahienaena's death in 1836, Kamehameha reformed. Lessons in government from William Richards led to a Declaration of Rights in 1839, and the institution of a constitutional monarchy in 1840.

Hawaiian independence survived threats from both the French (in 1839) and the British (in 1843). The former were diffused after concessions were made permitting certain French goods and Catholic missionaries into Hawaii. The British incident involved one Lord George Paulet who, acting on his own initiative, occupied the fort at Honolulu and claimed Hawaii for the British crown. His superiors and Queen Victoria herself were vastly unamused and control was handed back to the king, along with profuse apologies.

Kamehameha III and Queen Kalama

LAND DIVISION Kamehameha III's single most significant act was to initiate the land division known as the Great *Mahele*. The concept of private ownership was alien to the Hawaiian people, who had

Sugar mills arose from cane fields

Many cane workers are Filipino immigrants

previously worked the land for the *alii* (chiefs), and later for the king. Encouraged by his foreign advisers, the king divided the Hawaiian lands into three portions: part to remain in the possession of the crown; part allotted to the government; and the remaining portion set aside for the Hawaiian people, though few of them followed the official claiming procedure. Just two years later, in 1850, *haole* (foreigners) were allowed to buy land freehold. Needless to say, many missionaries and their families were at the front of the line when the Hawaiians happily sold off their unaccustomed property.

KING SUGAR The first sugar cane plantations in Hawaii appeared on Kauai as early as 1835, but it was not until the California Gold Rush in the late 1840s that there was much demand for Hawaiian sugar. Though this initial interest was short-lived, the disruption to the sugar supply from the southern states during the Civil War was a further boost for the Hawaiian crop.

What had become painfully obvious by the mid-1800s was the dramatic and seemingly irreversible demise of the Hawaiian people. From an estimated population of around 300,000 at the time of Captain Cook, the Hawaiians now numbered a mere 50,000. The plantations required a massive, cheap labor force, but the Hawaiians were both too few in number and disinclined to abandon their traditional lifestyle to slave for the *haole*. The plantation owners' solution was to import workers from abroad.

The first contract laborers from China arrived in 1852, to be followed in 1878–1887 by some 12,000 Portuguese from the Azores and Madeira, many of whom were skilled workers and hence joined the *luna* (overseer) class. After a shaky start, large-scale immigrations from Japan began in the 1880s when the emperor relaxed the restrictions on Japanese emigration after a visit from Kalakaua.

Typical plantation conditions were grim. A backbreaking 12-hour day, six days a week, was the norm. Pay was low, facilities minimal, and restrictive regulations abounded. There were severe penalties for desertion. Many of the early immigrants, particularly the Chinese, returned home at the end of their contracts. But, equally, many stayed and moved into business. In all, approximately 395,000 immigrants came to Hawaii to work in the cane fields between 1852 and 1946. Their common experience forged lasting cross-ethnic links.

The thorny question of some form of reciprocity agreement with the U.S. to protect the fledgling Hawaiian sugar industry was first discussed in the 1850s. Naturally, plantation owners supported the plan, which would allow Hawaiian sugar to be exported duty-free to the U.S. in return for similar trading concessions on U.S. goods coming into Hawaii.

ANTI-U.S. FEELING Reciprocity did not appeal to Kamehameha IV, who had succeeded to the throne in 1854. An anglophile who distrusted the Americans, the king was wary of closer ties with the U.S., preferring to keep his options open.

In 1864, Kamehameha V overturned the liberal constitution of 1852, and also reduced the powers of the American-influenced legislature while attempting to invest further authority in the crown. He died without naming an heir in 1872, the last of the Kamehameha dynasty, and the new king was elected from another branch of the family.

King David Kalakaua (1836–1891)

The reign of the "People's King," King William Lunalilo (1873–1874), was brief but popular. When Lunalilo came to the throne, the whaling industry was a fraction of its former size, and he recognized the necessity for reciprocity with the U.S. to secure Hawaii's economic future. There were serious discussions about what form the Hawaiian concessions should take, and at one point it was suggested that Hawaii might offer the Americans rights to develop Pearl Harbor as a naval base, but public concern over U.S. influence saw the plan dropped.

THE MERRIE MONARCH King David Kalakaua, Lunalilo's successor, was no Kamehameha, but he was a

The last Hawaiian royal, Queen Liliuokalani (1891–1893)

powerful force and greatly beloved by his countrymen. He visited Washington to promote negotiations in 1875, and the Reciprocity Treaty was implemented the following year. The king made quite a hit in the U.S., but he was a great deal less popular with the American community in Hawaii. His autocratic rule, coupled with heavy taxes imposed on planters and businessmen, led to considerable resentment among the *haole* (foreigners), an influential group of whom banded together to form the pro-American Hawaiian League.

Kalakaua's lavish lifestyle, which included building the Iolani Palace and traveling on a world tour, was balanced by a genuine concern for Hawaiian history and culture. He revived the *hula* (native dance form), compiled a book of Hawaiian legends, and generally restored the Hawaiians' pride in their national heritage. But the country's coffers were empty, and the businesslike Hawaiian League stepped in with a list of demands that led to the Bayonet Constitution of 1887. Kalakaua was forced to concede considerable power to the League-influenced legislature; the vote was restricted to a coterie of wealthy or landowning figures, mainly the *haole*; and the Reciprocity Treaty was renegotiated, giving the U.S. title over Pearl Harbor.

ROYALTY OVERTHROWN Kalakaua died on a visit to San Francisco in January 1891, to be succeeded by his sister, Lydia Liliuokalani. A passionate nationalist, Queen Liliuokalani and her supporters were determined to reassert royal authority and preserve "Hawaii for the Hawaiians." Court intrigues abounded, and two years later Liliuokalani announced her intention to do away with the 1887 constitution. In a hastily convened session of the Annexation Club, led by Lorrin Thurston (a founding member of the Hawaiian League), a group of some 30 U.S. businessmen resolved to replace the queen with their own candidate.

They turned to the U.S. Minister to Hawaii, John Stevens, who summoned the USS *Boston* without consulting Washington. On January 16, 1893, 160 U.S. marines occupied strategic sites around Honolulu, and the following day the queen was forced to abdicate. The Hawaiian monarchy, after less than a century in power, was replaced by a provisional government headed by American plantation owner Sanford B. Dole.

When news of the American-led coup against the Hawaiian monarchy reached President Grover Cleveland, he was appalled and dispatched an emissary, James Blount, to assess the situation. Blount, who found an indignant ex-queen Liliuokalani and a resentful populace, reported to Cleveland that "a great wrong has been done to the Hawaiians."

FROM REPUBLIC TO U.S. TERRITORY Both Cleveland and Blount favored reinstating the monarchy, but the provisional government in Honolulu ignored Washington and declared the Republic of Hawaii in July 1894, elevating Sanford Dole to president. In 1895 Liliuokalani plotted a counterrevolution, but it was nipped in the bud by the provisional government, the coconspirators were rounded up, and the ex-queen was put under house arrest in the Iolani Palace. In 1898, the new Republican president, William McKinley, signed an annexation agreement, and the islands officially became a U.S. territory in 1900.

THE HAWAIIAN ECONOMY By the early 20th century, economic power was concentrated in the "Big Five" sugar companies, which soon began to diversify into shipping, ranching, and land development. James Drummond Dole founded the Hawaiian Pineapple Company in 1901, and soon the pineapple industry was second only to sugar. Immigrants flowed into Hawaii to work the plantations, until 75 percent of the workforce was Asian. By the time immigration from Japan was ended in the 1920s, 42.7 percent of the Hawaiian population was of Japanese descent. Further demand for labor was answered by 100,000 Filipino immigrants, who arrived between 1907 and 1941.

Besides the plantations, Hawaii's biggest revenue earner was the U.S. military, which had started arriving

Hawaiian pineapple power

in force from the beginning of the century. Pearl Harbor was dredged and equipped to service the Pacific Fleet, and the army occupied the huge Schofield Barracks complex in central Oahu. Tourism also began to play an important role, as luxury liners steamed into Honolulu Harbor, and the 1920s leisure classes danced and drank the tropical nights away in Waikiki's grand hotels. Air transportation arrived in the 1930s, and the first fare-paying air passengers flew in aboard the *Hawaii Clipper* from San Francisco on April 8, 1935.

WORLD WAR II The Japanese attack on Pearl Harbor on December 7, 1941 brought America into the war and also marked the start of another period of profound change in Hawaiian society. Martial law was immediately declared. There was some initial unease about the Japanese population, and internment was forced on some. When the AJA (Americans of Japanese Ancestry) 100th Battalion was formed in 1942, over 10,000 Hawaii AJAs applied for 3,000 places. Renamed the 442nd Regimental Combat Team, the AJAs fought with distinction in Europe, North Africa, and the Pacific to become the most highly decorated World War II unit in the U.S. forces.

The war did more to Americanize Hawaii's various ethnic communities than half a century of annexation. New industry combined with a newly unionized workforce eroded the power of the "Big Five"—C. Brewer, Castle & Cooke, Alexander & Baldwin, Theo Davies, and Amfac, Hawaii's biggest landowners and businesses, all originally sugar based—and Hawaii's servicemen and women pursued higher education under the Veterans Act. As racial and economic barriers came tumbling down, they began to demand a voice in Hawaii's future.

HAWAII BECOMES A STATE The postwar economy boomed and many lobbied for the benefits of statehood. Hawaii was admitted as the 50th state in the Union on August 21, 1959. That same year the first regular jet air service to the mainland was started, and tourism and the construction industry associated with it boomed. As international competitors forced the sugar and pineapple industries into decline, tourism grew to match military spending as Hawaii's chief source of revenue; attempts to diversify the economy through science and technology have been modestly successful. In 1994 the U.S. Congress apologized for the war-time annexation of Kahoolawe and returned the island to the people.

USS West Virginia *at Pearl Harbor*

Kahuku Point
Kawela Bay
Kawela
83
Kahuku Sugar Mill
Kahuku
COMSAT
Olio
Sunset Beach
Kahikilani (Washington Stone)
Malaekahana State Park
Banzai Pipeline
Waimea
Waimea Bay
Puu O Mahuka Heiau State Monument
Mormon Temple
Laie
Polynesian Cultural Center
Kawailoa Beach
Waimea Valley Adventure Park
Koolau Range
Kahuku Forest Reserve
Hauula
Kauai Channel
Haleiwa Beach
Haleiwa
Kaiaka Bay
Kawailoa Forest Reserve
Mokuleia Beach
Anahulu
Kaena Point
Keana Point State Park
Kuaokala Forest Reserve
Mokuleia
Waialua
Kamoolaa
99
Yokohama Bay
Leilehua Plateau
Makua
Waianae
Mokueleia Forest Reserve
Dole Plantation
Kaneana Cave
Makua Keaau Forest
4038ft Kaala
Schofield Barracks
Sacred Birth Stone
Botanic Garden
Ewa Forest Reserve
Waionae Kai Forest Reserve
Schofield Barracks
Wahiawa
Kepuhi Point
Makaha
Forest Reserve
1784ft Kokekole Pass
Waikele
Makaha
Mountains
Waipio Acres
Ewa Forest
Waianae Regional Park
Waianae
Kunia
Pokai Bay
3126ft Puu Kaua
Milani Town
Honouliuli Forest Reserve
Waiawa
Pacific Palisades
H2
Maili
Waipo
Maili Point
93
Hawaii Plantation Village
Pearl City
Nanakuli
Waipahu
Aiea
Nanakuli Beach Park
H1
USS *Bowfin* Submarine Memorial
USS *Missouri* Memorial
USS *Arizona* Museum
Pearl Harbor
Makakilo
Ewa
Hickam Air Force Base
H1
Honolulu International Airport
Hawaii Raceway Park
Ewa Beach
Barbers Point/ Kalaeloa
Barbers Point/ Kalaeloa Beach Park
Mamala Bay
0 5 10 km
0 5 miles
A B C
1 2 3 4

Vintage aloha *shirts now command high prices in Honolulu's trendy clothing stores*

Oahu

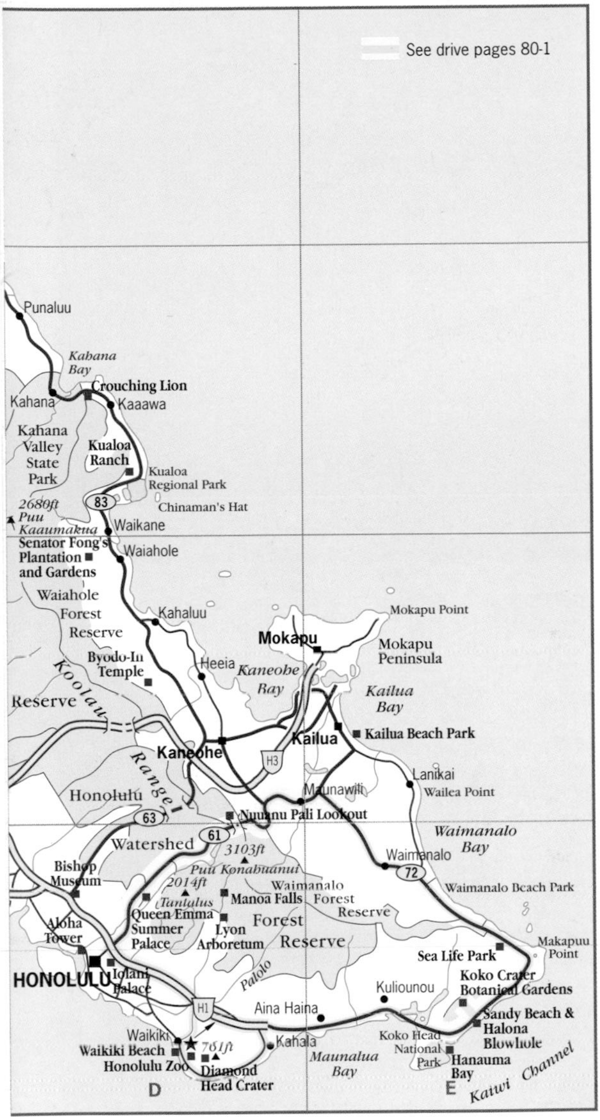

See drive pages 80-1

Punaluu
Kahana Bay
Crouching Lion
Kahana
Kaaawa
Kahana Valley State Park
Kualoa Ranch
Kualoa Regional Park
83
Chinaman's Hat
2680ft Puu Kaaumakua
Waikane
Senator Fong's Plantation and Gardens
Waiahole
Waiahole Forest Reserve
Kahaluu
Mokapu Point
Mokapu
Mokapu Peninsula
Byodo-In Temple
Heeia
Kaneohe Bay
Kailua Bay
Koolau Range
Reserve
Kailua
Kailua Beach Park
Kaneohe
H3
Lanikai
Wailea Point
Honolulu
Maunawili
63
Nuuanu Pali Lookout
Waimanalo Bay
Watershed
61
3103ft
Waimanalo
Bishop Museum
Puu Konahuanui
72
2014ft
Tantalus
Waimanalo Forest Reserve
Waimanalo Beach Park
Manoa Falls
Queen Emma Summer Palace
Lyon Arboretum
Forest Reserve
Aloha Tower
Makapuu Point
Sea Life Park
HONOLULU
Iolani Palace
Palolo
Koko Crater Botanical Gardens
Kuliounou
H1
Aina Haina
Sandy Beach & Halona Blowhole
Waikiki
Koko Head National Park
Waikiki Beach
761ft
Kahala
Maunalua Bay
Hanauma Bay
Honolulu Zoo
Diamond Head Crater
Kaiwi Channel
D
E

THE GATHERING PLACE The second oldest and third largest of the main Hawaiian islands, the island nicknamed the Gathering Place, is also the most populous, most developed, and most visited volcanic dot in the middle of the Pacific. A mere 604 square miles in area, the island is home to some 80 percent of Hawaii's 1.2 million people, and the capital, Honolulu, welcomes around 4.5 million visitors a year.

However, although Oahu lives up to its nickname, these statistics do not tell the whole story. Sometimes dismissed as a tourist ghetto by its detractors, Oahu has room to spare. Of the mountainous interior, 46 percent is just too steep to develop, and the heavily populated urban areas are confined to the southern portion of the island. Yet less

Makapuu Beach

ISLAND HIGHLIGHTS

LONG WEEKEND ITINERARY

Day one: Waikiki Trolley (suggested stops Hawaii Maritime Museum, Foster Botanical Garden, and Chinatown). Relax on Waikiki Beach or visit the aquarium.
Day two: USS *Arizona* Memorial. Aloha Tower Marketplace for lunch. Historic Honolulu Walk.
Day three: rent a car for the Southern Drive.
Day four: hike to Diamond Head Bay. Shop at the Ala Moana Center.

than half an hour from the concrete and glass heart of Honolulu, there are stunning azure-blue bays harboring more than 350 different types of tropical fish, terrific body-surfing beaches virtually deserted on weekdays, and a choice of upcountry hiking trails.

ATTRACTIONS Few visitors avoid Honolulu. It is, after all, the main gateway to the islands, and its high-rise skyline seems to reach up and draw the jumbo loads of pale vacationers down into its sunny embrace. For many visitors the charms of Waikiki—luxury shopping, fine restaurants, well-appointed beachfront accommodations, and a lively nightlife—prove equally magnetic, and some never venture farther afield. But Oahu is well worth exploring and rewards tourists with a plethora of quiet beaches, beautiful gardens, and more exotic attractions, from the popular Sea Life Park at Waimanalo to the South-Sea-Island delights of Laie's Polynesian Cultural Center.

TOPOGRAPHY AND CLIMATE Public transportation on Oahu is better than anywhere else on the islands, and private bus companies serve several of the more far-flung attractions, but independent travelers should still consider renting a car. The simple island road plan is dictated by local geography, namely Oahu's two mountain ranges. The Koolau Mountains, which rise behind Honolulu, run almost the length of the windward (east) coast, tailing off opposite the famous surfing beaches of the north coast. Here, the frenetic activity in the water is in complete contrast to the laid-back, hippy-surfer attitude of Haleiwa, the only settlement of any size in this part of the island. South of Haleiwa, the Central Plain is given over to diversified agriculture and pineapple plantations, while the Waianae Mountains reach over 4,000 feet before tipping down to the rugged west coast. As a rule of thumb, the windward coast is wetter, particularly in the November–March rainy season, and things get drier as you move west.

Honolulu and Waikiki

SHELTERED BAY The tenth largest city in the United States, Honolulu sprawls in the lee of the Koolau Mountains, extending its concrete arms from the Diamond Head end of Waikiki all the way around to the industrial jumble beyond Pearl Harbor. This is the financial center of the mid-Pacific, a top vacation destination and springboard to the Neighbor Islands, and the home of America's only royal palace.

The origins of Honolulu's success can be found on the downtown waterfront, where the original *hono-lulu*, or "sheltered bay," lies at the foot of the landmark Aloha Tower. The finest natural anchorage in the islands was put on the map by English seafarer Captain William Brown in 1792–1793, and became a useful mid-Pacific stop for sailing ships plying the ocean between the Americas and Asia. The port settlement boomed with the arrival of whalers and New England missionaries in the 1820s, prompting King Kamehameha III to move the Hawaiian capital here from Lahaina, Maui in 1845.

Downtown Honolulu covers a few compact blocks. The historic financial district is sandwiched between the harbor and Iolani Palace, and provides a buffer zone between the old mission headquarters and present-day Chinatown (rebuilt after a devastating fire in 1900), where the whalers once caroused along Hotel Street.

PEARL HARBOR To the west, beyond the airport, are the lagoons of Pearl Harbor, where there were oyster beds until they were dredged out in the early 1900s. As the home port of the U.S. Pacific Fleet, this key naval base was the target of the infamous Japanese aerial attack that brought America into World War II.

Window cleaners hang out against a life-size whale leaping up a wall in Ala Moana

Life on the ocean wave

ONE WEEK ITINERARY
Days one to three: as for long weekend itinerary (see panel opposite).
Day four: Haleiwa, the Northern Beaches, and Waimea Valley Adventure Park. Polynesian Cultural Center *luau*.
Day five: Punchbowl Crater and Tantalus Drive. Lunch at the Contemporary Museum. Lyon Arboretum and Manoa Falls Walk.
Day six: Kodak *Hula* Show (Tue–Thu), Honolulu Zoo and Diamond Head.
Day seven: relax on Waikiki Beach. Shopping at Ala Moana Center.

Kaneohe
Kailua
Manoa Falls
Honolulu Watershed Forest Reserve
1870ft Napuumaia
Kekoalele Ridge
Pali Highway
Rainforest Drive
63
Kalihi Valley Park
Lyon Arboretum
Kalihi
61
Kalihi Valley
1414ft Waolani
Dowsett Highlands
2014ft Tantalus
Manoa
Upper Manoa
Likelike Highway
Kapalama
Alewa Heights
Oahu Country Club
Queen Emma Summer Palace
Nuuanu
Nuuanu Valley Park
Rainforest
Roundtop Forest Reserve
Waoiani
Nuuanu
Pacific Heights
Punchbowl Lookout
Kamehameha Heights
1046ft Roundtop
Royal Mausoleum
Makiki Heights
Manoa
Contemporary Museum
Pagoda Lookout
Tantalus Drive
Nuuanu Avenue
Kapalama
Pali Highway
Pauoa
Bishop Museum
Lanakila
Punchbowl Crater National Memorial Cemetery of the Pacific
Makiki
Punahou
Aiea
H1
N King Street
Vineyard Blvd
Lunalilo Freeway
Kalihi
Kuan Yin Temple
Foster Botanical Garden
Cathedral of Our Lady of Peace
Chinatown Cultural Plaza
Honolulu Academy of Arts
S Beretania Street
S King Street
Dillingham Blvd
China
Washington Place
Dole Cannery Square
State Capitol
Thomas Square
Nimitz Highway
Iwilei
Oahu Market
Iolani Palace
City Hall
Neal S Blaisdell Center
Kapiolani
Kalakaua Ave
Honolulu International Airport, Pearl Harbor
92
Kawaiahao Church
Mission Houses Museum
Downtown
Aloha Tower
Ala Moana Shopping Center
Kapalama
Kapalama Basin
Honolulu Harbor
Hawaii Maritime Center
Kakaako
(The Falls of Clyde)
Ala Moana Blvd
Ward Warehouse
Ward Center
Ala Moana Beach Park
Sand Island
Honolulu Channel
Kakaako Waterfront Park
Sand Island State Park
Mamala Bay
Mokouea Island
A B C
1 2 3 4

Honolulu and Waikiki street plan

Waikiki Beach surfboard lockers

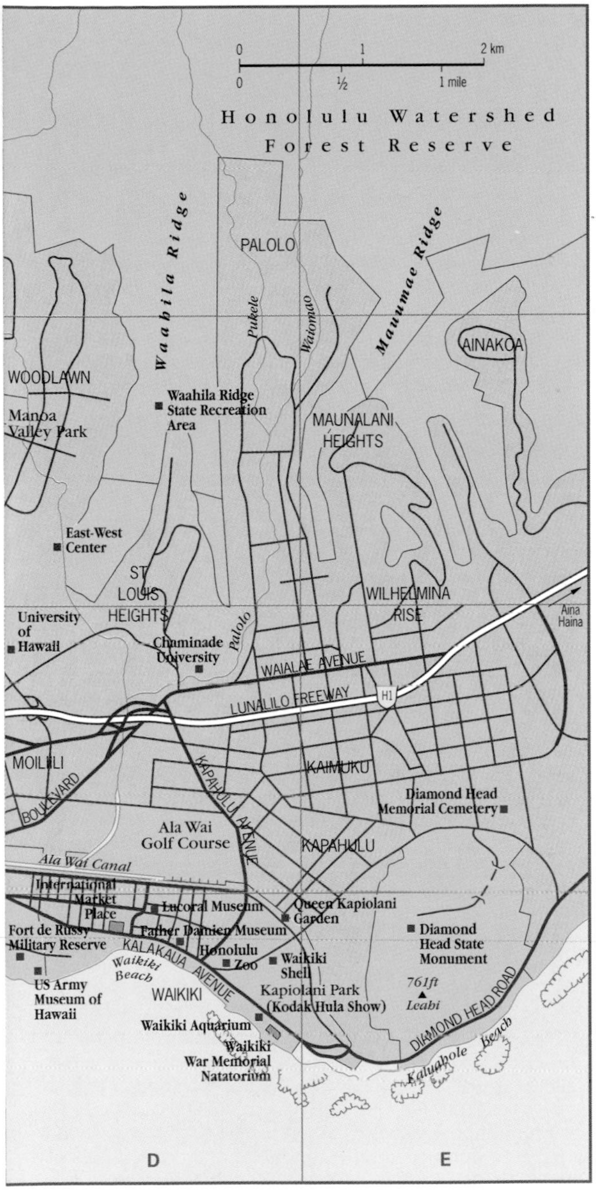

"SPOUTING WATER" East of downtown Honolulu, there is an area which the Hawaiians called "Spouting Water." This former swamp, with its 1½-mile-long beach guarded by Diamond Head, is better known as Waikiki. Long before mass tourism, Queen Kaahumanu surfed here, and the 19th-century Scottish writer Robert Louis Stevenson "talked story" in a little grass hut. Drained and reclaimed, the square-mile resort boasts some 31,000 hotel rooms and over 200 restaurants, plus diversions galore. It may not be everyone's cup of coconut milk, but it is a crowd-pleaser through and through.

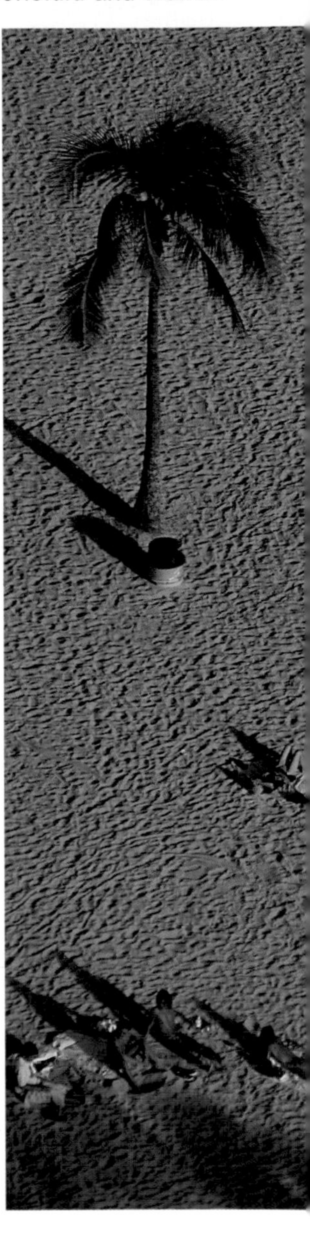

Catching the last rays of the day

Aloha Tower

PRINCESS BERNICE PAUAHI
Destined to marry into the royal family, Princess Bernice Pauahi defied her family and married American banker Charles Reed Bishop instead. The couple dedicated their considerable energies to the preservation of Hawaii's cultural heritage. Princess Bernice also founded the Kamehameha Schools to provide a first-rate education for students of Hawaiian or part-Hawaiian blood. These are still funded by the Princess Bernice Pauahi Bishop Estate, which controls vast tracts of Honolulu and the outer islands.

Honolulu is a crossroads of Asian cultures

▶ Aloha Tower 54B1

Pier 9, Downtown
Open: Sun–Thu 9–9, Fri–Sat 9 AM–10 PM. Admission free
Bus 19, 20, 47; Waikiki Trolley Stop 7

The 10-story Aloha Tower was the tallest building in town when it was completed in 1926, a welcome beacon on the quayside overlooking Honolulu Harbor where the cruise ships of yesteryear were greeted by a bevy of hula girls with fragrant *lei* (garlands). Although long since dwarfed by modern skyscrapers, the tower still affords splendid views of downtown and the harbor from its outdoor observation decks. Orientation boards point out local landmarks, and there is a bird's-eye view of the four-masted sailing ship *Falls of Clyde* directly below. The surrounding Aloha Tower Marketplace, decked out in a nautical turquoise and white trim, has a range of attractive boutiques and waterfront restaurants.

▶▶▶ Bishop Museum 54A2

1525 Bernice Street, Honolulu (tel: 808/847-3511; web: www.bishop.hawaii.org)
Open: daily 9–5; Planetarium, daily shows at 11 and 2, and Fri–Sat at 7 (reservations required).
Admission: moderate. Bus 2; Waikiki Trolley Stop 10

This notable State Museum of Natural and Cultural History was founded in 1889 by Charles Reed Bishop, the husband of Princess Bernice Pauahi, great-granddaughter of King Kamehameha I. The princess was an enthusiastic collector, and her peerless cache of Hawaiiana formed the basis for the museum's very impressive catalog of Hawaiian and Pacific artifacts (some 187,000 pieces), widely regarded as the finest in the world.

In the Victorian main building, exhibits in the Polynesian Hall cover the island cultures of Melanesia and Micronesia in the Pacific southwest. Artifacts range from flutes and fish hooks to jewelry, finely carved from human bone, and elaborate costumes constructed with great skill and flair from animal, vegetable, and even mineral components.

The three floors of the Hawaiian Hall delve into every aspect of Hawaiian history, society, and culture. Beneath the skeleton of a 55-foot sperm whale, hoisted to its present position as a tribute to the whaling industry in 1902, displays unravel the complexities of the ancient social hierarchy alongside magnificent ceremonial capes, each made from the feathers of up to 80,000 birds. There are Stone Age tools and utensils, and sections on war, immigrant heritage, and traditional crafts. In addition to frequent guided tours, daily demonstrations feature the likes of *lei*-making and quilting.

Beyond the main halls, look for the exhibitions in the Castle Building, *hula* performances in the Atherton Hall, and daily shows in the Planetarium.

▶ Chinatown 54B2

West of Nuuanu Avenue, between Ala Moana and Vineyard Boulevards
Bus 2, 19, 20, 47; Waikiki Trolley Stop 11

A stone's throw from the bustling dockside where the first Chinese indentured laborers would have landed in the 1850s,

Honolulu's Chinatown is a compact and evocative grid of colorful Asian markets, stores selling Chinese medicines and joss sticks, noodle shops, and Asian restaurants. Open-air activities and cultural performances take place in the Chinese Cultural Plaza on North Beretania Street. Nearby, a statue commemorates the "Father of Modern China," Sun Yat-sen, who founded the revolutionary Hsing Chung Hui secret society in Honolulu in 1895, before overthrowing China's Manchu dynasty in 1911.

The Bishop Museum houses a fine collection of Hawaiiana

One of the best ways to explore the area and come to grips with its colorful history is to take a guided walk run by the Chinese Chamber of Commerce, 42 North King Street (tel: 808/533-3181).

▶ Contemporary Museum — *54C3*

2411 Makiki Heights Drive, Honolulu (tel: 808/526-0232)
Open: Tue–Sat 10–4, Sun 12–4. Admission: moderate
Bus 15

Try to visit this elegant museum around lunchtime to have a bite in the excellent Contemporary Café. The permanent collection of modern art (predominantly Hawaiian) is augmented by temporary exhibitions. Take a turn around the pretty gardens, and do not miss David Hockney's 1983 stage model for the Ravel opera *L'Enfant et les Sortilèges*, a theatrically lit, naive-style woodland environment housed in the Milton Cades Pavilion.

CHARLIE CHAN

Honolulu's Chinatown was home to Charlie Chan, the world-famous Asian sleuth in Earl Derr Biggers' best-selling crime stories. Biggers drew the inspiration for his hero from a real-life Hawaiian-Chinese detective, Chang Apana, who died in 1933.

The fully rigged Falls of Clyde

LOCAL DIRECTIONS
If, when asking directions of local people, you are told to walk "Diamond Head, two blocks" for your destination, it means head toward that mountainous landmark. There are three other local direction terms that are less easy to understand: *makai* (toward the sea), *mauka* (toward the mountains), and *ewa* (west toward the Ewa Plain beyond Pearl Harbor).

Heading makai *in the lee of Diamond Head*

►► Diamond Head 55E1

Diamond Head State Monument, Diamond Head Road
Open: daily 6–6. Admission free

The crest of Diamond Head, Honolulu's most arresting natural landmark, towers over the southern end of Waikiki Beach. The headland, site of an ancient Hawaiian *heiau* (temple), gained its *haole* (foreign) name from a band of British soldiers who found calcite crystals here in 1825, and mistook them for diamonds.

For a great view of Honolulu, follow Diamond Head Road into the crater. A strenuous trail leads up from the parking lot, through a tunnel and up to the summit.

► Dole Cannery Square 54A2

650 Iwilei Road, Downtown
Open: daily 9–5. Admission free. Free bus from Waikiki (schedule, tel: 808/548-6601); Bus 19, 20;
Waikiki Trolley Stop 8

Although the Dole canning factory has closed, and the huge pineapple-shaped water tank no longer exists, the Square still entertains visitors with a multimedia presentation devoted to Jim Dole and his pineapples (see page 151), and a display of pineapples from all over the world.

▶ Damien Museum — 55D1

130 Ohua Avenue, Waikiki (tel: 808/923-2690)
Open: Mon–Fri 9–3. Admission: donation

Behind St. Augustine's Catholic Church on Kalakaua Avenue, this simple museum houses a smattering of memorabilia and a video presentation about Father Damien de Veuster. De Veuster came to Hawaii as a theology student in 1864. From 1873 until his death from leprosy (Hansen's disease) in 1889, he devoted his life to tending the lepers of Kalaupapa (see pages 116–117).

▶ East–West Center — 55D3

1601 East–West Road, Honolulu (tel: 808/944-7111; web: www.ewc.hawaii.edu)
Open: Mon–Fri 8–4:30. Admission free

Inaugurated to promote relations between the U.S. and Asian-Pacific nations, the East–West Center's chief attraction is its setting on the University of Hawaii campus at Manoa. The Imin Conference Center was designed by I.M. Pei, architect of the pyramid at the Louvre in Paris. Also on the campus is the Thai Pavilion donated by the King of Thailand, and the Center for Korean Studies, inspired by the Kyongbok Palace in Seoul.

▶▶ Foster Botanical Garden — 54B2

50 North Vineyard Boulevard, Downtown (tel: 808/533-6335)
Open: daily 9–4. Tours Mon–Fri at 1.
Admission: inexpensive. Bus 4; Waikiki Trolley Stop 11

In 1853, William Hillebrand, a young German doctor, leased this leafy 14-acre plot from the Crown, built a home, and planted several of the exotic trees that tower over visitors today. Look for the explosive flowers of the cannonball tree, the panama-hat tree, specialty orchids, heliconias, palms, ferns, and the boulder-strewn Prehistoric Glen.

▶▶▶ Hawaii Maritime Center — 54B1

Pier 7, Honolulu Harbor (tel: 808/536-6373)
Open: daily 9–5. Admission: moderate. Bus 19, 20, 55, 56, 57; Waikiki Trolley Stop 7; free parking

Start a visit to this world-class maritime museum with an audio-guided tour of the main hall (personal stereos provided). Exhibits trace the islands' seagoing history, from early Polynesian rafts to the heyday of steamships, by way of models and all manner of nautical knick-knacks. Beside the museum is the restored *Falls of Clyde*, the world's last fully rigged, four-masted sailing vessel. Built in Glasgow in 1878, it once plied the San Francisco–Honolulu route.

▶▶ Honolulu Academy of Arts — 54B2

900 South Beretania Street, Downtown (tel: 808/532-8100)
Open: Tue–Sat 10–4:30, Sun 1–5.
Admission: moderate. Bus 2; Waikiki Trolley Stop 5

Housed in a charming, 1927 Mediterranean-style building, the Academy is a pleasure to explore. The Asian section, including author James Michener's collection of Japanese *ukiyo-e* prints, is one of the finest in the U.S. Notable Western artworks include paintings by Picasso, Gauguin, and Van Gogh, plus sculptures by Rodin. The popular Garden Café here is well worth a visit (see page 199).

The Hawaii Maritime Center creates a vivid picture of Hawaii's maritime past

LEGEND OF DIAMOND HEAD

The Hawaiian name for Diamond Head is Leahi ("Brow of the Ahi"). Ancient Hawaiian legends say it was named by the fire goddess Hiiaka, who thought it resembled the profile of a yellowfin tuna (*ahi*). The Hawaiians venerated the site and constructed a *heiau* (temple) here, probably on the western slopes. Kamehameha I is reputed to have both worshiped at the temple site and, after his victory over Oahu's chieftain Kalanikupule, at the Battle of Nuuanu Valley in 1795, presided over some of the last human sacrifices in Hawaii.

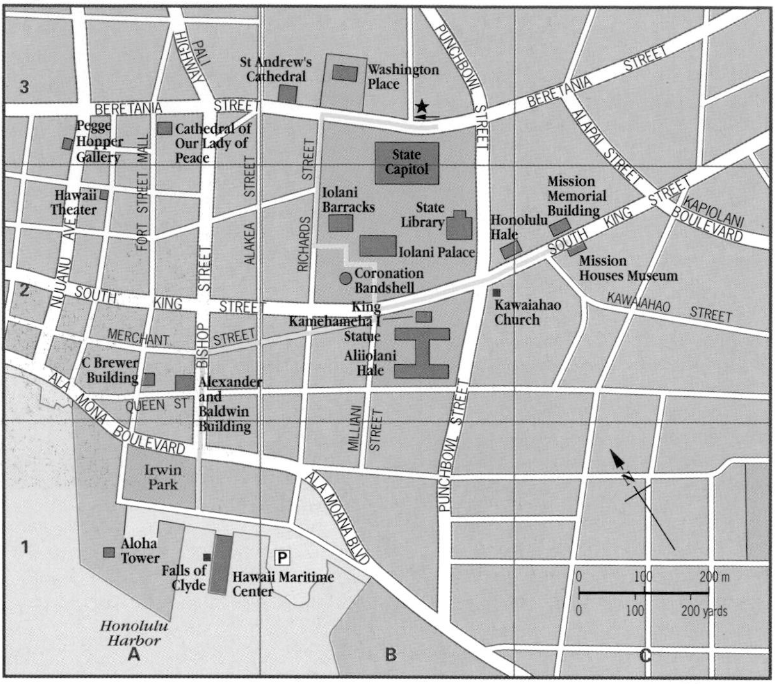

Walk

Historic Honolulu

This walk offers a full half-day of sightseeing through the historic heart of downtown Honolulu. If you want to include a visit to the Iolani Palace, do remember to make reservations in advance (see page 62).

Start at the **State Capitol** (from Waikiki take Bus 2 or Waikiki Trolley Stop 6 to South Beretania Street). Surrounded by a moat and flanked by pillars that represent palm trees, the 1969 Capitol building gathers its architectural inspiration from Hawaii's volcanic origins. A striking 600,000-tile mosaic in shades of ocean blues dominates the central courtyard. From the Capitol, head across Beretania Street to **Washington Place**, an elegant Greek Revival mansion of the 1840s that was built by Queen Liliuokalani's in-laws. It now houses the governor's official residence.

St. Andrew's Cathedral

A resplendent Kamehameha the Great

Next to Washington Place, the neo-Gothic **St. Andrew's Cathedral** was built in the 19th century, partially from stone cut in England and then shipped around the Horn. Above the porch a stained-glass window depicts the church's founders, King Kamehameha IV and Queen Emma. From here, take Richards Street, across from Washington Place, to the side entrance into the grounds of the **Iolani Palace**. A royal palace for 10 years from 1882 until it was stormed by U.S. troops in 1893, ending the monarchy, it takes its name from the Hawaiian for "Hawk of Heaven," the highest symbol of royal authority. The American Florentine-style building has been carefully restored and furnished with many original pieces (see page 62).

Leave from the Iolani's main gate and turn left along South King Street, crossing Punchbowl Street. On the left, the Mediterranean Revival-style city hall, **Honolulu Hale**, was opened in 1929. Farther along King Street, and used as a City Hall annex, is the gracious red-brick **Mission Memorial Building**, its façade lined with elegant white columns beneath a triangular tympanum. Built in honor of the New England missionaries, the Mission Memorial faces the original Sandwich Islands Mission buildings, now a museum.

Cross King Street to the **Mission Houses Museum**, the oldest surviving Western-style buildings in the islands. The buildings were erected by New England missionaries here at the headquarters of the Sandwich Islands Mission, and offer a fascinating insight into life in the islands from the 1820s to the end of the missionary era (see page 64).

Leave the museum and cross Kawaiahao Street to the churchyard gate of **Kawaiahao Church** (see page 63). Though the missionaries arrived in Honolulu in 1820, the construction of this Protestant church was not completed until 1842.

If you have had enough exploring for one day, Waikiki Trolley Stop 13 is across the street. If not, walk west along King Street to the **Kamehameha Statue** across from the Iolani Palace. Set on the lawn in front of the Aliiolani Hale, this replica gold-caped statue of Kamehameha I is a famous downtown landmark (the original remains are on Kamehameha's home island of Hawaii).

Now take Merchant Street on the far side of the Aliiolani Hale, off Milliani Street, walk the two blocks to Bishop Street, then turn left and continue to the **Alexander and Baldwin Building** at 822 Bishop Street. This venerable building belongs to one of Hawaii's "Big Five" trading companies. Admire its splendid carvings, glazed tiles depicting Hawaiian marine life, and the plethora of oriental motifs.

Continue down Bishop Street to the waterfront. To the right, the **Aloha Tower Marketplace** offers shopping, eateries, and great views from the tower itself (see page 56). To the left is the excellent **Hawaii Maritime Center** (see page 59), opposite Waikiki Trolley Stop 7.

IOLANI BARRACKS
Within the Iolani Palace grounds lies the Iolani Barracks building, a toytown castle with mini crenellated battlements and arrow slits, which now houses the ticket kiosk, visitor center, and a gift shop piled high with Hawaiiana. To the left of the palace façade, the Royal Coronation Bandstand, erected for the coronation of King David Kalakaua and Queen Kapiolani in 1883, now hosts free concerts by the Royal Hawaiian Band every Friday at 12:15. Behind the palace, a statue of Queen Liliuokalani honors Hawaii's last monarch.

►► Honolulu Zoo 55D1

151 Kapahulu Avenue, Waikiki (tel: 808/971-7171)
Open: daily 9–4:30. Admission: inexpensive; children under 5 free. Bus 4; Waikiki Trolley Stop 2

Honolulu Zoo occupies a 42-acre site in Kapiolani Park. The old-fashioned enclosures, currently being refurbished, are being phased out and replaced with natural habitat displays, such as the African Savannah area, with hippos and Nile crocodiles, antelopes, lions, giraffes, and chimps. The zoo is home to more than 1,250 animals, including giant Galapagos tortoises (the first bred in zoo conditions), kangaroos, and gibbons; there is a reptile house, plus the rare *nene* goose, Hawaii's state bird.

►►► Iolani Palace 54B2

South King Street, Downtown (tel: 808/522-0832)
Open: Wed–Sat 9–2:15 (no children under 5).
Admission: moderate. Bus 2; Waikiki Trolley Stop 6

Hailed as "America's only royal palace," the Iolani was founded in 1879 and completed three years later under the direction of King David Kalakaua, Hawaii's "Merrie Monarch." The palace has been restored and the koa-wood interior is full of grand furnishings, Bohemian crystal, French porcelain, and portraits of the Hawaiian kings and queens that recall King David's love affair with foreign royalty and its trappings. Guided tours (reservations are advised) reveal fascinating nuggets of royal history and palace gossip.

► Kapiolani Park 55D1

Kalakaua Avenue, Waikiki
Open site. Admission free. Bus 4; Waikiki Trolley Stop 2

When King David Kalakaua dedicated the park in his wife's name in 1877, he declared "this breezy plain a place of innocent refreshment for all who wish to leave the dust of the town streets." The 300-acre park east of the Waikiki hotel district is still a popular recreation area. The park is home to Waikiki Shell Honolulu Zoo and the Kodak *Hula* Show (see panel), and also hosts numerous events.

The Iolani Palace, completed at a cost of $360,000 in 1882

Kamaaina grannies join in the fun at the Kodak Hula Show...

▶ Kawaiahao Church 54B2

957 Punchbowl Street, Downtown (tel: 808/522-1333)
Open: daily 9–1, Services 8 and 10:30 AM Sunday
Admission free. Bus 2, 4; Waikiki Trolley Stop 13

Kawaiahao is built from blocks of coral rock—around 14,000 of them weighing some 1,000 pounds apiece. It was completed in 1842, on the site of the first Christian church, and services are still held there. Two prominent Hawaiians are interred in the graveyard: King William Lunalilo, the "People's King," and the Reverend James Kekela, Hawaii's first native Christian minister.

▶ Kuan Yin Temple 54B2

170 North Vineyard Boulevard, Downtown
Open: daily 8:30–2. Admission free
Bus 4; Waikiki Trolley Stop 11

The smell of incense wafting down the street near the Foster Botanical Garden greets you long before you catch sight of this ornate little temple, with its traditional curving roof, and red and gold trimmings. A statue of Kuan Yin, the Buddhist goddess of mercy, presides over the altar and carved and gilded pagodas contain the figures of many other deities.

▶▶▶ Lyon Arboretum 54C4

3860 Manoa Road, Honolulu (tel: 808/988-0456)
Open: Mon–Sat 9–3. Admission: donation

These glorious gardens lie tucked in a cleft of the Manoa Valley cliffs. Winding paths traverse steep hillsides and there is a Fern Valley en route to Inspiration Point, which affords splendid views over the flowering trees. The Aeroid Valley path leads to plantations of colorful gingers and heliconias. Touring the gardens is quite a hike in itself, but if you still feel energetic, the start of the Manoa Falls walk (see page 69) is near the arboretum's entrance.

... and their daughters show how it should be done

KODAK HULA SHOW

A Waikiki institution, this popular *hula* show has been running since 1937. It is still great fun, with the added bonus that it is free. Be sure to arrive early in summer since the line snakes around the park. (Kapiolani Park, Tue, Wed, and Thu at 10 AM.)

WAIOLI TEA ROOM
Feeling thirsty after a morning's trek around the Lyon Arboretum? Hungry after the hike to the Manoa Falls? On the road back to town, look for the intersection of Manoa Road and Oahu Avenue, where the Salvation Army's Waioli Tea Room (3016 Oahu Avenue, tel: 808/988-5800. *Open* Mon–Sat 9–4, Sun 12–4) serves salads and sandwiches, with tables on the veranda. You can also see the old grass shack in which author and traveler Robert Louis Stevenson is supposed to have lived during his stay in Waikiki in the 1880s.

UP IN THE HILLS
Anyone renting a car in Honolulu should explore the hills behind the city. From Puowaina Drive (the road up to Punchbowl Crater), Tantalus Drive winds its way up into the Koolau Mountains, changes its name to Round Top Drive, then makes a grand circuitous tour through the lush rain forest and classy residential heights of the city. There are several viewpoints, public paths, and hiking trails en route, and the Contemporary Museum (see page 57) makes a good lunch stop on the way back.

▶▶▶ Mission Houses Museum *54B2*

553 South King Street, Downtown (tel: 808/531-0481)
Open: Tue–Sat 9–4 (tours every hour 9:30–11:30 and 1–3), Sun 12–4 (tours every hour 1–3). Admission: moderate
Bus 2 from Waikiki; Waikiki Trolley Stop 13

When the first New England missionaries arrived in Hawaii in 1820, they established their headquarters here in Honolulu. This small group of historic buildings, its exhibits, and guided tours trace the lifestyle of the missionaries and their relationship with their native hosts. Among the period furnishings of the 1821 frame house, built of precut timber shipped from New England, is a rocking chair that belonged to Queen Kaahumanu, whose conversion to Christianity was a major coup for the mission brothers. The Hale Pai (printing office), completed in 1841, displays a working press that was used to print Hawaiian and English tracts and books.

▶▶ Punchbowl Crater National Memorial Cemetery of the Pacific *54B2*

2177 Puowaina Drive, Honolulu
Open: daily 8–5:30 (until 6:30 Mar 2–Sep 29). Admission free. Bus 2 to Beretania and Alapai streets, then Bus 15

The national cemetery, located in the crater of an extinct volcano whose name (Puowaina) means "Hill of Sacrifice," contains the graves of 25,000 servicemen and women who fought in World War II, Korea, and Vietnam. The site is dominated by the Columbia Memorial, where the Courts of the Missing flanking the monumental staircase list a further 26,000 military personnel whose bodies were never recovered. Behind the 30-foot-high statue of Columbia is a chapel, and galleries on either side illustrate major World War II battles in the Pacific.

A road leads up from the cemetery to a lookout point that affords spectacular views from Pearl Harbor across Waikiki to Diamond Head.

The Columbia Statue at Punchbowl Crater National Memorial Cemetery of the Pacific

"Suitably masked and flippered, the bride wore a white one-piece, while the groom was attired in tuxedo and board shorts. After the ceremony, the happy pair swam away to a reception held aboard a 65-foot pirate schooner, accompanied by the priest, his parrots, and 15 close friends." It could only happen in Hawaii.

The big day Hawaii's wedding industry is booming. Around 43 percent of the marriages performed in the state are for visitors from the mainland or overseas, and providing both partners are over 18 and hold a valid Hawaiian marriage license (see panel), getting married in Hawaii is easy. Most large hotels have their own wedding coordinator, and offer special packages with extras such as a champagne breakfast in bed or a sunset sail for the newlyweds.

Pirates and *paniolo* On Oahu, the Reverend Howie Welfeld of **Above Heaven's Gate** (tel: 808/259-5429; web: www.hawaiiweddings.com) is a big fan of alfresco weddings in what he calls "the Lord's Outdoor Cathedral"; couples employing his services can tie the knot on his schooner *Lotus Flower* or even under water! At **Kualoa Ranch** (tel: 800/231-7321; web: www.kualoa.com), the happy pair can head off *paniolo*-style (cowboy-style) into the Koolau Mountains with a blue-jeaned minister for a short ceremony followed by a barbecue reception.

Surfboards to temples On Kauai, **Wedding in Paradise** (tel: 808/246-2779; www.paradiseservices.com) are the local experts. On Maui, options include a surfboard ceremony orchestrated by **Royal Hawaiian Weddings** (tel: 800/659-1866; www.mauiweddings.com), or weddings at a Tibetan temple arranged by **A Wedding Made in Paradise** (tel: 808/879-3444 or 800/453-3440). On the Big Island, **Paradise Weddings Hawaii** (tel: 808/883-9067 or 800/428-5844) fulfills the motto "Intimate to Outrageous" by organizing weddings in helicopters and submarines, on horseback, or even on Harley Davidson motorcycles.

For most couples, however, a traditional wedding in a Hawaiian setting is the order of the day. And for Hawaii's professional wedding organizers, no wedding is too big or too small, too grand or too simple, or even too weird!

MARRIAGE RULES

Hawaiian marriage licenses can be purchased from the Department of Health, Marriage License Office (1250 Punchbowl Street, Honolulu, HI 96813), or from a marriage licensing agent on any of the Neighbor Islands (details available from hotels and from wedding organizers). A birth certificate, driver's license, or some other form of identification will be required. The names and birthplaces of both partners' parents must be filled in on the form. If either partner has been married before, he or she must state the date, county, and state (or country) in which the divorce was finalized.

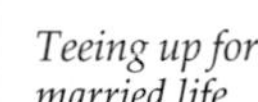

Teeing up for married life

Queen Emma Summer Palace in the hills above Honolulu

KAMEHAMEHA IV
The high regard in which Kamehameha IV held British royalty dated from a trip he made to Europe as a young prince in 1849–1850. A stop in England resulted in a meeting with Queen Victoria, who later agreed to be a godmother to his son, Albert Edward (named after Victoria's husband Prince Albert). On returning to Hawaii via the U.S., the 15-year-old prince was mistaken for a black servant and ejected from his train carriage by the conductor. The incident left a lasting impression, and Kamehameha IV consistently favored British interests over those of the U.S.

▶▶ Queen Emma Summer Palace *54B3*

2913 Pali Highway (tel: 808/595-3167)
Open: daily 9–4. Admission: moderate. Bus 4 from Kuhio Avenue
This modest summer retreat, perched on the Nuuanu hillside with its shuttered windows aligned to catch the slightest breeze, is a short drive from downtown Honolulu. The materials for the two-bedroom wooden home were shipped from Boston in the mid-1800s, and the Victorian furnishings include memorabilia of the British royal family, with whom Queen Emma and her husband, Kamehameha IV, maintained a cordial if long-distance acquaintanceship.

▶ Royal Mausoleum *54B3*

Nuuanu Avenue, Honolulu. Open site. Admission free
During Kamehameha V's reign, the royal graveyard in the grounds of what is now Iolani Palace was deemed overcrowded, so the burial site was moved to the lower reaches of the Nuuanu Valley in 1865. All the Kamehameha kings except Kamehameha I are buried in this attractive plot, as are King David Kalakaua and Queen Liliuokalani.

▶▶ U.S. Army Museum of Hawaii *55D1*

Fort de Russy, Kalia Road, Waikiki (tel: 808/438-2822)
Open: Tue–Sun 10–4:30. Admission free (charge for audio tours)
This well-laid-out and informative museum is housed in a former coastal artillery battery. Tours begin with an introduction to Hawaiian history and warfare. Alongside other assorted Hawaiiana are a selection of vicious-looking barbed spears and *pua*-wood clubs inset with sharks' teeth.

Photographs, memorabilia, models, and video presentations detail World War II in the Pacific, with coverage of the Pearl Harbor attack and the exploits of the famous AJA (Americans of Japanese Ancestry) battalion, which saw action in Europe, North Africa, and the Pacific. Further exhibits turn to more recent conflicts in Korea and Vietnam.

▶▶ USS *Arizona* Memorial *50C1*

Pearl Harbor (Exit 15A from H-1 West) (tel: 808/422-0561)
Open: Visitor Center, daily 7:30–5; daily programs, Sep–May

8–3, Jun–Aug 7:45–3. Admission free. Bus 20 and 47 from Waikiki direct; or 8, 19, or 58 to Ala Moana Center and transfer to 48, 49, 50, or 52

At 07:55 on December 7, 1941, two waves of Japanese fighter-bombers dropped out of the sky above Oahu and pulverized the American war machine massed on the "Gibraltar of the Pacific." The catalog of military gaffes—planes parked wingtip to wingtip, and disarmed at night to prevent sabotage—defies belief, and the losses were catastrophic. President Roosevelt described it as a "day of infamy," and the attack brought the U.S. into World War II.

The USS *Arizona* sank at her moorings on Battleship Row, and 1,102 members of her crew rest with her on the bottom of Pearl Harbor. The memorial was dedicated on May 30, 1962, to all service personnel killed in action during the attack. Visits to the striking white concrete structure that spans the 106-foot-wide and 608-foot-long hull begin at the *Arizona* Memorial Center on the dock. After a film presentation, which includes clippings from prewar newsreels as well as actual footage shot during and after the attack, there is a boat trip out to the memorial. The full visit takes approximately 75 minutes, and tickets are issued on a first-come-first-served basis. Arrive early to avoid crowds. The Visitor Center has basic refreshment facilities and information.

SALVAGED SHIPS

From the film footage and photographs showing the aftermath of the Japanese attack on Pearl Harbor, it is hard to believe that anything could have been salvaged from the scrapheap of twisted metal, shattered masonry, and burning hulks. Amazingly, all but three (the USS *Arizona, Oklahoma,* and *Utah*) of the 130 vessels in the harbor at the time of the attack were salvaged and later saw action. Much of the damage to the base was superficial, and fortunately the Pacific Fleet's vital aircraft carriers were not in port.

▶ USS *Missouri* Memorial *50C1*

Pearl Harbor (Exit 15A from H-1 West) (tel: 808/423-2263 or 1-888/877-6477; web: www.ussmissouri.com). Open: daily 9-5, 1 hour tours. Admission: moderate.

On September 2, 1945, the 58,000 ton USS *Missouri*, the last battleship built by the U.S. Navy, hosted the historic surrender ceremony in Tokyo Bay ending World War II. She was mothballed but then reactivated, and saw service as recently as the Gulf War, but was retired again in 1992. In 1999, the 887-foot "Mighty Mo" was towed to Hawaii, moored near the USS *Arizona* Memorial, and opened to the public.

The roll call of servicemen lost in the Pearl Harbor attack in 1941

The memorial building above the sunken USS Arizona

The USS Bowfin *at Pearl Harbor*

►► USS *Bowfin* Submarine Museum and Park 50C2

11 Arizona Memorial Drive, Pearl Harbor
Open: daily 8–5. Admission: moderate. Bus 20 and 47 from Waikiki direct; or 8, 19, or 58 to Ala Moana Center and transfer to 48, 49, 50, or 52

This museum makes a welcome harborside diversion for visitors to the *Arizona* Memorial who may have a wait between ticket collection and access to the center. It gives a history of submarines and tours of an actual World War II submarine, and visitors can have a free stroll around its missile garden park.

The waterfront park positively bristles with hardware, from torpedo shells and gun batteries to an amputated conning tower and a captured Japanese suicide submarine. From the dock, you can go below deck into the cramped confines of the USS *Bowfin*, nicknamed the "Pearl Harbor Avenger" for her role in sinking 44 enemy vessels during nine tours of duty.

Waikiki Aquarium and Sea Life Park both provide a fascinating window on the tropical waters of Hawaii

►►► Waikiki Aquarium 55D1

2777 Kalakaua Avenue, Waikiki (tel: 808/923-9741)
Open: daily 9–5. Admission: moderate (children under 12 free)

The third-oldest public aquarium in the U.S. (founded 1904) lies right on the ocean shore and is just the place to come to grips with the exotic marine life of the Hawaiian Islands and South Pacific. Indoor and outdoor exhibits bring visitors face to face with denizens of the deep and not-so-deep, and interactive displays track the journeys of marine creatures across the Pacific to Hawaii.

Here you can meet the endangered Hawaiian monk seal, investigate the myriad life forms of the coral reef at the Reef Machine exhibit, and ogle the predatory sharks at Hunters on the Reef. Then take in a couple of shows at the SeaVisions Theater and learn about the life cycle of the *mahimahi* (dolphin fish) at the Mahimahi Hatchery, before trawling The Natural Selection gift shop for fishy gifts and other marine-related souvenirs.

Walks

Two short walks around Honolulu

These two walks in the hills above Waikiki are easily accessible from Honolulu. They take in beautiful views, colorful trees and flowers, and glimpses of native birdlife.

Manoa Falls

This short but worthwhile hike through the lush hillsides of Mount Tantalus will take only an hour or so for the round trip, and begins at the top of Manoa Road, just beyond the Lyon Arboretum. A pair of sensible shoes and good mosquito repellent are advisable.

From the road, the marked path leads into the cool, verdant woodlands. At the first fork in the path, keep left and then navigate the main stream with the help of stepping stones. The trail clambers through the woods across a chaos of mossy boulders and twisted tree roots edged by ferns. A massive exposed network of roots serves as a slippery stairway before the path narrows, traverses a bamboo copse on duckboards, and winds up to the base of the falls, which cascade down the bare cliff face in a plume of white foaming water.

Waahila Ridge

This trail makes another short walk above Honolulu, beginning from the Waahila Ridge State Recreation Area up in St. Louis Heights. Take St. Louis Drive and Peter Street up to Ruth Place, and park in the State Recreation Area. It can get very hot and breezy up here, so bring water and sunscreen.

From the parking lot, the first leg of the hike is a strenuous 10-minute uphill climb through the ironwood forest. Then the trail alternately scales the peaks and plunges down the troughs of the narrow, 2-mile ridge top. There are bird's-eye views across the Manoa and Palolo valleys on either side, but some of the prettiest things to be seen are the colorful wild flowers that grow in abundance up here. In addition to the blankets of miniature passion-flower vines, hibiscus-like yellow-orange *ilima* flowers, and tuffets of spiky purple valerian, there are tunnels of gnarled trees tortured into bizarre shapes by the wind.

Manoa Falls

Souvenir city: Waikiki's International Marketplace

Shopping

The shop-'til-you-drop contingent will find plenty of fun in the malls, markets, galleries, and gift shops of Waikiki and Honolulu.

Waikiki Waikiki's Kalakaua Avenue is the home of two major shopping places: the **Royal Hawaiian Shopping Center**, whose three buildings are filled with 150 designer boutiques, discount stores, perfumeries, T-shirt outlets, and dining places; and the six-story **Waikiki Shopping Plaza**. Just down the block, the **International Marketplace** spreads its wares over a collection of open-air stalls beneath a banyan tree. This merchandise is strictly kitsch, but is still good for a browse. On **Kalakaua Avenue**, you can upgrade your luggage at Louis Vuitton, drop in on Chanel, and check out the latest designer-wear from Italy.

Honolulu Outside Waikiki, just across the Ala Wai Canal, Honolulu's biggest and best mall, the **Ala Moana Center**, contains 200-plus stores and Hawaii's largest food hall. The well-known department stores—Sears, J.C. Penney, and the Hawaiian chain store Liberty House—are here, as well as designer outlets and souvenir sellers. Closer to downtown, the **Ward Center** (1200 Ala Moana Boulevard), and neighboring **Ward Warehouse** (1050 Ala Moana Boulevard), with a more arts and crafts bias, both offer shopping, dining, and easy access via the Waikiki Trolley route (Stop 17).

Downtown's latest shopping area is the attractive, harborfront **Aloha Tower Marketplace** complex, where the inevitable boutiques are augmented by elegant household shops selling Hawaiian quilts and furnishings crafted from native woods. Farther west, the **Chinatown** district offers a cornucopia of Asian shops and markets, plus recently rediscovered and cleaned-up **Nuuanu Avenue**, nicknamed "Gallery Row," which is a showcase for Hawaii's vibrant contemporary arts scene.

KAMAKA ALL

What have Tiny Tim, Laurel and Hardy, astronaut Scott Carpenter, and just about every celebrated Hawaiian slack key guitarist got in common? They have all owned a Kamaka ukulele. These *koa*-wood Stradivariuses of the ukulele world are handcrafted by the family firm of Kamaka Hawaii, Inc., under the direction of the sons and grandsons of its founder, Sam Kamaka Sr., who turned out the first Kamaka ukes from the basement of his home in 1916. Kamaka ukulele are on sale in good music shops, and aficionados are always dropping in for a chat at the family factory at 550 South Street, Honolulu.

Arts and crafts For high-quality Hawaiian-made souvenirs of the arts and crafts variety, the best choice and some of the fairest prices are often found in museum gift shops throughout the islands. The **Iolani Palace, Mission Houses Museum**, and **Bishop Museum** all offer a selection of *kukui*-nut jewelry, Hawaiian quilting kits, *koa*-wood carvings, Hawaiian books, and specialty guides. The Iolani Palace is particularly good on things royal; the Mission Houses Museum sells Hawaiian foodstuffs such as coffee and tropical fruit jellies, as well as inexpensive prints produced from period plates on the original mission press; and the **Honolulu Academy of Arts** shop sells all sorts of handicrafts by local artists, including pottery and glassware.

Clothes Probably the most classic Hawaiian souvenir is the *aloha* shirt. This boxy, short-sleeved tradition introduced in the 1930s is on sale everywhere, from the hotel foyer to hippie beach stalls. The female equivalent, the sacklike *muumuu*, is also a popular buy. **Hilo Hattie** has become a byword in the islands for the greatest choice of *aloha* wear, general resort-style clothing, and good souvenirs; there is a store at Ala Moana, while the Honolulu branch provides free transportation from Waikiki, and is on the Waikiki Trolley route (Stop 9). Another tourist shopping spot is the **Maui Divers' Jewelry Design Center**, which specializes in jewelry made from Hawaiian coral and shells (Waikiki Trolley Stop 4). If you want to buy your *aloha* wear from the same places that the locals buy theirs, try the **J. C. Penney, Liberty House** or **Reyn's** chain stores. Alternatively, for vintage (and expensive) *aloha* shirts go to **Bailey's**.

A Taste of Hawaii Macadamia nuts, a local specialty, are widely available. So are jams, jellies, and preserves made from guavas, pineapples, and mangoes, and coffee from the Big Island's Kona Coast. You'll find these items in gift stores, though better deals can be found in supermarkets, and Long's Drugs (a chain of discount stores).

LOOKING FOR *LEI*?
Then make tracks for Chinatown's Maunakea Street. Here, dozens of shops and street stalls offer the best choice of *lei* in town, from the intricate and rare to the simply fragrant. Maunakea Street is also the place to buy tropical blooms such as gingers, anthuriums, proteas, and orchids. Several flower shops can arrange delivery to the mainland U.S.

Honolulu's malls are filled with designer shops and U.S. stores

TOP ENTERTAINMENTS
Keep an eye out for acts such as the excellent singing duo The Brothers Cazimero, who play at various venues; crooner Don Ho at the Waikiki Beachcomber, (tel: 808/923-3981); and others such as Hapa, Olomana, Kapena, and the Makaha Sons. Comedian Frank De Lima plays at the Hawaiian Waikiki Beach Hotel (tel: 808/922-2511); and the pick of local and mainland entertainment can be seen at the restored Hawaii Theatre (tel: 808/528-0506).

Nightlife

As yet another spectacular tropical sunset turns the Pacific horizon to fire, the *mai-tais* begin to flow,the bands tune up, and the great Waikiki entertainment scene shifts into high gear for another night on the town. Among the entertainment possibilities are cabaret and dinner shows, Hawaiian *luau*, dance clubs, comedy clubs, and karaoke lounges where the patrons noisily provide the entertainment. Weekly listings of diversions on offer are published in the Friday edition of the *Honolulu Advertiser*, and in free publications such as *This Week* and *Honolulu Weekly* (widely available in hotel lobbies and on the street). The latter are also a good source of discount entry and free drinks coupons.

A little cocktail music For a sundowner accompanied by ocean views and a little local music, the classiest spot on "The Strip" must be the Halekulani Hotel's **House Without a Key** (2199 Kalia Road, tel: 808/923-2311), which has some of the best old-style Hawaiian music on the island. The upscale **Sheraton-Waikiki** (2255 Kalakaua Avenue, tel: 808/922-4422; www.sheraton-waikiki.com) features local singer-musicians in three bars and *hula* at the poolside; and there is always an entertaining show at the **Hilton Hawaiian Village's** open-air **Tapa Bar** (2005 Kalia Road, tel: 808/949-4321; web: www.hilton.com).

For something a little more lively, whoop it up with margaritas and tortilla chips at **Compadres Bar & Grill** (Building 3, Ward Center, 1200 Ala Moana Boulevard, Honolulu, tel: 808/591-8307).

Dinner shows and *luau* Polynesian-style dinner shows are perennial favorites with visitors to Oahu, and probably the most impressive on the beach is the

Party time Polynesian-style in Waikiki

entertaining **Sheraton Princess Kaiulani's Polynesian Revue** (120 Kaiulani Avenue, tel: 808/971-5300), with earlybird and 8 PM seatings. **Waikiki Beachcomber's** (2300 Kalakaua Avenue, tel: 808/971-4321) is a good family show with the added attraction of magician John Hirokawa, while the **Outrigger Main Showroom** (2335 Kalakaua Avenue, tel: 808/922-6408) features the Society of Seven show band, which spices up its act with impressions and comedy routines.

Out of town, on the Windward Coast, the **Polynesian Cultural Center** (Kamehameha Highway, Laie, tel: 808/293-3333) offers the most spectacular revue of them all with a cast of hundreds.

Terrible liberties have been taken with the traditional Hawaiian *luau* (see pages 16–17), and vacationers expecting a genuine Hawaiian experience may well be disappointed. Yet commercial *luau*, accompanied by music and *hula*, are very popular with people who enjoy a crowd. Oahu's leading *luau* operations are **Paradise Cove Luau** (tel: 808/842-5911) and **Germaine's Luau** (tel: 808/949-6626).

Dance the night away At the top end of the market is the chic **Aaron's Atop the Ala Moana** (Ala Moana Hotel, 410 Atkinson Drive, tel: 808/955-4466), where visiting celebrities go. **Rumours** (Ala Moana Hotel, 410 Atkinson Drive, Honolulu, tel: 808/955-4811), stays open until 4 AM every Friday and Saturday. **Studebaker's** (500 Ala Moana Boulevard, Honolulu, tel: 808/526-9888) is in Restaurant Row. If you prefer dancing in the old-fashioned way to music from the 1940s, 1950s, and 1960s, try the **Esprit Lounge** (Sheraton Waikiki Hotel, 2255 Kalakaua Avenue, tel: 808/922-4422), where the resident band covers a wide and impressive range of rock, disco, and big-band favorites from these decades.

Honolulu is one of the biggest cities in the U.S. and at night it certainly looks it

HONOLULU SYMPHONY ORCHESTRA

The Honolulu Symphony Orchestra strikes a more classical note from its base at the Neal Blaisdell Concert Hall, 777 Ward Avenue, Honolulu (box office, tel: 808/591-2211; administration office, tel: 808/527-5400). The symphony's August–May season covers a wide range of classical music and pop, and also hosts Hawaiian artists and special holiday concerts. Outdoor concerts at the Waikiki Shell in Kapiolani Park are a favorite summer feature.

Kau-kau *wagon*

THE PLATE LUNCH
A typical Hawaiian hybrid, the plate lunch is said to have its origins in World War II, when lunch wagons trundled around feeding workers on site. These cramped portable kitchens, known as *kau-kau* wagons, still exist, parked in city lots or down at the beach. They dish up plates of *teriyaki* beef and/or chicken, barbecue ribs, a fish dish such as *mahimahi* (dolphin fish), macaroni salad, and the requisite "two scoops rice." The plate lunch is generally no culinary masterpiece, but it is fast, filling, and inexpensive.

Waterfront dining

Eating and drinking

Honolulu's eclectic restaurant scene leaves very few gastronomic stones unturned. You can eat your way around the globe, from China to California, a pizza to Pacific Rim (see panel), Creole to continental, and Thai to Tex-Mex, all within a short walk of most hotel lobbies. The choice often starts in the hotel itself with, for example, a courtyard café, a seafood grill, and a chic dining room serving French, Italian, or New American/Pacific Rim cuisine.

Home cooking The most difficult ethnic cuisine to find amid this wealth of international influences is authentic Hawaiian food. Several commercial *luau* and dinner shows (see page 72) offer tame Hawaiian dishes with distinctly American trimmings, but visitors who want the real thing in Waikiki should try chef Gary Strehl's excellent Hawaiian buffet at the **Hawaii Prince Hotel**. Alternatively, for home cooking, Honolulu's best local restaurant is **Ono Hawaiian Foods** (see page 199), where you can enjoy a mountainous plate lunch (see panel).

Asian influences The greatest influence on the local cuisine after all-American is Japanese. *Teriyaki* beef, *teriyaki* chicken, *teriyaki* fish, even *teriyaki* hamburgers, are tried and tested island favorites, though some palates may find meat treated this way cloyingly sweet. *Sushi* is also popular, as is *saimin*, a Japanese clear soup made with noodles, scallions, and fish or meat.

Chinese cuisine is also a strong influence. Chinatown is obviously the place to go if you want authentic *dim sum*. There are also good Chinese restaurants in Waikiki, and Korean, Vietnamese, and Thai restaurants are also well represented.

Where to go Most major hotels offer a choice of dining options, from buffets and family-style eateries to elegant candle-lit "signature" restaurants. Shopping centers are a good source of affordable restaurants and snack stops. The **Ala Moana Center's Makai Market** food court has 18 eateries serving up a diverse range of cuisines. The **Royal Hawaiian Shopping Center** in Waikiki, and the **Ward Center** and **Ward Warehouse** on Ala Moana Boulevard also provide a successful mixture of shops and restaurants. The **Aloha Tower Marketplace** enjoys a waterfront setting; and Honolulu's **Restaurant Row** is nearby at the downtown end of Ala Moana.

Several of Waikiki's top hotels combine superior cuisine with enviably romantic settings. A table on the terrace overlooking the ocean at the Halekulani Hotel's **Orchids** restaurant should ensure an unforgettable evening; or, if you are really feeling extravagant, try the sumptuous **La Mer**, in the same hotel, or **Hoku's** at the Kahala Mandarin Oriental.

What to expect On the whole, restaurant dress in Hawaii is casual, although one or two restaurants request that men wear a jacket. Reservations are advisable at all good restaurants. Most restaurants have smoking and non-smoking sections, so make your preference clear when booking. Service is rarely included on the bill; a 15 percent tip is the norm.

Thirsty work There is nothing quite like a day on the beach for building up a thirst, and Waikiki boasts hundreds of drinking venues, from pool bars to pubs. Most serve cocktails, American and imported beers, and Californian wines at resort prices. Local bars are often more reasonably priced than hotels, although daily specials and Happy Hours offer a few bargains, and every decent Hawaiian bar should offer a selection of *pupu* (bar snacks).

PACIFIC RIM CUISINE
Hawaiian regional cuisine, as it is often known in the islands, draws its inspiration from Hawaii, Asia, and Europe, marrying fresh local ingredients with cooking styles from around the world. Renowned local chefs include Peter Merriman, Roy Yamaguchi, Alan Wong, and Jean-Marie Josselin.

Genuine luau *are hard to find*

Turn-of-the-century elegance at the Sheraton Moana Surfrider

Accommodations

With well over 90 hotels providing around 30,000 hotel rooms, Waikiki offers its visitors a tremendous choice of accommodations ranging from relaxed family-style facilities, quiet "boutique" hotels, and condominiums with full kitchens to luxurious beachfront properties.

On the one hand, there is the Hilton Hawaiian Village's resort within a resort, boasting over 3,000 rooms in five separate high-rise buildings in a complex of pools, bars, restaurants, and entertainment areas. At the opposite end of the scale are intimate "boutique" hotels with elegant surroundings but few facilities.

Although nowhere in Waikiki is more than a 10-minute walk from the beach, location is important and, not surprisingly, accommodations on the beach command higher rates. An unimpeded panorama of the sparkling Pacific from an oceanfront room adds between 10 and 15 percent to the price of an identical room with a garden or mountain (inland) view.

Peak-season rates run from mid-December to March, with slight variations on either side. Some hotels also raise their prices during the June–August summer season. And remember Hawaii's 10 percent room tax.

Value for money Waikiki hotels are seldom a bargain, and there are no chain motels to soften the blow for budget travelers. However, most of the hotels offer competitive package rates for stays of a week or more, including extras such as car rental. Check what is on offer with a knowledgeable travel agent. Many larger hotel groups, such as the Hilton, Sheraton, and the islands' own Outrigger and Aston groups (with 20 and eight hotels in Waikiki respectively), have toll-free reservations numbers in the mainland U.S.

The Hawaii Prince Hotel rises up behind Ala Wai Yacht Harbor in Honolulu

Every major hotel has a swimming pool for catching a few rays and working on that tan

Make sure the hotel's facilities will suit your needs. Most hotel rooms are equipped with air-conditioning, T.V., and phone, and nonsmoking rooms are usually available on request. A swimming pool, different dining options, and an activities desk providing advice on local sights and tours are frequently available, as well as children's programs and free evening entertainment.

Condominiums Waikiki's wide range of condominium accommodations are an attractive option if you are staying for awhile, and for families and groups of friends. These privately owned apartments are usually part of a high-rise development that may or may not offer facilities such as a pool, concierge, and maid service. Minimum stay is usually three to seven days, particularly during the peak season. The Hawaii Visitors and Convention Bureau can supply a comprehensive list of its member properties throughout the islands (see page 192). A number of moderately priced hotels offer efficiencies (hotel rooms equipped with basic cooking facilities), another money-saving option.

Beyond Waikiki Although Waikiki offers the greatest choice of accommodations, there are alternatives to The Strip. Just 5 miles east of Waikiki is the **Kahala Mandarin Oriental** (see page 195), a luxurious beachfront retreat with dolphins swimming in a lagoon; and there is golf, tennis, and riding at the **Turtle Bay Hilton & Country Club**, on the windward coast at Kahuku (see page 195). Peace and quiet are promised at the **J. W. Marriott Ihilani Resort & Spa** on the leeward coast, which has deluxe facilities, a championship golf course, tennis courts, watersports, three restaurants, and shopping (see page 195). Look for more affordable bed-and-breakfast accommodations on the windward coast.

COLONIAL AND ATMOSPHERIC

For style that stands out by a mile, there are two *grandes dames* of the Waikiki hotel scene. The senior is the elegant, colonial-style Sheraton Moana Surfrider, built in 1901 around a banyan-shaded courtyard, where the well-heeled patrons take afternoon tea or a cocktail on the veranda. The rival Royal Hawaiian, a splendid, overelaborate Spanish Moorish Revival edifice built in 1927, has been nicknamed the "Pink Palace" because of its rosy paintwork. This former playground of Douglas Fairbanks and Mary Pickford still offers some of the best dinner shows and most fabulously decorated public rooms in town.

SPECIALIZED TOURS
Several other types of tours are available on Oahu in addition to bus trips. In Honolulu, Punchbowl Walking Tours (tel: 808/946-6383) offers a historical stroll around Hawaii's top visitor attraction, the National Memorial Cemetery of the Pacific. For an overview of the whole island from Diamond Head to the inaccessible mountain back-country, nothing beats the bird's-eye view from a seaplane run by Island Seaplane Service (tel:808/836-6273: email: seaplane@lava.net).

Practicalities

Airport transfers Honolulu International Airport lies a 15-minute drive northwest of downtown and 30 minutes from Waikiki. The international and interisland terminals are linked by the free **WikiWiki Shuttle**. Reasonably priced **buses** to Waikiki hotels depart every 20 minutes or so from the median strip outside the arrivals areas. Round-trip tickets are available; the Waikiki–airport trip should be reserved 24 hours in advance. There is always a plentiful supply of **taxis**, including capacious family-size limousines.

Car rental All the major car-rental companies have offices at the airport and many are found in Waikiki. For further details, see pages 184–185.

Crime Sadly, crime does exist in paradise, but the main danger for tourists is petty theft, so do not carry large amounts of cash; do not leave valuables unattended on the beach or in easily identifiable rental cars; and keep to brightly lit streets after dark.

The Bus and the Waikiki Trolley Honolulu and all of Oahu has the best public transportation service in the islands. "**The Bus**" serves 65 routes covering most of the island, and it is a bargain. Buses stop only at marked bus stops, and the number and destination are written on the front. One-price tickets (there is a reduction for students, and children under six go free) are issued on board and cover single continuous trips in one general direction, including transfers (tell the bus driver your destination). Payment must be made with exact money; no change is given. For specific route information, tel: 808/848-5555 between 5:30 AM and 10 PM; for recorded information on how to get to more than 50 top attractions and places of interest, tel: 808/296-1818, followed by code 8287.

The touristy **Waikiki Trolley**, though hardly a bargain, is convenient and easy to use. These open-sided, rubber-wheeled trolleys depart from outside the Royal Hawaiian Shopping Center every 15 minutes from 8 AM to 4:30 PM on a two-hour circuit of Waikiki and downtown Honolulu, stopping off at all the major sights. Passengers are free to get off where they choose and to stay there for as little or as long as they like. In addition to its one-day passes, the Trolley also offers a four-day Multi-Day Pass. For further details tel: 808/593-2376.

Tourist information Information for Oahu and the other islands can be obtained in advance from the **Hawaii Convention and Visitors Bureau**'s U.S. mainland or overseas offices (see page

The Honolulu Police Department gives friendly advice to tourists

The WikiWiki Shuttle links the terminals at Honolulu International Airport

192), or direct from the main information office at the Waikiki Business Plaza (2270 Kalakaua Avenue, 7th Floor, Honolulu, HI 96815, tel: 808/923-1811; web: www.visit.hawaii.org), Monday to Friday 8–4:30. Most Waikiki hotels have a selection of maps and brochures in their reception areas covering the island's main sightseeing attractions, dinner shows, and tours. Larger establishments may have an information desk offering assistance with inquiries and a reservations service.

Tours Dozens of operators offer tours of Oahu. Two of the best known are **E. Noa Tours** (tel: 808/593-8211; web: www.enoa.com) and **Polynesian Adventure Tours** (tel: 808/833-3000; web: www.polyad. com), both of which offer a range of downtown Honolulu and around-the-island tours as well as visits to specific attractions, in air-conditioned buses or minibuses. (See also panel opposite.)

BRINGING THE KIDS
Hawaii is very child friendly and is perfect for family holidays. The biggest problem is likely to be too much sun, so an ample supply of strong sunscreen is essential. Many of the larger hotels run *keiki* (kids) programs. For a modest fee, or even for free during the summer, kids can learn to *hula*, make *lei*, build sandcastles, or try a host of other activities.

The Waikiki Trolley plows a regular route through Waikiki

Southern Oahu

See map on pages 50–51.

This leisurely day-long driving tour from Waikiki explores the eastern corner of Oahu. Leave plenty of time for sightseeing along the 60-mile circular route, which takes in a royal retreat, the Sea Life Park, surfing beaches, and a crater garden.

From Waikiki, take Kapahulu Avenue off Kalakaua Avenue, and follow the signs to the H-1 freeway. Take H-1 west to Exit 21B, exit onto the Pali Highway (HI-61), and drive uphill for about 3½ miles before beginning to look for the red and yellow HCVB signpost (on the right, but difficult to see) outside the **Queen Emma Summer Palace**. This upcountry retreat of one of Hawaii's most beloved queens has just five rooms leading off its broad central hall. Royal furnishings and ornaments include splendid *koa*-wood beds, feathered *kahili* (royal standards) and jewelry, plus poignant reminders of Emma's only child, Prince Albert Edward, who died at age four. (See also page 66.)

Back on the Pali Highway, continue for about 3 miles to the exit for the **Nuuanu Pali Lookout**. This was the scene of Kamehameha I's victory over the king of Oahu's army in 1795. It is said that the defenders jumped or were pushed over the sheer cliff, which affords a magnificent view over the Kailua and Kaneohe bays.

Beyond the lookout, HI-61 cuts through the Pali Tunnels and descends toward the windward coast. Take the Kalanianaole Highway exit (HI-72) and head southeast via Waimanalo (8 miles) to **Sea Life Park** (tel: 808/259-7933). One of the island's top attractions, Sea Life Park combines a little gentle education about the marine world with a host of great shows, and there are fascinating exhibits in the free **Whaling Museum**. The on-site family-dining restaurant is a convenient place to stop for lunch. (See also pages 87 and 88.)

Sea Life Park ocean view

Stunning Hanauma Bay

Continue on HI-72 for approximately 2 miles to the right turn onto Kealahou Street, and follow signs to the Koko Crater. Inside the crater are the **Crater Botanical Gardens** (tel: 808/537-1708), a relatively new outpost of the Honolulu Botanical Gardens. The 200-acre site is being planted with desert-loving plants such as cacti, aloes, and other hardy types (*Open:* daily 9–4. *Admission free*).

Return to HI-72; **Sandy Beach** is almost directly across the main road. This beautiful white-sand beach is famous for its splendid though treacherous surf, so if the waves are up do not swim unless you are an expert. However, it is a great place to unfurl a beach towel and escape the car. Just down the coast is the **Halona Blowhole**, where waves forced up a narrow lava tube spout like a giant geyser.

Still hugging the coast, continue on HI-72 until it reaches **Hanauma Bay**, a gorgeous aquamarine inlet encircled by the walls of a sunken volcano. This is one of the places on the island that most people want to visit, so in order to preserve its fragile marine ecostructure visitor numbers are restricted. There is fabulous snorkeling around the reef, home to more than 150 types of brilliantly colored tropical fish so tame they approach the flippered and masked visitors.

Return to Waikiki via HI-72/H-1 (15 miles) or follow the signs to Diamond Head for a scenic detour.

Hitching a ride

WAIMEA VALLEY AND ADVENTURE PARK
After a couple of slow days on the beach, let off steam at Waimea Adventure Park—a real favorite with children. There are ATV (all-terrain vehicle) rides along wilderness trails to the top of the valley. There is also an ATV Mini-Challenge obstacle course, downhill mountain-bike tours, and kayak trips down the Waimea River (see panel opposite).

Central Oahu and the North

►► Banzai Pipeline 50B4

Ehukai Beach Park, Kamehameha Highway (HI-83), northeast of Waimea

Flanked to the west by Waimea Bay, and to the northeast by Sunset Beach, Banzai Pipeline must rate as the most evocatively named surfing beach in the world. It is also, along with its immediate neighbors, one of the best. Winter waves can reach heights of around 30–40 feet, and international competitions are held here regularly. In summer the tamed ocean can resemble glass, but these are tricky waters, so snorkel and swim with care. (See also pages 84–85.)

► Dole Plantation 50B3

64-1550 Kamehameha Highway (HI-99), 2 miles north of Wahiawa (tel: 808/621-8408)

Open: daily 9–5:30. Admission free

Surrounded by the pineapple fields of James Drummond Dole's original plantation, this is the home of pineapple power. The Dole Plantation Visitor Center is a gift shop laden with pineapple-themed souvenirs, from beach bags and potholders to T-shirts and confectionery. There are fresh pineapples for sale whole, sliced, or juiced (but none of them a bargain). Other diversions include horseback-riding and an international pineapple garden.

►►► Haleiwa 50B3

Kamehameha Highway (HI-83)

Little more than an hour's drive from Waikiki, but light years away in style, this delightfully laid-back north coast settlement displays the casual signs of surfer culture everywhere—faded Billabong T-shirts and thongs, sun-bleached locks, and trucks loaded with boomboxes and boards. Spread haphazardly along HI-83, clapboard buildings with creaky *lanai* house all sorts of boutiques and galleries with fluttering tie-dye creations and shell jewelry on display. You can rent a bike or a surfboard, charter a deep-sea fishing boat, cool down with one of the

Winter is the time hard-core surfers visit the north shore to catch the big waves of the Banzai Pipeline

Vacationers enjoying the golden sands at Sunset Beach, Haleiwa

famous shave ices (Hawaii's answer to the snow cone) from the Matsumoto Store, pick up sandwiches from a delicatessen, eat a plate lunch from a *kau-kau* wagon on the beach, or dine at a linen-clad table overlooking the marina. The one thing you shouldn't do is hurry. It's just not cool, man.

► Wahiawa Botanic Garden *50C3*

1396 California Avenue, Wahiawa (tel: 808/421-7321)
Open: daily 9–4. Admission free

These leafy botanic gardens—27 acres of rain forest—lie a short distance east of the highway, and make a good reason to stop off in Wahiawa. They are planted with spice trees from the Indies (smell the bark of the cinnamon tree), tropical conifers, palm trees, lobster-claw heliconias, bird-of-paradise plants, brownleas with their orange pom-pom flowers, and many other native varieties. From the upper level, paths lead down into a shaded ravine. This lower area is still being developed, so watch your step on the mini-trek past palms, ferns, and brightly colored banks of impatiens. There is an information desk and an explanatory booklet with maps to guide visitors around the gardens.

►►► Waimea Valley and Adventure Park *50B4*

59-864 Kamehameha Highway (HI-83 east of Haleiwa)
Open: daily 10–5:30. Admission: expensive
Guided tours are available; narrated tram rides leave every 20 minutes from the entrance; for information tel: 808/638-8511

A lush 1,800 acres, reaching back into the Waimea Valley, this park offers something for just about everyone. Landscaped botanic gardens lead gently up to the falls themselves, with plenty of stops along the way. The colorful blooms provide photo opportunities galore, and garden lovers can take guided tours. An arboretum contains more than 5,000 varieties of plants, many of them endangered. More than 30 species of birds live in the park, special exhibits add a historical angle, and there are interactive areas such as the Kauhale Kahiko, where visitors can learn about traditional crafts, Hawaiian food, and medicinal plants. Do not miss the entertaining *hula* show, and do join in the Hawaiian games; and try to time your arrival at the falls for a cliff-diving demonstration.

PUU O MAHUKA HEIAU
For a wonderful view of the north coast, its jagged volcanic fingers inset with white-sand beaches stretching off either side of Waimea Bay, turn off the highway onto Pupukea Road, just east of Waimea. The road winds up to Puu O Mahuka Heiau, an ancient Hawaiian temple site, where locals still leave offerings of fruit, flowers, and shells on the piles of ancient stones. It is said that the *heiau*, one of the largest on Oahu, was used for human sacrifices, and that three English sailors from HMS *Daedalus* were slaughtered here in 1794.

Cliff diving at Waimea Falls

The Hawaiians have been surfing for a thousand years. Images of surfers can be found among ancient petroglyphs carved into the volcanic rocks of the Big Island, and age-old mele *(chants) celebrating surfing exploits, and* pohuehue *(prayers for perfect waves) have been passed from generation to generation.*

SURF OR BOOGIE?
Waikiki remains one of the best places in the world to learn how to surf. There are around a dozen long-ride breaks between Diamond Head and the Hilton Hawaiian Village. In addition to reliable year-round surfing conditions, locals and board rental operators are usually around to offer advice. If you want to ride a wave, but don't rate your chances on a surfboard, boogie boards are a fun alternative. These 3-foot-long foam boards, which support the upper body while leaving the legs free to kick, are inexpensive to buy or can be rented for a nominal fee.

Duke Kahanamoku

"Sliding on a wave" The Hawaiian word for surfing was *hee nalu*, or "sliding on a wave," an apt description of this demanding sport with its vital combination of grace and power. The *mele* tell of hotly contested competitions, animated betting, and sizable wagers won and lost, as well as days when the surf was up and the fields lay unattended as the Hawaiians rode the great winter waves that have their origins in the stormy Arctic.

When Captain Cook and his men arrived by sea, the Hawaiians paddled out on their surfboards to greet them, and the first Europeans to see these standing, wave-riding Hawaiians were fascinated and impressed in equal measure. Farmers and fishermen were not the only *hee nalu* addicts. Women and children of all ages took to the water whenever possible, and the *alii*, or Hawaiian royalty, reserved some of the best surfing beaches for themselves. Royal surfing beaches, such as Queen Kaahumanu's favorite Waikiki, were *kapu* (forbidden) to commoners, and trespassers could be punished with death.

The "Father of Modern Surfing" By the end of the 19th century, however, surfing was a dying art. The combined influences of the all-work-no-play missionary era and increasing Westernization had taken their toll. The writer Jack London is often credited as the man responsible for reviving interest in the sport through articles written after his stay in Waikiki in 1907. The *haole* (foreigners') Outrigger Canoe Club, founded in 1908, and the Hawaiians' own Hui Nalu club, both helped to preserve the Hawaiian surfing and outrigger traditions. But the man who really put surfing on the map, and took it all over the world, was Duke Kahanamoku (1890–1968), the acknowledged "Father of Modern Surfing."

A pure Hawaiian raised in Waikiki, "The Duke" first hit the headlines in 1912, when he took an Olympic gold for the 100-meter freestyle swim at the Stockholm Games. Between 1912 and 1932, Kahanamoku's Hawaiian crawl style added a further two gold, two silver, and four bronze medals to his personal haul. Meanwhile, The Duke starred in films and acted as Hawaii's unofficial "Ambassador of *Aloha*," introducing surfing to Australia, Europe, and the U.S. eastern seaboard, before being elected Sheriff of Honolulu for 13 consecutive terms from 1934 to 1960.

Surf's up! From humble beginnings, surfing is now a world-class sport with a generous purse. The professional circuit has spread from the Americas to Australia, Europe, and

South Africa, but most of the world's monster ridable surf is still found in Hawaii—more precisely on Oahu's north shore. Waimea Bay is one of the hosts for winter surfing classics such as the Hawaiian Pro and Triple Crown (see panel). Even if no official competition is in progress, when the surf is up spectators take positions on shore to watch the daring few paddle out on their big wave boards. At the relative calm of the "lineup," the surfers judge the swell and pick their moment to ride some of the most thrilling waves the ocean can produce.

Modern technology has brought about a revolution in surfboard design. The *koa*-wood boards of the ancient Hawaiians, which measured between 18 and 20 feet and could weigh in at around 150 pounds, have been replaced by lightweight fiberglass shells filled with polyurethane foam, and measuring only 8 to 12 feet in length. Skegs (rudder-like fins) can be selected for increased maneuverability in different wave conditions. And the search for the perfect hydrodynamic board goes on as the prize money rises.

Throughout the islands, the local press, radio stations, and even television news broadcasts offer up-to-the-minute surf reports.

Riding the big blue

SURFING CHAMPIONSHIPS

Hawaii's top winter surfing classics, the Hawaiian Pro and Triple Crown of Surfing, take place from mid-November to mid-December at several locations along Oahu's north shore. They make a great day out even for non surfers. The actual competition days depend on how the waves are shaping up over a set time period, so check the local papers for details. Another hot date in the surfing calendar is mid-February's Buffalo's Big Board Classic at Makaha on the leeward coast.

Oahu's north shore attracts the world's best surfers

KUALOA RANCH
This family-owned cattle ranch on HI-83 south of Kaaawa, opposite Kualoa Regional Park, has now diversified into the adventure-tour market and offers activities ranging from horseback-riding and ATV trail rides to diving, movie-set tours, jet-skiing, snorkeling, and even helicopter trips. Reservations should be made in advance; prices vary according to the activity, tel: 808/237-7321.

Japanese heritage is celebrated at the Byodo-In Temple

The Windward Coast

► Byodo-In Temple 51D2

47-200 Kahekili Highway (HI-83), Kaneohe (tel: 808/239-8811)
Open: daily 8:00–4:30. Admission: inexpensive

Tucked behind the rolling lawns of the Christian cemetery in the Valley of the Temples is a traditional-style Japanese Buddhist temple, set in a peaceful dell backed by the volcanic folds of the Koolau Mountains. Completed in 1968 to mark the centenary of the arrival of the first Japanese immigrants in Hawaii, its design is based on the famous 900-year-old Phoenix Hall of Byodoin at Uji, Japan. The ocher-painted buildings with their yellow trimmings and graceful curving roofs are surrounded by gardens and carp ponds, and guarded by rather predatory pecking peacocks.

►► Kualoa Regional Park 51D3

HI-83 south of Kaaawa
Open: daily 7–7. Admission free

This popular windward-coast beach park has a long, grassy strip backing the beach, good swimming and snorkeling, and facilities that include picnic tables, toilets, and campsites. It can get windy, but that is good news for kite-flyers. The distinctive little **Chinaman's Hat** island, just offshore, is accessible at low tide.

►►► Malaekahana State Park 50C4

HI-83, just north of Laie
Open: daily 7 AM–dusk. Admission free

Hidden behind a swath of coastal woodlands, this secluded beach park is invisible to the average passerby. There is a beautiful, narrow stretch of white sand facing Goat Island (a pint-sized offshore seabird sanctuary), picnic tables and barbecue grills in the woods, a spacious grassy area and campsite facilities (reservations necessary, tel: 808/293-1936. There is a $7 entrance fee for people over seven years old).

Music and dance at the Polynesian Cultural Center

▶ Mormon Temple 50C4

55-600 Naniloa Loop (off HI-83), Laie
Open: Visitor Center, daily 9–8. Admission free

The first Latter Day Saints (Mormon) mission arrived in Hawaii in 1850, and moved to Laie in 1864. The town's population is 95 percent Mormon, and its temple, the first to be built outside the mainland U.S., is the second most visited after that in Salt Lake City, Utah. Dedicated in 1919, the square, white, wedding-cake structure stands in impressively landscaped grounds. Fresh-faced young Mormon guides patrol the grounds. Non-Mormons are not allowed to enter the temple.

▶▶ Whaling Museum 51E1

HI-72, Waimanalo
Open: daily 9:30–5, Fri until 10 PM. Admission free

This free museum, part of the Sea Life Park complex, gives a fascinating account of whaling history. Its displays are laid out beneath the 38-foot-long skeleton of a sperm whale that was washed up off Barbers Point in 1980. Informative (and occasionally pithy) signboards, photographs, models, and memorabilia detail the dangers that the whalers—and the whales—faced. There are also many fine examples of scrimshaw carvings, the traditional folk art made by sailors in the long empty hours on board (see panel).

▶▶ Polynesian Cultural Center 50C4

55-370 Kamehameha Highway (HI-83), Laie
(tel: 808/293-3333 or 800/367-7060; web: www.polynesia.com)
Open: Mon–Sat 12:30–9. Admission: expensive
Ticket options offer admission only; admission and show; and admission, show, and a choice of buffets

One of Oahu's top attractions, the Polynesian Cultural Center opened in 1963 and has been playing to packed houses ever since. It features traditional-style buildings and entertainment from the seven main Polynesian nations of Tahiti, Fiji, Tonga, the Marquesas, Samoa, New Zealand's Maoris and, of course, Hawaii. The center is set in attractive landscaped grounds, and the interactive village settlement areas highlight traditional building styles and crafts. Canoe tours paddle around the 42-acre site, and a giant IMAX film show explores Polynesian history.

The all-singing, all-dancing, 90-minute evening show, a Polynesian revue with fire-dancing and other high-octane pursuits, features 100-plus performers, many of whom are Pacific Island students at the neighboring Brigham Young University—Hawaii.

SCRIMSHAW KNICKKNACKS

Faced with long months at sea and intermittent work, many whalers whiled away the hours whittling scrimshaw masterpieces from whales' teeth and jawbones. The scrimshaw collection at the Whaling Museum contains dozens of expertly carved pieces, including children's toys and games such as cribbage boards, intricately decorated canes and knife handles, sewing kits and pastry cutters intended as presents for girlfriends and wives. The famous whalebone stays that enforced the hourglass figures of Victorian and Edwardian women were made not from bone but from baleen, a tough, flexible material found in the whale's mouth.

Turtle watch at Sea Life Park

"WHOLPHIN"

What's in a "wholphin?" Astonished marine biologists at Sea Life Park were treated to a scientific wonder on May 15, 1985. One of the park's female bottlenose dolphins gave birth to a calf that was half-bottlenose dolphin (*Tursiops truncatus*) and half-false killer whale (*Pseudorca crassidens*). Christened Kekaimalu, the 600-pound, almost 10-foot-long "wholphin" is about a third larger than an average dolphin and has 66 teeth compared to a dolphin's 88 and a whale's 44. Being a native Hawaiian, she also dances the *hula* in daily shows.

Sea-lions can only be found at the Sea Life Park

►►► Sea Life Park — 51E1

41-202 Kalanianaole Highway (HI-72), Makapuu Point (tel: 808/259-7933)
Open: daily 9:30–5, Fri until 10 PM. Admission: expensive
Free round-trip transportation six times daily from several Waikiki hotels; telephone for schedules

A noted marine research facility and a top attraction, the park takes visitors straight to the heart of the matter just inside its gates as they descend the curving ramp that circles the 300,000-gallon Hawaiian Reef Tank. Giant windows reveal more than 2,000 marine specimens, from moray eels and rays to the bizarre scalloped hammerhead shark with its eyes literally out on stalks. There are striped convict tangs, horned unicorn fish, sex-changing wrasses and the tongue-twisting *humuhumunukunukuapuaa*, Hawaii's multi-colored state fish.

Bottlenose dolphins, sea-lions, and penguins perform regularly in the Hawaii Ocean Theater. At Whaler's Cove, the replica whaling ship Essex offers a view of the park's dolphins and whales through sunken porthole windows. This is also the place to spot a "wholphin," the park's rare (if not unique) bottlenose dolphin/false killer-whale hybrid (see panel). Other attractions include a touch pool, a seabird sanctuary, a penguin habitat, a sea-lion feeding pool, a turtle lagoon, and a care center for Hawaiian monk seals.

Guided tours (40 minutes) are offered five times daily, and include a close-up look at animal-training techniques, and a visit to the maternity tanks, not open to the general public (telephone for schedules). Friday night is "Kamaaina Night," when visitors can enjoy dinner and an evening of Hawaiian music at the park's Sea Lion Café.

►► Senator Fong's Plantation and Gardens — 51D2

47-285 Pulama Road (off HI-83), Kaneohe
Open: daily 10–4 (last tram at 3). Admission: moderate

Since his retirement, former U.S. Senator Hiram Fong (the first Asian-American senator in Congress) has devoted his energies to tending this lush 725-acre estate. Open-sided trams make 45-minute guided tours of the extensive rain-forest gardens and orchards, where more than a hundred different varieties of tropical fruits and nuts are cultivated.

The West

Heading *ewa* (west) of Honolulu, H-1 streaks past the industrial jumble of Aiea, the old sugar town of Waipahu, and sprawling Ewa almost as far as the Ko Olina resort, a surprising oasis for golf and spa lovers at the southern end of the Waianae Coast, Oahu's arid leeward side. The old Farrington Highway, a slow local traffic and truck route, parallels H-1 all the way, and then continues as HI-93 north up the coast for 17 miles through a smattering of virtually tourist-free local towns. The road disintegrates into a track at Yokohama Bay, renamed for the Japanese cane workers who came to fish here.

This is largely undiscovered Oahu. Traditionally poor and with a bad reputation, the Waianae Coast has vigorously resisted development, but there are some fine sandy beaches at Maili and Makaha, and a long, clean sand strip at Kaena Point State Park, where the road runs out. The challenging surf attracts some of the island's real hot shots, and February's Buffalo Big Board Surfing Contest at Makaha is a major event on the surfing calendar.

ON THE BEACH
There is good tide pooling at the far end of the Kaena Point State Park Beach, where wave action has also eroded several natural arches in the rocky cliffs on this northwestern tip of Oahu. Diamond Head Beach Park is close enough to Waikiki to be convenient but far enough away that you can escape the crowds. A strip of pristine white sand runs along the bottom of a cliff below Diamond Head, and there are always wind-surfers to provide entertainment.

►► Hawaii Plantation Village *50C2*

94-695 Waipahu Street, Waipahu (Waikele/Paiwa Street exit off H-1) (tel: 808/677-0110)
Open: Mon–Fri 9–3, Sat 10–3. Tours on the hour
Admission: moderate

Somewhat off the beaten track for most visitors, but well worth searching out, this little historical park in the shadow of the old sugar mill has preserved a real chunk of Hawaiian history. There is a small but interesting museum displaying artifacts and memorabilia from the heyday of Hawaii's sugar industry. Clothing, tools, domestic utensils, photographs, and even the dog tags the immigrants were forced to wear by their employers paint a vivid picture of hardship and fortitude. There is also a guided tour of a plantation settlement, with a genuine period store, camp office, infirmary, and workers' houses in as many styles as there were nationalities: Chinese, Portuguese, Japanese, Puerto Rican, Okinawan, and Filipino.

Makaha Beach on Oahu's Waianae Coast

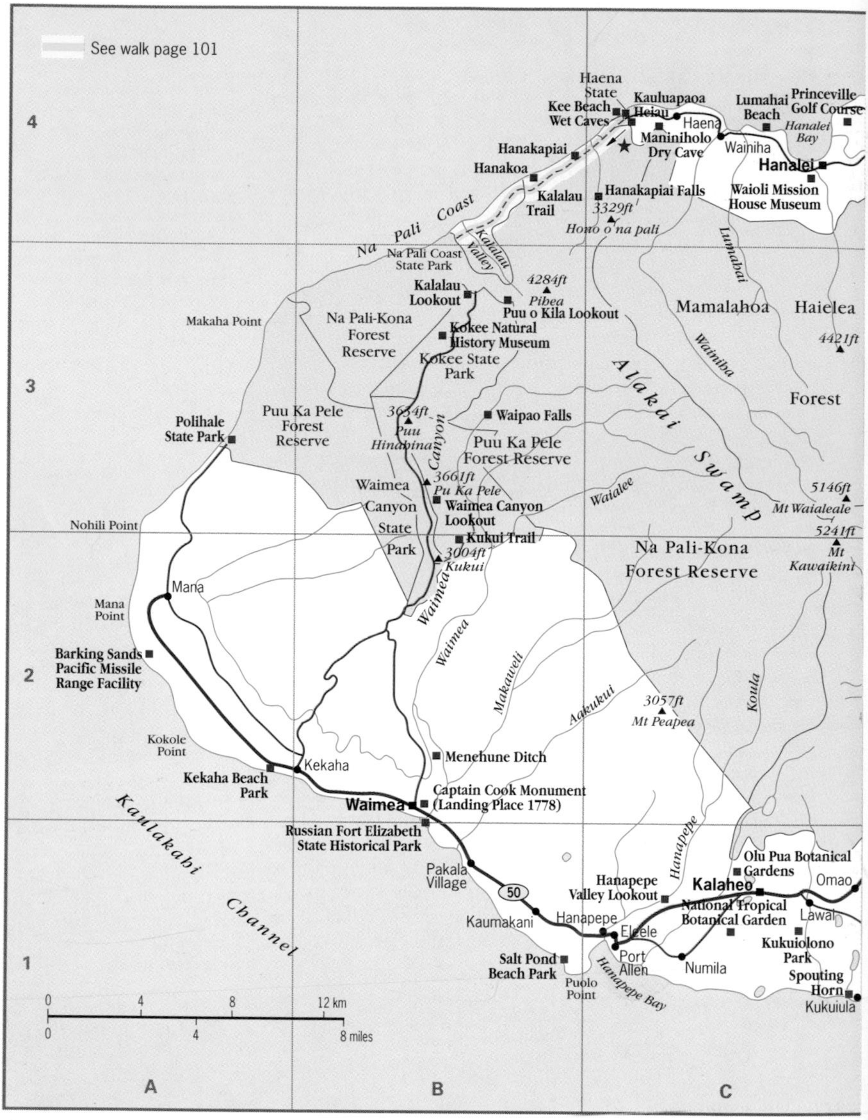

See walk page 101

Haena State
Kee Beach
Wet Caves
Kauluapaoa Heiau
Haena
Maniniholo Dry Cave
Lumahai Beach
Princeville Golf Course
Hanalei Bay
Wainiha
Hanalei
Hanakapiai
Hanakoa
Kalalau Trail
Hanakapiai Falls
3329ft
Hono o na pali
Waioli Mission House Museum
Na Pali Coast
Na Pali Coast State Park
Kalalau Valley
Lumahai
4284ft
Pibea
Kalalau Lookout
Puu o Kila Lookout
Mamalahoa
Haielea
Makaha Point
Na Pali-Kona Forest Reserve
Kokee Natural History Museum
Kokee State Park
Wainiha
4421ft
Alakai Swamp
Forest
Puu Ka Pele Forest Reserve
3654ft
Puu Hinahina
Waipao Falls
Polihale State Park
Canyon
Puu Ka Pele Forest Reserve
3661ft
Pu Ka Pele
Waimea Canyon State Park
Waimea Canyon Lookout
Waialee
5146ft
Mt Waialeale
Nohili Point
Kukui Trail
5241ft
Mt Kawaikini
3004ft
Kukui
Na Pali-Kona Forest Reserve
Mana
Mana Point
Waimea
Waimea
Barking Sands Pacific Missile Range Facility
Makaweli
Aakukui
3057ft
Mt Peapea
Koula
Kokole Point
Menehune Ditch
Kekaha
Kekaha Beach Park
Captain Cook Monument (Landing Place 1778)
Waimea
Russian Fort Elizabeth State Historical Park
Kaulakabi Channel
Hanapepe
Olu Pua Botanical Gardens
Pakala Village
Hanapepe Valley Lookout
Kalaheo
Omao
50
National Tropical Botanical Garden
Lawai
Kaumakani
Hanapepe
Eleele
Kukuiolono Park
Salt Pond Beach Park
Port Allen
Numila
Spouting Horn
Puolo Point
Hanapepe Bay
Kukuiula

0 4 8 12 km
0 4 8 miles

4 3 2 1
A B C

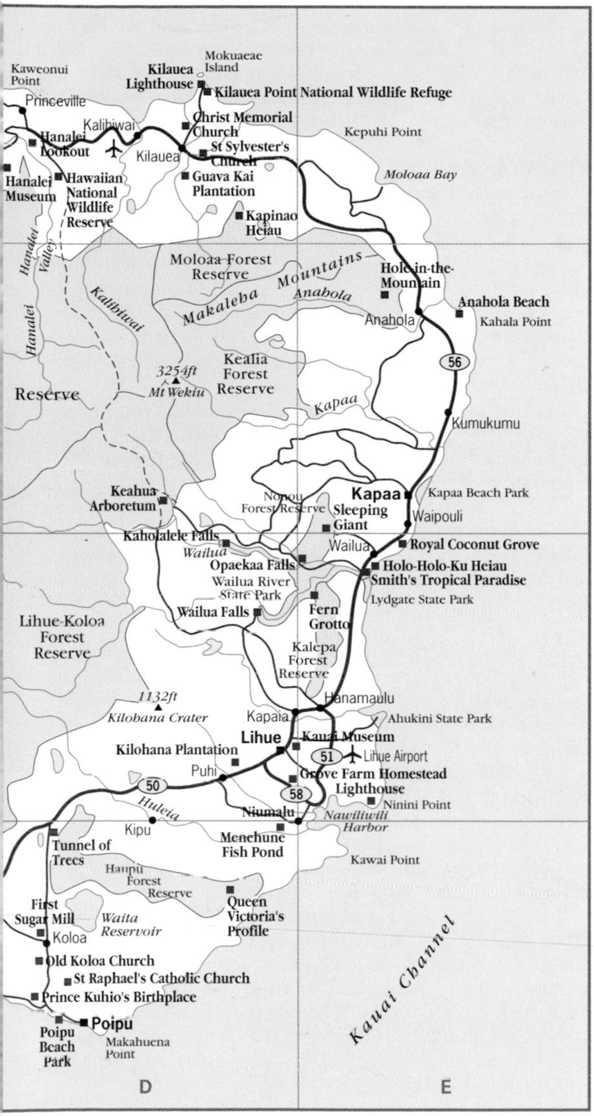

Kauai

►►► ISLAND HIGHLIGHTS

THE GARDEN ISLE Lush and beautiful Kauai was named the Garden Isle by admiring 19th-century visitors, and it can still do justice to the name. The island is swathed in a rich mantle of luxuriant greenery, from the flanks of its ancient mountains to its rippling lowland cane fields and vivid emerald checkerboards of taro patches. Kauai, the oldest of the main Hawaiian islands and the result of a single massive volcano, has an unmistakable maturity to its grandeur. Several million years of rain, wind, and waves have sculpted dramatic sea cliffs and broad valleys, and the latter have been cultivated for almost 1,000 years. From the 5,148-foot central crown of Mount Waialeale, "the wettest spot on earth"—with an average annual rainfall of 444 inches—several rivers and dozens

TAKE A HELICOPTER Helicopter tours offer unparalleled access to the remotest corners of Kauai's mountainous heartland and the Na Pali Coast. They swoop above twisting chasms, dangle within a few yards of 1,000-foot-high waterfalls in the misty heights of Mount Waialeale, hover over high valleys, and flit around the whole island pointing out landmarks. Reservations should be made in advance (use every ploy in the book to secure a window seat). For further information, contact: Ohana Helicopter Tours, Lihue (tel: 808/245-3996); Island Helicopters, Lihue (tel: 808/245-8588).

Brilliant emerald-green taro fields in the Hanalei Valley

of streams and waterfalls have furrowed the mountainsides and carved the monumental Waimea Canyon. Meanwhile, offshore reefs have been ground away to create the island's fine white-sand beaches, which are backed by the ever-encroaching jungle.

RESORTS AND ATTRACTIONS Despite stealing an evolutionary march on the younger islands to the south, Kauai has been somewhat more reticent in the tourism stakes. Its charms are low-key and scenic, though there is no lack of luxury and style. The three main resort areas—Poipu in the south, Kapaa-Wailua on the east coast, and Princeville-Hanalei in the north—boast accommodations ranging from comfortable seaside condos and bed and breakfasts to luxurious hotel suites. Backpackers are equally welcome.

Activities on Kauai include horseback-riding, biking, some of the most spectacular hiking in the islands, kayaking, and boat trips, as well as sport fishing. You have your choice of glorious golf courses (see pages 24–25). Natural beauties are augmented by the historic homes of early missionaries and plantation owners, and one of the state's best museums, in Lihue, the island's capital. And Kauai is *the* place to take a helicopter tour (see panel).

A BIT OF HISTORY Kauai may have been inhabited up to 500 years before the other Hawaiian islands—even the Big Island—by early Polynesians, who were possibly Kauai's legendary "little people," the *menehune* (see panel on page 100). Several ancient sites, including irrigation ditches and stone-walled fishponds, have been attributed to the *menehune*. Though most of them are supposed to have sailed away to preserve their bloodline from contamination by the first Tahitian immigrants, a few are said to have missed the boat and continue to live on in Kauai, hiding out in the hills.

The Tahitians settled Kauai's fertile valleys, building stone terraces into the hillsides and cultivating taro, sweet potatoes, and bananas. Captain Cook noted several coastal settlements around Waimea Bay when he landed on Kauai on January 20, 1778 (see pages 36–37). Waimea later developed into a busy port, the center for the sandalwood trade in the early 19th century and a whaling station in the 1840s.

TAKEN BY STEALTH During the great Kamehameha I's campaign to unite the islands at the end of the 18th century, Kauai was twice saved from invasion fleets by the weather. In 1810 the Kauai king, Kaumualii, managed to negotiate a face-saving agreement with Kamehameha to relinquish his role as monarch and become instead the governor of the island.

In 1815, Georg Anton Schaeffer, who was sent to salvage a wrecked ship belonging to the Russian-American Company, secured permission from Kaumualii to build a fort at Waimea and to raise the Russian flag. The construction of Fort Elizabeth in 1817 alarmed Kamehameha who, fearing the threat of Russian annexation, expelled Schaeffer from Kauai. The unfortunate Kaumualii was eventually kidnapped by Kamehameha II and forced to marry Kamehameha I's widow, Kaahumanu, thus firmly securing Kauai for the Hawaiian kingdom.

MISSIONARIES AND PLANTATIONS The first missionaries arrived in Kauai in 1821, and the first sugar plantation in the Hawaiian Islands was established at Koloa by New Englanders in 1835. They were joined by German Lutheran planters in the 1850s, and by Asian and Portuguese immigrant laborers, and thousands of acres of sugar cane were planted in the south of the island.

MODERN KAUAI Kauai's strong agricultural tradition has enabled the island to retain much of its quiet rural aspect and lifestyle. Most of the population lives on the "Coconut Coast," between Lihue and Kapaa on the east of the island. Beyond here, villages are small and friendly, served by mom-and-pop stores and farmers' markets. A coastal road loops around three-quarters of the island before running into the impassable Na Pali Cliffs, and there are no shortcuts across the interior. Here, remote areas such as the Alakai Swamp have been preserved by their very inaccessibility as rich and rare sanctuaries for plant and bird life, some of it unique to this lovely island.

ON LOCATION
Hollywood has had a long love affair with Kauai ever since some canny location scout decided the Garden Isle would make a splendid backdrop for "Bali-Hai" in the smash-hit film *South Pacific*. After Mitzi Gaynor washed that man right out of her hair on the North Shore's Lumahai Beach, Elvis Presley came along for some *Blue Hawaii* at the Coco Palms Resort, Jessica Lange squealed her way through a remake of *King Kong*, and dinosaurs rampaged around the primordial Na Pali Coast in Spielberg's *Jurassic Park*—to name but a few.

Wailua Falls

The Fern Grotto

APPROXIMATE DRIVING TIMES FROM LIHUE

- Kapaa: 20 minutes
- Kilauea: 45 minutes
- Kokee: 1 hour 30 minutes
- Poipu: 30 minutes
- Princeville and Hanalei: 1 hour
- Wailua: 15 minutes
- Waimea Canyon: 1 hour 15 minutes

History in Lihue

The East Coast

►► Coconut Coast and Lihue *91E2*

The **Coconut Coast**, a stretch of the island's east coast, takes its name from a 19th-century coconut grove near Wailua. Kapaa, Wailua, and neighboring Waipouli together form "Garden Island Central," a seaside strip of tourist-oriented hotels and restaurants, plus two popular shopping malls in the attractive Coconut Marketplace complex and the Kauai Village respectively. Wailua also has a fine 18-hole municipal golf course.

To the south is **Lihue**, Kauai's chief town, located midway along the coastal highway (see panel for driving times). Lihue's airport is the main gateway to Kauai, but the town has little for the visitor save the excellent Kauai Museum (see opposite page) and the Kukui Grove Shopping Mall (2 miles southwest), which has department stores, supermarkets, and an information booth.

►► Fern Grotto *91E2*

Wailua Marina
Open: daily, regular departures with Waialeale Boat Tours (tel: 808/822-4908) and Smith's Motorboats (tel: 808/821-6892). Admission: moderate

This extravagantly fern-draped grotto is one of the most popular attractions on the island and the most touristy. To reach it, visitors are ferried on flat-bottomed river boats along the only stretch of navigable river in the Hawaiian Islands. The 1½-hour, 6-mile round trip is accompanied by local entertainers. Bring a raincoat.

►►► Grove Farm Homestead *91D2*

Nawiliwili Road, near Lihue (tel: 808/245-3202)
Open for tours by reservation: Mon, Wed–Thu 10–1.
Admission: moderate

A visit to the old Wilcox homestead gives a fascinating insight into Hawaiian plantation life. Tours (by reservation

only) are limited to preserve the 80-acre property, which was founded in 1864 by George Wilcox, one of eight sons born to Hanalei missionaries Abner and Lucy Wilcox. The comfortable family home is still furnished with original antiques. Although sugar has been abandoned, the present farm is self-sufficient, relying on its orchards, cattle pasture, timber, and a vegetable garden.

Grove Farm Homestead in the foothills above Lihue

▶▶▶ Kauai Museum 91D2

4428 Rice Street, Lihue (tel: 808/245-6931)
Open: Mon–Fri 9–4, Sat 10–4. Admission: moderate
Rated second only to the prestigious Bishop Museum in Honolulu, this small museum is a must for those with an interest in local history and Hawaiiana. The collections and informative storyboards trace the development of the islands from the Stone Age to the plantation era and also cover immigrant workers, Kauai's leading families, geology, and natural history. There is a very good museum shop for gifts and souvenirs.

▶ Keahua Arboretum 91D3

7 miles along HI-580 from Wailua
Open site. Admission free
This country park, which is a great place for a picnic, sits up in the hills above Wailua. There are mountain views, open meadows, and picnic benches in the shade, plus a swimming hole with a rope swing on the Keahua Stream.

▶ Nawiliwili Harbor 91E2

Waapa Road, off Nawiliwili Road (HI-58) south of Lihue
Nawiliwili is a small working harbor and marina on a sheltered bay at the mouth of the Nawiliwili Stream. There are kayaks for rent here, and Island Adventures (tel: 808/245-9662) offers guided kayak tours up to the **Menehune Fishpond** (see panel) and to the lush backwater country where parts of *Raiders of the Lost Ark* were filmed. Sport-fishing operators True Blue Charters (tel: 808/245-9662) are also based here.

SHRIMP PAY

There are two notable *menehune* sites on the south coast of Kauai. The first is the neat semicircular Menehune Fishpond in the Huleia River valley behind Nawiliwili Harbor; there is a good view of it from a point on Hulemalu Road. The other is Kiki a Ola, or the Waimea Ditch, an earthwork near the Waimea River, reached from Menehune Road (off HI-50 at Waimea). The ditch is said to have been built for Ola, an ancient chief of Waimea, who paid the *menehune* workers in shrimp.

WAILUA VALLEY
The Wailua Valley was cultivated by Kauai's *alii* (chiefs) in ancient times, and there are a number of historic sites in its vicinity. Along the upriver trail, once known as the King's Highway, the remains of several *heiau* (temples) can still be seen, while *kapu*-breakers (taboo-breakers) could find refuge at the *puuhonua* (sanctuary) that occupied part of what is now Lydgate State Park. Royal women would make their way down to the shore at Wailua to give birth at the *pohaku-hoo-hanau*, or royal birthing stones, near the Coco Palms Resort, still closed after extensive hurricane damage.

►► Opaekaa Falls 91E2

HI-580, 1½ miles west of Wailua
Open site. Admission free
The picturesque Opaekaa Falls plunge down the cliff face in a veil of mist to a deep pool hedged in by forest, and are a favorite destination for visitors. Across the street from the parking lot there is a good view of the Wailua River and the river boats making their way upstream to the Fern Grotto (see page 94).

► Smith's Tropical Paradise 91E2

174 Wailua Road, off HI-56 (gardens, tel: 808/821-6895)
Open: gardens, daily 8:30–4; luau, *Mon, Wed, Fri 7–9 (pageant only, 7:30). Admission: gardens, moderate;* luau, *expensive*
Situated on 30 prime acres at the mouth of the Wailua River, Smith's Tropical Paradise has three strings to its bow. The first is river boats, which make their way at a leisurely pace up to the Fern Grotto from the dock (see page 94). The second and third are a botanical garden and a *luau* (feast), which share the same landscaped site. Tram tours circle the gardens and central lagoon, taking in Polynesian-style villages and a mature display of local and exotic plants and trees. The evening *luau* features a pageant, and *kalua* pig cooked in the traditional way in an *imu* (underground oven).

►► Wailua River and Falls 91D2

The 12-mile-long Wailua River starts life on the slopes of Mount Waialeale. The slow-flowing lower portion of the river is a good spot for a half-day's boating, and kayaks can be rented from a number of operators on the main highway. KBTC (4-746 Kuhio Highway/HI-56, tel: 808/822-7447) throws in useful extras such as a cooler for drinks, tarpaulin, dry bag, and so on.

About five miles north of Lihue, off HI-583, the river's south fork plummets down the 80-foot **Wailua Falls**. It is said that ancient Hawaiian chiefs used to dive into the pool from the top of the falls to test their courage. Today, it is not even recommended to attempt the trail down.

A floating carpet of water lilies is the centerpiece of Smith's Tropical Paradise

The Hawaiian lei *(garland) is pure* aloha*, a traditional symbol of friendship and affection given in greeting or farewell, and is often presented as a gift to celebrate a special occasion.*

Lei *are traditional adornments for these girls at a* keiki hula *contest*

Origins The origins of the *lei* are a mystery, though some believe the custom began during the days of the earliest European explorers, when plants were presented as gifts. Today, *lei*-making is one of the islands' most visible craft forms, adorning the necks of tourists and *hula* dancers, *kamaaina* grannies and grinning politicians, not to mention the Kamehameha I statue in downtown Honolulu, which is festooned in dozens of multicolored *lei* on May 1, Hawaii's official Lei Day.

The basic *kui*-style *lei*, which is made of either fragrant plumeria flowers or carnations strung end to end, is child's play, but wondrous *haku*-style *lei*, intricate braids of greenery and flowers, are skilled works of art. Many hotels offer demonstrations and simple *lei*-making lessons. For *lei* galore, head for Maunakea Street in Honolulu's Chinatown; better still, attend a prestigious local *hula* competition, such as the springtime Merrie Monarch Festival on Hawaii.

Flowers and shells Each Hawaiian island has its own special *lei*. On Oahu, look for the orange ruffle of an *ilima*-flower *lei;* on Maui it is the rosy-pink *lokelani*. Kauai's *lei* are scented by little square *mokihana* berries, which smell of anise and were used by the ancient Hawaiians to perfume their clothes. Hawaii has adopted Madame Pele's feathery red *lehua* blossoms, while Lanai has a twist of orange *kaunaoa*. Molokai combines the silver-green leaves of the *kukui* (candlenut) tree with its small white flowers, though many visitors prefer a polished *kukui* nut necklace as a permanent souvenir of the islands. Barren Niihau harvests the beach for *lei*-making purposes. The "Forbidden Island's" delicate shell *lei*, made from tiny white and speckled *pupu* shells, make expensive but lasting souvenirs of a trip to the *aloha* islands.

A *LEI* FOR EVERY SEASON
A *lei* is a thing of beauty, and a scented sensation. In addition to plumeria and carnations, two of the most sweet-smelling types of flower used in *lei*-making are heady tuberoses and *pikake* (the Hawaiian name for jasmine). White ginger flowers exude a delightfully subtle fragrance, while some types of orchid have a delicate vanilla scent. The aromatic leaves of the *maile* vine are popular, and the locals favor the unusual *puakenikeni lei*, which not only smell divine, but gradually change color as well.

Lei-*making is an art form*

NEWELL'S SHEARWATERS
During October and November, hundreds of Newell's shearwaters flock to Kauai's north shore. These endangered, pigeon-sized black-and-white seabirds fly only at night, so they easily become confused and disoriented by bright lights (to which they are attracted), and frequently crash into buildings and telephone wires. Locals rescue dozens of dazed birds from the roadside every year.

OH *POI*
The soggy wetlands below Hanalei Scenic Lookout are the perfect place to grow taro. The brilliant green fields of this tropical plant dominate the panorama and make for what must be the islands' most spectacular agricultural scene, but the green leaves, however impressive, are just for show. The important part is the tuberous root below water level. This was the main staple for old Hawaiians, and for centuries their progeny have pounded the root into a glutenous purple paste called *poi*. Although it is one of the most nutritious carbohydrates known and no *luau* is complete without it, it is also practically tasteless, and it's best eaten with something else.

The North Shore

► Guava Kai Plantation — 91D4

South of Kuhio Highway (HI-56), Kilauea
Open: daily 9–5. Admission free
With 480 acres of guava trees yielding around 14 million pounds of fruit a year, it is no wonder that this plantation is called the "Guava Capital of the World." Introduced from South America in 1791, the delicious pink-fleshed guava makes excellent jams, jellies, and sweet syrups. The fresh juice is even better and can be sampled for free in the plantation shop, which also sells guava preserves and other foodstuffs. There is a short "nature trail" through a garden where bird-of-paradise flowers, gingers, taro, bananas, pineapples, and other food plants grow behind an intoxicatingly scented gardenia hedge.

►►► Hanalei — 90C4

Approaching Hanalei from the east on HI-56, stop off at the **Hanalei Scenic Lookout** just beyond Princeville for a preview of the green and fertile Hanalei Valley. The valley, backed by 3,500-foot-high mountains streaked with waterfalls, has been cultivated for centuries. Its colorful patchwork of taro fields and wetlands, irrigated by the Hanalei River, is one of the last refuges of the Hawaiian coot, and is busy with ducks, gallinules, golden plovers, and dozens of visiting waterfowl.

The road continues down to the Hanalei Bridge, a narrow span with a sharp right-angled bend at the far side that discourages tour buses. Here, Ohike Road strikes off into the valley and the 917-acre **Hanalei National Wildlife Refuge**. Birdwatchers can walk or drive along the track, but the farm land is private property.

Sleepy downtown Hanalei straggles along the main street in a collection of old wooden houses. There are galleries, cafés, and restaurants in the attractive open-air **Hanalei Center**, where the Old School House has filled its former classrooms with surf and sailboard stores, boutiques, and craft shops. The **Ching Young Village** across the way contains much of the same and also has a supermarket. The town has several adventure-tour operators, offering bicycle rental, kayak outings, and boat trips along the magnificent Na Pali Coast.

Aku Road, adjacent to Ching Young village, leads down toward **Hanalei Bay**, where whaling boats and traders once anchored. Turn right for the beach park and pier.

Kauai's mountainous interior rises above Hanalei Bay

Kee Beach at the northern end of the Na Pali Coast

This can be a good surfing spot, and kayak tours leave from the mouth of the Hanalei River.

On the road out of town to Haena and Kee Beach is the little green and white shingle **Waloll Huiia Church** (1912) and a timber-framed **Mission Hall**, completed in 1841. Inside the American Gothic-style church, pretty stained-glass windows cast a cool, green light. The bell tower contains the original mission bell brought from Boston in 1843. The mission house lies across the park and is now a museum (see page 100).

▶▶ Kee Beach *90C4*

At the end of the road on the Na Pali Coast is pretty Kee Beach, part of Haena State Park. Along the route from Hanalei are several small bridges and a couple of popular beaches in Lumahai (the "*South Pacific* Beach") and the surfers' favorite, Makua, also known as "Tunnels Beach." Just across the Limahuli Stream, look for the entrance to the Maniniholo Dry Cave, which was hollowed out of the cliff face by ancient surf.

Kee and the neighboring beaches are protected by reefs, and are great for swimming and snorkeling; they also have basic facilities. The challenging Kalalau Trail along the Na Pali Coast (see page 101) starts at Kee Beach, and returning hikers are all too grateful to flop down on the sand and dip their weary toes in the lagoon. On a less intrepid note, paths lead up through the undergrowth to the ruins of the Kauluapaoa Heiau where, it is said, the *hula* dance form was first enacted in honor of the goddess Laka.

LIMAHULI GARDENS

Next to the entrance to Haena State Park a sign points to the Limahuli Gardens, an outpost of the National Tropical Botanical Gardens. Flanked by 2,000-foot forested cliffs, this 17-acre site in the isolated Limahuli Valley is stunningly beautiful. Limahuli Gardens support important areas of native forest, as well as a more conventional garden of colorful interlopers such as heliconias and gingers. The stone-terraced hillsides, constructed by ancient Hawaiians as far back as 700 years ago, have been repaired and recultivated. (Tours by reservation only, Tue–Fri and Sun from 9:30–4 PM; tel: 808/826-1053.)

Kilauea lighthouse

THE LAST OF THE *MENEHUNE*

Legend tells of the last trek of the *menehune* to self-imposed exile on the Na Pali Coast through the Kalalau Valley. Two princesses died on the way, giving their names to the Hanakoa and Hanakapiai valleys. Some *menehune* stayed behind, however: a 19th-century census recorded 65 living in the Wainiha Valley!

Spectacular views of the Na Pali Coast are within a few minutes climb from the roadhead at Kee Beach

▶ Kilauea — *91D4*

This old sugar village lies just off the main road and has a brace of churches: the little coral-rock Christ Memorial Church, and St. Sylvester's. A clutch of shops on the road to Kilauea Point includes the delectable Kong Lung Store (purveyor of designer furnishings, knickknacks, and fashions) and a delicatessen. A 1913 lighthouse boasting the world's largest clamshell lens overlooks the cliffs and coves of **Kilauea Point National Wildlife Refuge**. Here, nesting colonies of boobies, shearwaters, albatrosses, and tropical birds cling to the precipitous cliffs, and whales can be spotted offshore in winter and spring.

▶▶▶ Na Pali Coast State Park — *90B3*

Rearing up from the ocean in a series of magnificent fluted and ridge-backed cliffs inset with deep, green valleys, the Na Pali Coast is breathtakingly beautiful. The remote and difficult-to-access Na Pali valleys were inhabited and cultivated right up until the early 20th century. The valleys can be reached only by boat, or via the 11-mile Kalalau Trail (see page 101). For views alone, nothing can beat a helicopter tour (see panel on page 92). There is also a spectacular lookout over the Kalalau Valley from Kokee State Park (see page 102).

▶▶ Waioli Mission House Museum — *90C4*

HI-56, Hanalei (tel: 808/245-3202)

Open: Tue, Thu, Sat 9–3. Admission: donation

The Reverend William Alexander and his family arrived at Hanalei in a double canoe from Waimea in 1834. Their first home was a thatched hut, but the pastor built a sturdier house in 1837. The descendants of their successors at the mission, the Wilcox family, restored this house in 1921, furnishing it with some original family possessions, from mission furniture and china to leather-bound volumes of uplifting reading material.

Walk

Na Pali Coast Kalalau Trail

Hala trees and lush tropical vegetation on the trail

The Kalalau Trail is surely one of the best short treks in the world. The challenging 11-mile, one-way trail cuts a strenuous path via five valleys from Kee Beach (see page 99) to the Kalalau Valley, about halfway along the Na Pali Coast.

Most people tackling the full trail are advised to make an overnight camping stop in the Kalalau Valley. Drinking water, sunscreen lotion, mosquito repellent, and wet-weather gear are essential equipment.

The first (and easiest) 2-mile section of the trail to Hanakapiai is a popular short hike. Beyond Hanakapiai it is necessary to have a permit, free from the State Parks Office, 3060 Eiwa Street, Lihue (tel: 808/274-3444. *Open:* Mon–Fri 8–2:15).

A reasonably fit walker can tackle the trail between Kee and **Hanakapiai** in about an hour. There are terrific views along the coast as the narrow path hugs the cliff sides, which are edged by banks of ferns, papaya trees, and groves of *hala* (screw pine). A worthwhile, although tough, 2-mile detour is possible from the beach by the mouth of the Hanakapiai Stream up to the 300-foot **Hanakapiai Falls**. You pass old taro terraces and mango trees to reach a great swimming hole below the falls.

Back on the trail, between Hanakapiai and Hanakoa (4 miles/2–3 hours), the main path climbs 800 feet before tumbling down into **Hoolulu Valley**. This is the hardest section. The scale of Hoolulu is awe-inspiring and there is plenty of shade as you trek on to **Waiahuakua**. The trail then drops down to **Hanakoa Valley**, another lush, shaded spot with an abundance of mountain apple, mango, and guava trees.

On the final 5-mile stretch to **Kalalau** (3 hours), the landscape and vegetation become more arid as the trail leaves the island's windward side. The Kalalau Valley, 2 miles wide and 3 miles deep, studded with freshwater pools, was a Hawaiian settlement. There is camping on the beach and near the trail.

***MOA* ON THE RUN**
On the drive up to Kokee you may be forgiven for thinking that there has been a mass breakout from the local chicken farm. However, the glossy brown fowl feeding at the roadside are not domestic hens, but wild jungle fowl, or *moa*, introduced by the Polynesians. *Moa* now survive only on Kauai, which has no mongooses. The mongoose, which has a penchant for birds' eggs, was introduced into Hawaii to control the rat problem in the 1880s, but the consignment for Kauai was tipped off the dock by the irate recipient of a mongoose bite, to the everlasting gratitude of the *moa*.

The South

▶ Hanapepe *90C1*

West of the Hanapepe Valley, which was featured in scenes from *Jurassic Park*, is the small plantation town of Hanapepe. It has also had its moment of screen fame, masquerading as outback Australia in the television version of *The Thorn Birds*. Here tin-roofed homes and false-fronted wooden shops bake quietly in the hot sun. There are a couple of small galleries, restaurants, and delicatessens where you can find picnic items for lunch at **Salt Pond Beach Park**, a sandy beach west of town with safe swimming, basic facilities, and picnic pavilions that provide shade and protection from falling coconuts.

▶▶ Kilohana Plantation *91D2*

HI-50, 1½ miles southwest of Lihue (tel: 808/245-5608)
Open: Mon–Sat 9:30–9:30, Sun 9:30–5; carriage rides Mon–Sat 11–6:30, Sun 11–5; reservations for wagon tours and Gaylord's, tel: 808/245-9593. Admission free; charge for carriage rides and wagon tours

Built in 1935 by a member of the Wilcox family as a private home, this brick and shingle manor house has been transformed into a collection of craft shops and galleries, with Gaylord's restaurant in the courtyard. Souvenir hunters can stock up on "Kauai made" products, Niihau shell *lei*, Hawaiian quilts, and more. The 35-acre grounds, which include tropical gardens and a working farm, can be explored on foot or by horse-drawn carriage. Wagon tours venture into the surrounding cane fields.

▶▶▶ Kokee State Park *90B3*

HI-550, 15½ miles north of Waimea
Open: Museum, daily 10–4. Admission free

An outing to Kokee encompasses two of Kauai's most spectacular sights. On the road up to the 4,345-acre state

A rainbow strikes the ridge above Hanapepe

The Wilcox sitting room at Kilohana Plantation

park there are lookouts to the views over the dramatic 10-mile-long Waimea Canyon (see page 108), and within the park itself the Kalalau Lookout gazes out from the 4,000-foot-high cliffs at the head of the Na Pali Coast's deepest valley.

At an altitude of 3,800 feet, Kokee's cool, forested heights seem a million miles from the hot sands of Polihale, which in reality are just 30 miles away down on the coast. Temperatures are around 12°F cooler than at sea level. The weather is changeable, and for the best views of the Kalalau Valley it is wise to make an early start, arriving at the lookout before 10 AM when clouds can close in.

At the park headquarters, the **Kokee Natural History Museum** contains collections of plants and geological specimens as well as samples of petroglyphs found on Kauai. It has an information center selling hiking maps, books, and souvenirs. There is also a restaurant, Kokee Lodge, which is the contact point for cabin rental in the park (see page 196).

The park's rugged terrain is crisscrossed by 45 miles of hiking trails. These range in length and degree of difficulty from a 15-minute nature walk near the museum to forest walks along unpaved jeep tracks (see panel) and arduous treks down into the precipitous gorges of the Na Pali Coast.

The Alakai Swamp is boggy and remote, and the hiking is demanding, as the area is frequently swathed in mist and rain. Rainwater from Mount Waialeale gathers in the giant caldera of Kauai's only volcano to form the 30-square-mile Alakai. But here, in these conditions unsuited to introduced species, native plant species continue to flourish, and rare birds—perhaps even the *oo aa*, which has not been seen for decades—flit among the stunted *ohia* trees, which barely reach knee height. Hikers in the Alakai must be well prepared, with wet-weather gear, drinking water, and decent maps. If you're contemplating a hike down to the Na Pali Coast, be aware that there are no facilities or quick routes out. Information can be obtained from the State Parks Service (tel: 808/274-3444).

TWO SHORT WALKS

For an easy-to-access short walk in Kokee, look no further than Camp 10 Road near the park headquarters, which winds its way through moss-covered *ohia* and fern forests. Another relatively easy hike is the first section of the Pihea Trail from the Puu O Kila Lookout, 5 miles beyond the park's headquarters. A mile out and a mile back, the walk takes about an hour and affords views of the 3-mile-long, 2-mile-wide Kalalau Valley and the Alakai Swamp. However, be warned: both trails get very slippery after heavy rains.

The air is cool at 4,000 feet on a muddy trail in Kokee State Park

Koloa still has the air of an old plantation town

▶ Koloa *91D1*

On the main road to Koloa (HI-520), a mile-long leafy tunnel of eucalyptus trees momentarily blocks out the view of cane fields. The former plantation town of Koloa was the center of the Kauai sugar industry, and the first successful plantation in Hawaii, with its sugar mill (now gone), was founded here in 1835.

The town's restored wooden stores and houses are clustered around the site of the old Ladd & Company mill. Nearby, Old Koloa Church reveals New England origins in its white-painted clapboard and classical-revival columns. Out near the existing sugar mill, off Weliweli Road, the 19th-century Catholic Church of St. Raphael is a more typically European stone-built affair. The mortar used in the original construction was made from pounded coral collected from the offshore reefs by hand and then hauled overland for 3 miles back to the church site.

▶▶▶ National Tropical Botanical Garden *90C1*

Off HI-50, Lawai Valley
Tour information and reservations, tel: 808/826-1053.
Admission: expensive

There are, in fact, two glorious gardens here. The NTBG's 186-acre Lawai Garden contains collections of tropical plants from around the world, including bromeliads, palms, and heliconias, with a special emphasis on rare and endangered Hawaiian species. The neighboring Allerton Garden, which was founded in the 1870s, is a masterpiece of garden design. Laid out around Queen Emma's oceanside summer cottage, the garden has meandering paths that link a number of plant-filled and individually landscaped outdoor "rooms," many of them ornamented with unique pools and fountains.

▶▶ Olu Pua Botanical Gardens *90C1*

HI-50, 1 mile west of Kalaheo (tel: 808/332-8182)
Open: daily, tours every hour from 9:30 to 2:30.
Admission: moderate

This is another lovely garden, with the added bonus of a 1930s plantation home designed by architect C.W. Dickey for the Alexander family. The 12½-acre landscaped site is full of unusual trees and plants, colorful hibiscus bushes (the state flower), and water lilies in a hibiscus-shaped pond. There is also a rain forest section

HURRICANE INIKI
Originating off the coast of Central America, hurricanes usually dissipate before they reach Hawaii, but on September 11, 1992, Hurricane Iniki caught Kauai head on. Winds gusting up to 227mph damaged 14,000 buildings, and the costs of rebuilding—all the major hotels have been refurbished—and property compensation have been enormous.

Baking white sands at Polihale State Park

where orchids flourish amid giant gingers, lobster-claw, and parrot's beak heliconias. The plantation house is decorated with exquisite Asian furnishings and porcelain, and overlooks a little Japanese garden.

►► Poipu *91D1*

A popular resort area on the sunny southern tip of the island, Poipu's string of crescent-shaped sandy beaches spreads 1½ miles along the coast. Accommodations range from deluxe beachfront resorts and well-appointed condominiums (none of them taller than a coconut palm) to bed-and-breakfast operations. There is great snorkeling, fishing, sailing, windsurfing, and scuba diving off the coast, plus golf, tennis, and horseback-riding for land-lubbers. Of the beaches, Poipu Beach Park is a favorite. In the grassy park, there are picnic tables and barbecue grills under the trees. Brennecke's store and restaurant across the way offers everything from a fish dinner and sandwiches to boogie-board rental and boat tours.

At the western end of Poipu, the tour buses roll up to watch the antics of **Spouting Horn**. It is best seen on a blustery day when the waves are driven powerfully through an old lava tube in the volcanic rock promontory, creating a massive geyser-like plume of spray with an eerie accompanying moan that sounds like whale song.

► Polihale State Park *90A3*

A 5-mile-long red dirt track leads through the cane fields to this magnificent beach in the driest corner of the island. Its sprawling dunes end abruptly in the towering buttresses of the Na Pali Coast, and the only shade is provided by spiky thorned *kiawe* trees. There are showers and barbecue grills; camping permits are available from the Division of State Parks (tel: 808/274-3444).

A plume of spray from Spouting Horn, Poipu

LAPPERT'S ICES

One of the most popular pit-stops in Koloa is the Lappert's ice-cream emporium. A home-grown family business founded in Hanapepe in 1983, Lappert now sells its exotic sorbets and diet-shattering rich ice creams throughout Hawaii. One generous serving is almost guaranteed to soothe frayed tempers and fractious children after a long drive or a day at the beach. Try the caramel-coconut-macadamia ice cream, or "Hana Road," with marshmallows, walnuts, and white-chocolate chunks.

Dip beneath the glassy surface of the Pacific Ocean, and you find a spectacular marine world set to rival—or even surpass—the diversity and beauty of Hawaii's scenery on land.

NIGHT DIVES
All sorts of nocturnal creatures desert their daytime hideaways to feed, stony corals appear to blossom against the backdrop of a darkened ocean, and the reef's colors are, if anything, magnified by flashlight beams, which also attract fish. For an unforgettable experience, try Kona Coast Divers on the Big Island of Hawaii (tel: 808/329-8802).

Unlike snorkeling, diving gives a three-dimensional view of the underwater world

Coral reefs The Hawaiian Islands form the most isolated archipelago in the world, and local marine life is every bit as unusual as the flora and fauna found on dry land. About a third of the marine species living in Hawaiian waters are endemic to the islands—fish and molluscs that have evolved on and around the offshore reefs and are found nowhere else in the world.

Hawaii's coral reefs have taken millions of years to develop in the mid-Pacific, where the water is relatively cool for coral. The hard corals, which form the basis of the reef, are the limestone exterior skeletons of polyps (soft-bodied relatives of sea anemones and jellyfish), and grow slowly but surely as each generation of corals builds on the skeletal remains of its ancestors. Hard coral reefs are generally found on the sheltered leeward sides of the islands, and are practical as well as beautiful. They act as a breakwater for the coast and make a safe anchorage for soft corals and shellfish, as well as creating the dazzling white-sand beaches that are the result of reef erosion.

Living color The bizarre but beautiful marine landscape, fashioned from corals and lava outcrops carved into pinnacles, archways, and dark caverns, is only the beginning of the wonders in store. Down beneath the waves, multicolor butterfly fish, neon wrasses, and striped convict tangs streak past masked divers like shivers of liquid color. Puffed-up and speckled balloon fish and parrot fish, which can bite off chunks of coral with their sharp, beaklike mouths, move at a more sedate pace. Stripy orange-brown lionfish shimmy by in a fluttering of lacy fins, while Moorish idols trail a delicate white streamer in their wake and surgeon fish swim about their business sporting tail spines that resemble scalpels.

One of the most colorful reef dwellers is Hawaii's state fish, the *humuhumunukunukuapuaa*, or painted triggerfish. Triggerfish are named for the sharp spine in their dorsal fin that can be used to scare off predators. Keeping a low profile, crabs, lobsters, and sinister moray eels lurk in convenient crevices.

In deeper water, yellowfin tuna, wahoo, amberjack, *mahimahi*, and marlin, swim with the sharks—black- and white-tipped sharks, hammerheads, and perhaps great whites—as they patrol their ocean territories. One peculiar resident here is the huge, toothless whale shark, the largest fish in the world. Another large creature is the blanket-sized manta ray, soaring through the ocean in a stunning display of grace and power.

Sighting a sea turtle is always a thrill. These primitive leviathans glide slowly above the coral beds and can grow shells more than 3 feet long. Another treat is the sudden arrival of a pod of spinner dolphins, performing effortless underwater acrobatics and chattering furiously in a welter of whistles and clicking sounds. In winter, divers can occasionally pick up the electrifying echo reverberations of humpback whale songs.

Snorkel and dive trips drop in on the under-water world

TOP SNORKEL AND DIVE SITES

- Cathedrals off Hulopoe, Lanai
- Haena State Park and Poipu, Kauai
- Hanauma and Pupukea Bays, Oahu
- Honolua Bay, Ahihi Bay, and Molokini, Maui
- Kealakekua Bay and Kahaluu Beach Park, Hawaii
- Mokuhooniki Island, Molokai

Snorkel and dive The best time for diving in Hawaii is in the summer, when the seas are calm and visibility is exceptional. Each island offers a choice of snorkel and dive sites (see panel), some suited to beginners and others requiring experience. Snorkeling equipment (flippers and masks) is available to rent on several busy public beaches and from many hotels. Local diving operators will offer scuba-diving courses with certified instructors, rent equipment out to certified divers, and run day- and night-diving expeditions for divers of all levels. Some can also rent underwater cameras and supply waterproof housings to fit many standard cameras and camcorders.

Waimea Canyon, the "Grand Canyon of the Pacific"

KUKUI TRAIL

The name "Waimea" means "red water," referring to the color of the Waimea River after heavy rain as flood waters carry away the rich red-brown soil. There is a strenuous but rewarding hike down the precipitous canyon sides to the river via the 2½-mile Kukui Trail. From the trailhead at the Iliau Nature Loop (Mile Marker 8.5), a steeply graded, knee-trembling path zigzags down to the canyon floor where it hooks up with the Waimea Canyon Trail leading back to Waimea (8 miles). Hikers should wear sturdy boots and carry drinking water and sunscreen.

▶ Russian Fort Elizabeth State Historical Park

90B1

HI-50, ½ mile east of Waimea
Open site. Admission free

Strategically placed at the mouth of the Waimea River, Georg Anton Schaeffer's Fort Elizabeth dominated the once-bustling port of Waimea. After Schaeffer was sent packing by King Kamehameha (see page 92), the Hawaiians occupied the European-design star-shaped fort until 1864, then demolished most of its 30-foot-thick walls and dismantled its guns. It is difficult to conjure up the full picture from the dark and dusty basalt rock ruins, but try to imagine the bay full of trading schooners and whaling ships. The views are suitably commanding.

▶ Waimea

90B2

This old port and whaling station, a mere shadow of its former self, is the last supply stop on the way up to the Waimea Canyon (see below) and Kokee State Park (see pages 102–103). The main road, flanked by some classic 1920s plantation-era buildings, runs straight through town. In the town center a monument commemorates Captain Cook, who first set foot on Hawaiian soil here on January 20, 1778, and the town throws off its dusty torpor once a year at the end of February for the Captain Cook Carnival.

▶▶▶ Waimea Canyon

90B3

Waimea Canyon Road (HI-550)
Open site. Admission free

Mark Twain called this the "Grand Canyon of the Pacific," and as the road climbs (over 1,000 feet in the first mile) and glimpses of the massive red, purple, and green cliffs appear, it is clear he was right. Measuring 10 miles long, more than a mile across, and over 3,000 feet deep, the canyon has been carved with deeply scoured valleys by centuries of wind and rain. Wooded gullies etched by waterfalls and streams burrow back into the multicolored volcanic rock, and rainbows sprout like fairy bridges. There are spectacular views from the Waimea Canyon Lookout, just beyond Mile Marker 10; serious hikers can tackle the Kukui Trail (see panel).

Niihau

THE "FORBIDDEN ISLAND" Separated from the west coast of Kauai by the Kaulakahi Channel, the "Forbidden Island" of Niihau is a tantalizing shadow on the horizon. The island was bought for $10,000 by Mrs. Elizabeth Sinclair in 1864, and it remains in the hands of her descendants, the Robinsons of Kauai.

CLIMATE AND WAY OF LIFE Bleak and arid Niihau (18 miles by 6 miles) is caught in the lee of neighboring Kauai, which siphons off most of the rain. The island is inhabited mainly by native Hawaiians, who make a living from cattle and sheep ranching, producing charcoal from *kiawe* trees, collecting honey, and gathering the shells to make precious Niihau shell *lei* (see page 97). There are no telephones, electricity, alcohol, or jails on Niihau. Most people live in simple wooden houses in the main village of Puuwai on the central west coast, and get around on horseback or by truck.

Hawaiian is Niihau's first language, though English is taught in the elementary school; children leave the island to attend high school on Kauai or Oahu. The people of Niihau are free to come and go, but the only way for an outsider to visit the island is as a guest of the Robinson family or via helicopter tours from Kauai operated by Niihau Helicopters (tel: 808/335-3500), which land at a remote spot far away from habitation.

Forbidding cliffs greet visitors to Niihau

BATTLE OF NIIHAU
One unwelcome guest on Niihau was a Japanese Zero pilot who was forced to ditch his plane after bombing Pearl Harbor. Having escaped his Hawaiian captors, the pilot retrieved a machine gun from his plane and held out for five days before local resident Benehakaha Kanahele went out to try to persuade him to give himself up. Kanahele was shot several times, but nevertheless managed to overpower the Japanese interloper. Kanahele was later awarded the Congressional Medal of Honor for his part in what became known as the "Battle of Niihau."

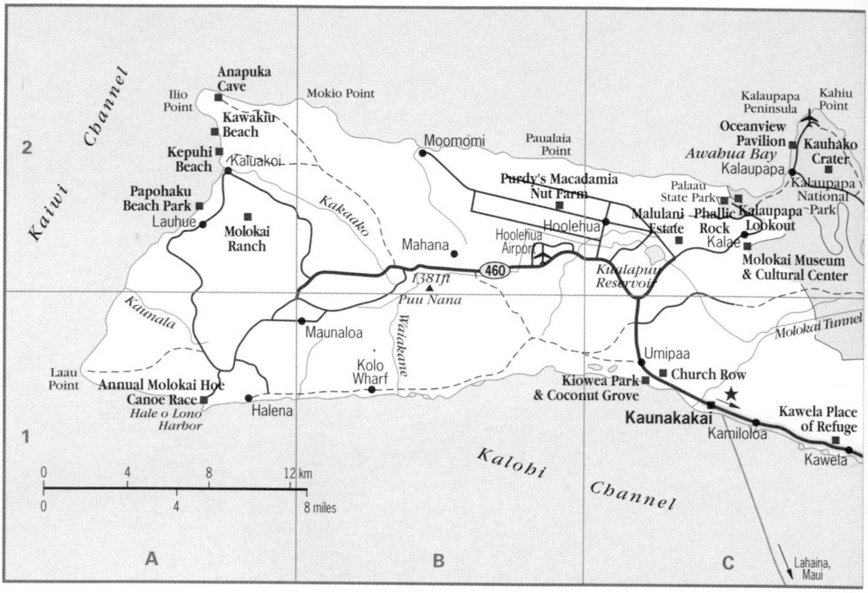

Ancient stone-walled fishponds line the south coast bays of Molokai

THE FORGOTTON ISLE
Once referred to as the Forgotten Isle and the Lonely Isle for its isolation, Molokai is now known as the "Friendly Isle". In 1778 Captain James Cook became the first Westerner to describe the island, but he found it too desolate and did not land; the first European to actually do so was Captain George Dixon, in 1786. In 1792 the island's population was estimated at 10,000, but this dropped to 1,000 early this century. Thanks to the Hawaiian Homes Act of 1921, which granted a 40-acre homestead to anyone who could prove over 50 percent Hawaiian ancestry, the population has now risen to 7,000.

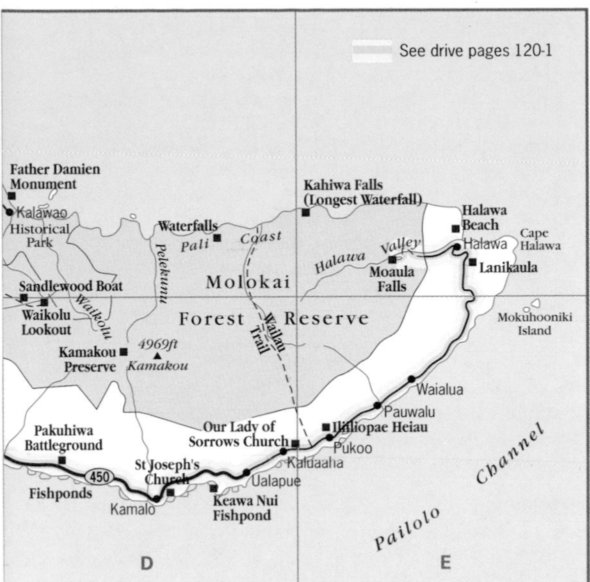

Molokai

THE FRIENDLY ISLE The third smallest of the main Hawaiian islands, Molokai measures a modest 38 miles by 10 miles. The absence of a natural harbor, which slowed development of the island, has actually worked in Molokai's favor. Although the island lies just 9 miles across the Pailolo Channel from Maui, and a 20-minute air hop from Honolulu, it is still 260 square miles of rare, unspoiled natural beauty and quiet rural charm.

The chief settlement, Kaunakakai, lies about midway along the single east–west main road on the central south coast. A laid-back country town, Kaunakakai (and indeed all of Molokai) does not have a single traffic signal or shopping center, and no building is taller than a coconut palm. The 7,000 residents, of whom around half are native Hawaiians (a higher proportion than on any other main island), are quite content to leave tourism to places such as Waikiki and Lahaina. Instead, they proudly point out the fact that over half their visitors are Neighbor Islanders who come to relax, play a little golf, go fishing or hunting, or simply enjoy the peace and quiet.

SCENERY AND CLIMATE The island was formed by two volcanoes—Kamakou in the east and Maunaloa in the west—linked together by a central plateau, and its scenery varies dramatically from one end to the other. Battered by wind, rain, and the relentless ocean, thewindward, northern slopes of Kamakou have been forcibly sculpted into dramatic 3,300-foot-high *pali* (cliffs). These are among the tallest sea cliffs in the world, and rise like an impenetrable moss-coated bulwark slashed by narrow valleys that glint with waterfalls.

The waterfalls are fed by rain clouds snared by the summit of Mount Kamakou (4,970 feet), at the heart of the mountainous East End. Here, in the cool depths of the forest reserve, there are areas of eerie, mist-clad swamp,

▶▶▶ ISLAND HIGHLIGHTS

Kalaupapa
pages 114–115

Kaluakoi and the West Coast Beaches
page 115

Palaau State Park
page 119

LIFE'S A BEACH
Molokai's low-key tourism scene translates to wonderfully deserted beaches. Moomomi Beach is on the northwest coast at the end of a 3-mile stretch of sand. Behind the beach, where rocks outnumber tourists, the massive Moomomi Dunes extend over 4 miles inland. Across the island, a dirt road leads to Kolo Wharf and a string of small sandy beaches. Note that rental cars are not allowed on dirt roads.

where primitive, stunted plants creep among lava boulders. At lower, and markedly warmer, altitudes, the steep hillsides falling down to the coast are swathed in rain forest, and there is a looping necklace of ancient stone-walled fishponds along the south shore.

The central plateau is given over largely to agriculture. The old pineapple plantation town of Kualapuu now experiments with coffee groves, fresh vegetables are a burgeoning business, and there is a macadamia nut orchard. To the west is open ranch country.

Molokai's West End receives a fraction of the East End's rainfall. Here, the island's only traditional resort, Kaluakoi, perches on the shore amid an emerald-green golf course that is flanked by beaches. Inland, the Molokai Ranch (the island's largest, with nearly 60,000 acres) offers a multitude of outdoor activities to guests staying at one of the three safari-camps nestled in the rolling grasslands overlooking the ocean, or in the Molokai Ranch Lodge (see page 119).

HISTORY Molokai was one of the first islands to be settled by the Polynesians (the fertile Halawa Valley in the East End was cultivated from around AD 650), but it was not always so friendly. During the 16th and 17th centuries neighboring islanders, wary of Molokai's powerful *kahuna* (priests), used to call Molokai the "Lonely Island" and avoided contact with it.

Captain Cook sighted Molokai in 1778 but did not stop. Kamehameha I did not allow the threat of the *kahuna* to interfere with his efforts to unite the islands, and took Molokai in 1795. The missionaries arrived in the 1830s,

Halawa Bay was a favorite surfing spot of Molokai's ancient alii *(chiefs)*

Kepuhi beach, Kaluakoi

sheep and cattle ranches were established in the 1840s, and Kamehameha V later secured the prime Molokai Ranch for himself, built a house near Kaunakakai, planted a coconut grove, and introduced axis deer, a present from the emperor of Japan.

In the mid-1800s, Hansen's disease, once widely known as leprosy appeared in Hawaii, possibly introduced by Chinese immigrant workers. A decision was made to isolate the victims on Molokai, casting them adrift off a remote and inaccessible cove on the Kalaupapa peninsula. In 1873, a Belgian priest, Father Damien de Veuster, arrived at the godforsaken colony and devoted his life to caring for the sufferers in one of the most famous true-life stories of Hawaii (see pages 116–117).

Sugar was introduced to Molokai in the 1870s, but the crop, and several later attempts to harvest cane, failed because of irrigation problems. In the 1920s, Del Monte and Dole set up pineapple plantations and associated fruit operations, which kept the island's economy afloat until the 1970s. Diversified agriculture is now the name of the game, though low-key tourism is essential to the island's shaky economy.

GETTING AROUND Molokai airport lies 8 miles northwest of Kaunakakai. Cars can be rented at the airport (reservations essential, especially at weekends). Molokai Charters offers boat tours (tel: 808/553-5852). Molokai Tours & Taxi (tel: 808/553-3369) offers offroad tours and taxi service. There is no public transportation available on the island.

Madame Pele's Ohia lehua *blossom*

SANDALWOOD
In 1810, Western traders discovered sandalwood in the Hawaiian Islands. The Chinese could not get enough of the fragrant timber, and the Hawaiians logged their forests until the last groups of mature sandalwood were destroyed in the late 1820s. Up in the Kamakou preserve, a deep depression alongside the trail is known as Ka Lua Na Moku Iliahi, "The Pit of the Sandalwood Ships." The pits were dug to resemble a ship's hold. Local people felled the sandalwood trees and filled the pit, then sold it as a job lot to trading vessels.

▶▶ Coffees of Hawaii — 110C2

Off HI-470 at Kualapuu
(tel: 808/567-9023 or 01-800/709-BEAN)
Open: Plantation Store daily 10–3; tours by reservation, Mon–Fri. Admission: Plantation Store, free; tours, expensive

Coffee is now grown instead of fruit on 450 acres of former Del Monte pineapple land around the plantation village of Kualapuu. There are free coffee tastings in the Plantation Store, which also houses a good souvenir shop. On weekdays, mule-drawn wagons tour the coffee groves, and there are also visits to the aromatic processing plant.

▶▶▶ Kalaupapa — 110C2

Several daily five-minute shuttle flights with Molokai Air Shuttle (tel: 808/567-6847)
Open: daily tours by reservation only, contact Damien Tours (tel: 808/567-6171); minimum age limit 15 years
Admission: expensive

The Kalaupapa peninsula, a volcanic afterthought tacked onto the central north coast of Molokai, at the foot of the *pali*, was reckoned to be the most isolated outpost of the Hawaiian kingdom in 1865 when Kamehameha V decided to quarantine those with Hansen's disease in a remote area far from the rest of the population.

Spectacular pali *(cliffs) tower over Kalaupapa's old leper colony*

Kayaking is one of the many activities available on Molokai

The first arrivals were literally tossed overboard in Kalawao Cove and left to struggle for survival. Later, Father Damien (see pages 116–117) moved the colony to the more hospitable western shore of the peninsula, where its inhabitants remained cut off from the world until the introduction of sulphone drugs, which arrest the effects of the disease, in the 1940s. Around 50 permanent residents remain by choice in the Kalaupapa village, now open for official tours.

The only land access to Kalaupapa is by foot or mule, via the steep 3-mile trail from Palaau State Park, near the Kalaupapa Lookout (see page 119). Hikers must make reservations in advance and will be met at the foot of the trail by Damien Tours for a guided visit.

▶▶▶ Kaluakoi and the West Coast Beaches *110A2*

At the end of the road on the west coast, the Kaluakoi resort offers hotel and condominium units, an 18-hole oceanfront golf course, tennis courts, a swimming pool, and an activities center (see panel).

There is a trio of terrific beaches close to Kaluakoi: the golf course actually borders lovely **Kepuhi Beach**; **Kawakiu Beach**, with excellent swimming, lies a short walk to the north; and **Papohaku Beach Park** (Mile Marker 15), to the south, boasts the largest white-sand beach in the state. Beyond a small shady park, where barbecue grills and picnic tables stand beneath *kiawe* trees, a strand of coastal woodland borders the dunes.

▶▶ Kamakou Preserve *111D1*

Off HI-470 at Mile Marker 4
Open: Permission from the Nature Conservancy (tel: 808/553-5236). Admission free

The Kamakou Preserve, a 2,774-acre tract of land on the slopes of Kamakou, was established by the Nature Conservancy in 1982 to protect one of the best remaining areas of native Hawaiian forest. A muddy jeep-track winds its way up through the forest past groves of eucalyptus where sandalwood once grew to a viewpoint on the edge of the Waikolu Valley. *Ohia* trees cling to the cliffsides and the rain forest harbors five endangered bird species, including the *olomao* and *kakawahie*, a thrush and a creeper respectively, both found only on Molokai. Near the top of the mountain, a slippery path-cum-boardwalk through moss-wrapped trees and bracts of *amau*, *hapuu*, and *uluhe* ferns leads up to the mysterious Pepeopae Bog.

OUTDOOR ACTIVITIES
Molokai can offer a host of outdoor adventures. Molokai Ranch Activities (tel: 808/552-2791; web: www.molokai-ranch.com) offers kayak trips, mountain biking, horseback riding and sailing. Molokai Charters (tel: 808/553-5852) offers day sails to isolated beaches for snorkeling and whale-watching (in season). Alternatively, try Bill Kapuni's Snorkel & Dive (tel: 808/553-9867). In addition to snorkeling, diving, and spear fishing, Maa Hawaii (tel: 808/558-8184) arranges a guide service for hikers and can organize rifle and bow-hunting excursions.

A colony created in 1865 on northern Molokai's remote Kalaupapa peninsula soon became one of the most godforsaken spots on earth. Its inhabitants, who suffered from the disfiguring and contagious condition once known as leprosy, were left to starve, reduced to little more than animals until a Belgian priest arrived in 1873.

RESTRICTED AREA
Though no longer a place of exile since its remaining inhabitants are now free to come and go as they please, the Kalaupapa peninsula is open to visitors by prior arrangement only. Today, some 50 people (all aged 60 plus) still prefer to stay on voluntarily, and the settlement will continue to be their home for as long as they wish. Sulphone drugs and other pharmaceutical developments have contained Hansen's disease, and former patients now run a guided tour program that was inaugurated in the late 1950s (see pages 114–115).

Hansen's disease Hansen's disease was first seen in Hawaii in the 1830s. The locals called it *mai pake*, "comes from China," and by the 1860s the disease was causing such concern that Kamehameha V agreed to the establishment of a quarantine colony. An isolated site was chosen on the north coast of Molokai, a barren, windswept peninsula bordered on three sides by treacherous seas and more or less cut off from the main body of the island by a natural barrier of towering cliffs. The peninsula was originally known as Makanalua, the "Given Grave."

The schooner *Warwick* transported the first boatload of sufferers to Molokai in January 1866, where they were tossed into the sea at Kalawao on the harsh east coast of the peninsula. Those who survived the waves and rocks were forced to live like wild animals, some constructing rude shacks on the shore or living in caves. There they preyed on new arrivals and fought for the few basic supplies that were occasionally dumped ashore. Fear of the disease was such that unrelated skin diseases were often misdiagnosed; bounty hunters roamed the Hawaiian kingdom wrenching sufferers and nonsufferers alike from their villages and families. The victims were then incarcerated in cages on the ships' decks, taken to Molokai, and dumped in the surf.

St. Joseph's Church at Kamalo

Our Lady of Sorrows Church at Kaluaaha, dated 1874

The Martyr of Molokai Four years before Norwegian scientist Armauer Hansen isolated the bacterium that causes the disease (thereafter known as Hansen's disease), Joseph Damien de Veuster arrived in Hawaii. Born in Tremeloo, Belgium in 1840, he attended the Catholic Seminary of the Sacred Heart in Louvain, before being posted to Hawaii. De Veuster was ordained at Honolulu's Cathedral of Our Lady of Peace in 1864 and was then sent to Puna on the Big Island of Hawaii.

By 1873, a few concerned missionaries had begun to organize a small-scale relief operation for the victims of Hansen's disease on Molokai. Father Damien heard about the mission on a visit to Maui and volunteered to go there for a few months to help out. His stay lasted 16 years.

The scene that greeted the priest had already sent several sickened volunteers scurrying back to civilization at the first opportunity. Although the mission distributed a few meager scraps of food and clothing, medical assistance was nonexistent, and physical contact with the unkempt and disfigured exiles was forbidden.

Father Damien flouted these rules. He bathed and dressed the suppurating wounds of the living and buried the dead himself. An accomplished carpenter, he built shelters, churches, orphanages, and hospitals, investing dignity and hope in the colony. It was moved to the more sheltered west coast of the peninsula, Kalaupapa or the "Flat Plain," and the priest lobbied government and mission agencies for supplies. A 3-mile trail carved down the *pali* in 1886 allowed mule trains to bring provisions, and Father Damien sold the produce of his vegetable plot for nails and bandages. Although many admired his extraordinary dedication and achievements, the good father also stirred up resentment among both mission and government circles.

The first tell-tale lesions of Hansen's disease appeared on Father Damien's body in 1885. Despite his illness, he continued his work to improve the lot of the people of Kalaupapa right up until his death, aged 49, in 1889. He was buried beside St. Philomena's, the church he built at Kalawao, although his remains were returned to Belgium in 1936.

HONORS AND DECORATIONS
What Father Damien would make of the present attention focused on him is hard to say. He rarely wore the Cross of the Royal Order of Kalakaua awarded to him in recognition of his selfless contribution to the plight of Hansen's disease sufferers on Kalaupapa, and later remarked, "The Lord has decorated me with his own particular cross—leprosy." Honored more recently by a statue erected near the State Capitol in Honolulu, the so-called Martyr of Molokai was also beatified by the Roman Catholic Church in 1995, the penultimate step before elevation to sainthood.

Statue of Father Damien beside St. Joseph's church

MOLOKAI RANCH TRAIL RIDES
A terrific way for guests to explore outback Molokai is on horseback with Molokai Ranch Trail Rides (tel: 808/552-2791). Local guides are full of information as the 1½-hour (or longer) rides follow trails across the private ranchlands above Kualapuu. There are views down the *pali* (cliffs) to the Kaluapapa peninsula and across to the sand dunes of Moomomi Beach.

▶ Kaunakakai 110C1

Reminiscent of an Old West trading post, Kaunakakai probably looks much as it did when *The Cockeyed Mayor of Kaunakakai* was a hit song in the 1930s. Among the false-fronted shops, Molokai Fish & Dive has an eclectic line of souvenirs and equipment for snorkeling, fishing, diving, and hunting. Down on the dock, you can watch canoe paddling youngsters, sample *poke* (raw fish) salad, and arrange sightseeing, diving, or sport-fishing trips.

A short drive (3 miles) west of town takes you to the half-dozen small chapels of picturesque **Church Row**. Across the street is the coconut grove which was planted by Kamehameha V in the mid-1800s.

▶▶ Maunaloa 110B1

The town that pineapple built: the firm of Libby, McNeill, and Libby literally shipped Maunaloa to Molokai in 1923. From a consignment of prefabricated houses, they constructed a plantation town among the pineapple fields. Although the pineapples have now gone, a restored Maunaloa retains its old-fashioned charm and neat rows of houses.

A colorful collection of fluttering windsocks and pennants heralds Maunaloa's famous diversion. Jonathan Socher's Big Wind Kite Store (tel: 808/552-2364) is the place to learn how to fly a *hula* dancer, a hibiscus flower, or a shark. Socher makes many of the kites on sale in his on-site workshop, and there are serious (and expensive) competition models and stunt kites, too (*Open:* Mon–Sat 8:30–5, Sun 10–2).

▶ Molokai Museum and Cultural Center 110C2

Off HI-470 at Kalae (tel: 808/567-6436)
Open: Mon–Sat 10–2. Admission: inexpensive

Rudolph Meyer arrived in Molokai from Hamburg, Germany, in 1850. He married a local chieftainess, had 11 children, farmed, managed Kamehameha V's Molokai Ranch, and still found time to take on more than a dozen public offices. Meyer experimented briefly with growing sugar, but without success. However, his old mill, which operated from 1878 to 1889 and was the smallest in Hawaii, has been restored to show the crushers and vats, the steam engine, and the clarifier.

As good as new, this engine once powered Hawaii's smallest sugar mill

View from the Kalaupapa Lookout

▶ Molokai Ranch 110A2

Molokai Ranch, Maunaloa (reservations tel: 808/552-2791 or 800/254-8871; web: www.molokai-ranch.com)
Open: all year; reservations

Originally formed by Kamehameha V in the 1850s, the Hawaiian Islands' second-largest ranch has 53,000 acres of rolling grasslands with three camps that provide deluxe accommodations, in either tents, yurts, or a deluxe lodge, with spectacular views over the ocean and neighboring islands. Activities from mountain biking and horseback riding to kayaking and snorkeling are available for paying guests. From November to May the general public can enjoy humpback whale viewing trips, and for the rest of the year fishing excursions are also on offer.

▶▶ Palaau State Park 110C2

Central north coast via HI-470

The chief reason to visit this 234-acre forested park on the crest of the *pali* (cliff) is for the eagle's-eye view it affords of Kalaupapa and the Makanalua peninsula, 1,500 feet below. The Kalaupapa Lookout is a five-minute walk through the woods from the parking lot.

Another path ends up at the **Phallic Rock**. It is no surprise that the ancient Hawaiians recognized this 6-foot protuberance as a fertility symbol. Infertile women, they say, need only stroke it...

▶▶ Purdy's Macadamia Nut Farm 110B2

Off HI-480, Hoolehua (tel: 808/567-6601)
Open: Mon–Sat 9:30–3. Admission free

Macadamia nut trees were first introduced to Hawaii in 1882 from Queensland, Australia, and the islands now produce a $44 million annual crop. Here on Tuddie Purdy's 1-acre, macadamia grove, after a short introduction, you can get down to the serious business of tasting. There is a slab of granite and a hammer to crack open the rock-hard shells. Tuddie also sells precracked roasted and salted kernels, as well as macadamia-flower honey, which you can sample on slivers of coconut.

CELEBRATING THE *HULA*
It is said that Maunaloa ("Long Mountain") was the birthplace of the *hula*, where the goddess Laka learned the dance from her sister Kapo. Laka traveled all around the other islands teaching the *hula*, and set up a sacred *hula* school at Haena on the island of Kauai. These days *hula* dancers from the Neighbor Islands come to Molokai on the third Saturday in May for Molokai Ka Hula Piko, a celebration of the birth of *hula*, and a day of free *hula* performances, Hawaiian music, and crafts.

Heavy duty tools to crack Macadamia nuts

Drive

From Kaunakakai to the East End

See map on pages 110–111.

A single road (HI-450) runs out from Kaunakakai along the coast to the Halawa Valley at the eastern tip of Molokai. Apart from great scenery, there are several low-key sites to visit along the way. History buffs wanting to visit the Iliiliopae Heiau, which is on private land, should contact Junior Rawlins Molokai Wagon Rides (tel: 808/558-8132).

Breathtaking views of where the Halawa Valley meets the Pacific Ocean

At the time of writing, the hiking route to the Halawa Valley's Moaula Falls is closed to the public because of a dispute about access, but check for developments with the Molokai Visitors Association (tel: 808/553-3876). Pack a picnic, fill up with gas (there are no gas stations en route), and allow a couple of hours to follow the scenic 30-mile road to Halawa at a leisurely pace.

The road heads out east toward Kamalo along the sea. Once, more than 60 ancient fishponds fringed Molokai's southeastern coast, lassoing the shallow waters in neat arcs of lava and coral boulders. Some of the fishponds date from the 13th century and are in use again for breeding mullet. **Keawa Nui** is the biggest, enclosing 54½ acres within its 2,000-foot seawall. Several other fishponds along the route are visible from the road.

At Kamalo (Mile Marker 10.5), **St. Joseph's Church** is a simple white-painted wooden church that was built by Father Damien in 1876. In addition to his work at the Kalaupapa colony, the priest also ministered to other settlers on the island. He built four churches outside Kalaupapa, of which only St. Joseph's and one other still stand. A statue of him stands by the entrance to the Gothic-style building.

A couple of miles farther on, the other Father Damien church, **Our Lady of Sorrows**, dates from 1874 but was rebuilt in 1966. There is a fine view from the open lawn past a giant wooden cross to the shallow waters of an ancient fishpond.

Just beyond Mile Marker 15.5 is Molokai Wagon Rides, which also offers horse-back riding from spectacular beach-front stables, through the island's largest mango grove, then inland, returning along the beach.

A 15 minute walk from the road over private land takes you to **Iliiliopae Heiau** (for directions see above), one of the largest (if not oldest) temple sites in Hawaii. The vast rock-strewn platform of the *heiau* stands 22 feet high and is surrounded by rain-forest jungle. Archeologists date the vast platform, which measures an astonishing 320 feet by 120 feet, between the 11th and 13th centuries. Powerful priests who carried out the most sacred and complex religious rites at Iliiliopae earned the island the name of *Molokai pule oo*, the "place of mature prayer."

Beyond Pukoo, the views along the rocky coast are tremendous. As the road climbs around hairpin bends into the Puu O Hoku ranchlands, look for **Mokuhooniki Island**, an offshore seabird sanctuary.

Panoramic views of the **Halawa Valley**, cut deep into the *pali* (cliffs), open up after Mile Marker 25. The valley was a major settlement site up until 1946, when a massive *tsunami* (tidal wave caused by an undersea earthquake or volcanic eruption) wiped out many of its farms. Now the jungle is reclaiming dozens of home and temple sites and choking terraces once irrigated by the Halawa Stream. At the mouth of the stream there is a small crescent-shaped beach. It is not safe to swim here, but the bay was a favorite surfing spot for the *alii* (chiefs).

A 2-mile trail crosses private property, so permission must be obtained before heading up the valley to the **Moaula Falls**. The pool beneath the falls is said to be guarded by a giant *moo*. Bathers should throw a *ti* leaf onto the pool to check the mythical lizard's mood: if the leaf floats it is safe to go in the water, if it sinks, steer clear.

Iliiliopae Heiau

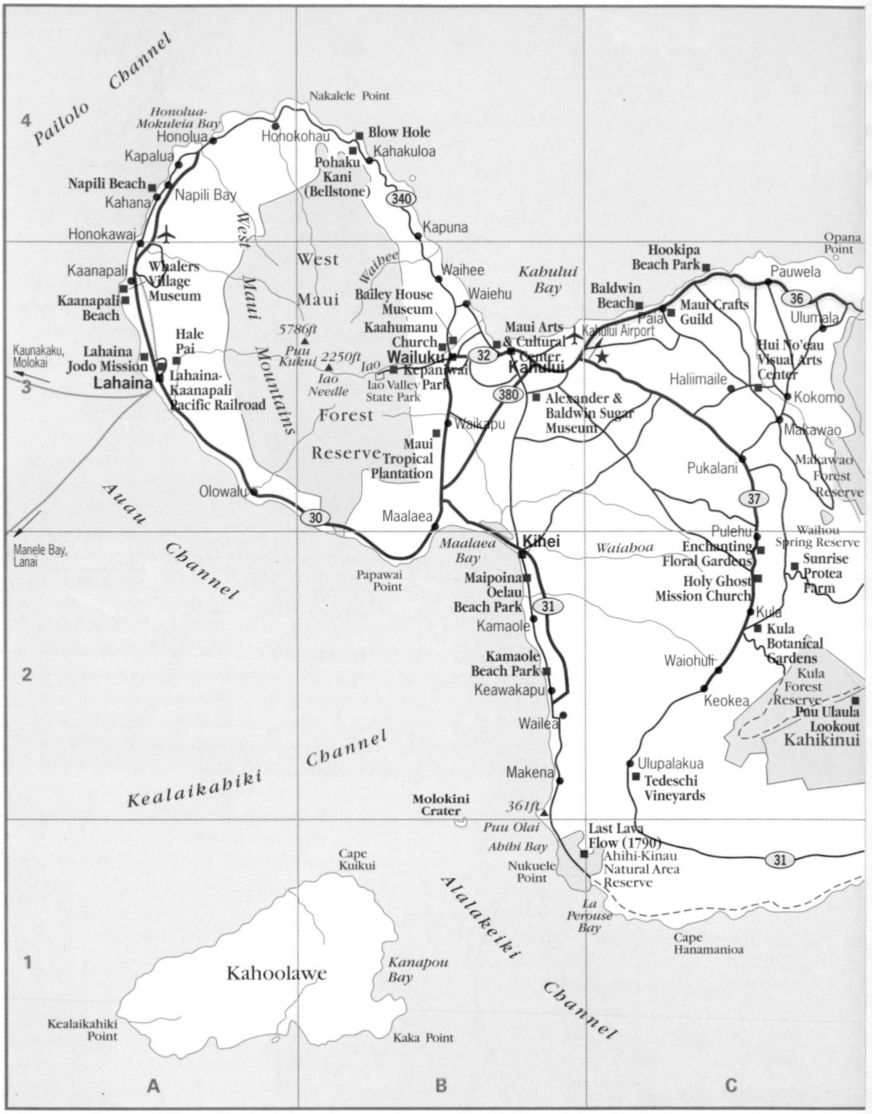

Pailolo Channel
Nakalele Point
4
Honolua-Mokuleia Bay
Honolua
Honokohau
Blow Hole
Kahakuloa
Kapalua
Pohaku Kani (Bellstone)
Napili Beach
Napili Bay
Kahana
340
Honokawai
West Maui Mountains
Kapuna
Kaanapali
Whalers Village Museum
West Maui
Waihee
Waihee
Kahului Bay
Hookipa Beach Park
Opana Point
Pauwela
Kaanapali Beach
Bailey House Museum
Waiehu
Baldwin Beach
Maui Crafts Guild
36
Paia
Ulumala
Hale Pai
5786ft
Kaahumanu Church
Maui Arts & Cultural Center
Kahului Airport
Kaunakaku, Molokai
Lahaina Jodo Mission
Puu Kukui
2250ft
Iao
Wailuku
32
Kahului
Hui No'eau Visual Arts Center
3
Lahaina
Lahaina-Kaanapali Pacific Railroad
Iao Needle
Kepaniwai Park
Iao Valley State Park
380
Alexander & Baldwin Sugar Museum
Haliimaile
Kokomo
Forest
Waikapu
Makawao
Reserve
Maui Tropical Plantation
Pukalani
Makawao Forest Reserve
Auau Channel
Olowalu
37
30
Maalaea
Waihou Spring Reserve
Manele Bay, Lanai
Maalaea Bay
Kihei
Waiaboa
Pulehu
Enchanting Floral Gardens
Sunrise Protea Farm
Channel
Papawai Point
Maipoina Oelau Beach Park
Holy Ghost Mission Church
31
Kamaole
Kula
Kula Botanical Gardens
2
Kamaole Beach Park
Waiohuli
Kula Forest Reserve
Keawakapu
Keokea
Puu Ulaula Lookout
Wailea
Kahikinui
Channel
Ulupalakua
Kealaikahiki
Makena
Tedeschi Vineyards
Molokini Crater
361ft
Puu Olai
Last Lava Flow (1790)
Ahihi Bay
Cape Kuikui
Nukuele Point
Ahihi-Kinau Natural Area Reserve
31
Alalakeiki
La Perouse Bay
Cape Hanamanioa
1
Kanapou Bay
Kahoolawe
Channel
Kealaikahiki Point
Kaka Point
A
B
C

Maui

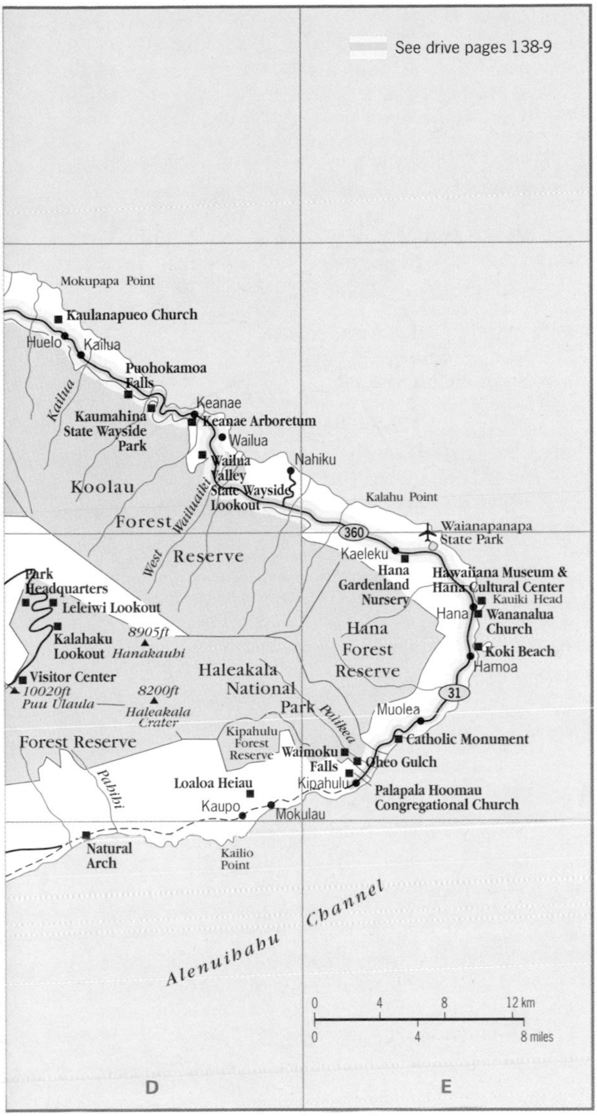

See drive pages 138-9

THE VALLEY ISLE The legendary demigod Maui, known for his feats of cunning and superhuman strength, lifted the sky so that humans could walk upright, slowed down the sun, and gave Hawaiians the secret of fire. His namesake island is almost as full of surprises as he was. Maui is the second-largest island in the Hawaiian archipelago, some 124 square miles bigger than Oahu but with just 10 percent of the population. Although Maui's tourist industry is well developed (it is number two in the tourism stakes, welcoming around 2 million visitors each year), the main resort areas of the island are confined to pockets along the sunnier, drier west coast and it is easy to escape into unspoiled, open countryside.

TRANSPORTATION
Public transportation is limited on Maui, so most visitors rent a car for a couple of days. Trans Hawaiian (tel: 808/877-7308) operates a shuttle between Kahului airport and locations in the Kaanapali resort area. Speedy Shuttle (tel: 808/875-8070) serves all Maui resort areas. Free shuttle buses operate within the Wailea resort area. The main center for information about car rental is the airport at Kahului.

PLANTATIONS
Competition from Asia has virtually destroyed the Hawaiian pineapple industry, once the biggest in the world. A few fields of pineapples remain under cultivation north of Lahaina on West Maui and southeast of Kahalui on East Maui. Most of the competition comes from the Philippines, and ironically it is Filipino labor that enables what is left of the industry to survive.

GEOGRAPHY Maui is shaped like a kneeling man craning down for a look at the offshore crater of Molokini and the uninhabited island of Kahoolawe, and was formed by two volcanoes linked by an isthmus. The head is mountainous West Maui, where Puu Kukui (5,788 feet) snags the clouds that feed its rain-forested slopes. The sheltered leeward (west) coast harbors the old whaling port of Lahaina and the popular resorts of Kaanapali and Kapalua.

Maui's commercial centers, modern Kahului and the older county seat of Wailuku, lie at the northern end of the neck, a low-lying valley that gives the island its soubriquet. Most visitors arrive at Kahului airport and then head across for Lahaina-Kaanapali, or to south Maui's Wailea-Makena resort areas.

East Maui is the kneeling man's torso, and at its heart is magnificent Haleakala (the "House of the Sun"), the largest dormant volcano in the world. At 10,023 feet, with a crater that could comfortably accommodate Manhattan, Haleakala is quite literally the high spot of the island and a "must see" on any tourist itinerary.

On Haleakala's gentle western slopes, the cane fields of the valley give way to upcountry ranchlands and flower farms. Cattle country extends around to the south via the Tedeschi vineyards, where Hawaiian pineapple and other wines are made, and eventually runs into the rainforest belt that circles the windward portion of the mountain. The road to Hana along the lush windward coast is another visitors' "must"—54 miles and 600 curves of twisting tarmac edged by forest and waterfalls on one side, and startling views of the deep-blue sea and the rocky and windswept shore on the other.

WARRIORS AND WHALERS When Captain Cook stopped at Hawaii, Maui was ruled by powerful Chief Kahekili. In the 1780s, Kahekili brought Oahu and Molokai under his control and proved a formidable opponent to the great Kamehameha I (who some say was his son). Kamehameha eventually took control of Maui after Kahekili's death in 1794, and later established a royal seat at Lahaina, where his sons held court until the 1840s.

The whalers beat the missionaries to Maui by about four years, and during the mid-1800s turned the sheltered harbor of Lahaina into the whaling capital of the world.

Silver-green pineapple fields on the north shore

Meanwhile, the missionaries did battle for the Hawaiians' souls and tried every means to counter the licentious and alcohol-fueled antics of the whalers.

After the royal court was moved to Honolulu and the whaling ships left town for good, Lahaina slipped back into obscurity and waited for a new foreign invasion in the form of tourism. In recent years its picturesque wooden buildings have been restored and refitted, and it has emerged as Maui's leading tourist town. Along Front Street, where tour operators hustle good-naturedly for the tourist dollar, there are plenty of boutiques and galleries, bars and restaurants, and self-conscious new owners of garish *aloha* shirts pack the sidewalks three or four deep in a lively and entertaining street parade.

VACATION ACTIVITIES The sheltered waters of Lahaina Harbor, where hundreds of whaling ships once rode at anchor, now buzz with sailing yachts and charter boats heading for Lanai or the snorkel and dive sites around Molokini. Other popular options are whale-watching excursions and deep-sea fishing charters. On Lahaina's main street you can book boat trips, or sign up for bus tours, surfing lessons, parasailing, helicopter flights, submarine adventures, horseback-riding, and even bicycle rides down Haleakala.

Perfect vacations on Maui come in all shapes and sizes. For some, the ideal is a long weekend relaxing by the pool of a Kaanapali hotel within a stone's throw of a wonderful restaurant; others may prefer to spend a week or more hiking on Haleakala or diving off Molokini. However, there is no doubt that for the locals and many repeat visitors *Maui no ka oi*, "Maui is the best."

The first Western visitors to Maui landed at rocky La Pérouse Bay

▶▶▶ ISLAND HIGHLIGHTS

Drive: The road to Hana
pages 138–139

Haleakala National Park
pages 140–141

Kaanapali-Kapalua
page 133

Lahaina–Kaanapali & Pacific Railroad
page 128

Molokini Excursions
pages 128–129

APPROXIMATE DRIVING TIMES FROM KAHULUI

- Haleakala: 1 hour 45 minutes
- Hana: 2 hours 30 minutes
- Kaanapali: 50 minutes
- Kapalua: 1 hour
- Lahaina: 45 minutes
- Wailea: 35 minutes

LOKO O MOKUHINIA
One of the most sacred sites of ancient Hawaii now lies buried beneath a baseball diamond in Lahaina's Maluulu O Lele Park. Once there was a sacred freshwater fishpond here, Loko O Mokuhinia, guarded by Princess Kihawahine (daughter of Maui's famous 16th-century chieftain, Piilani), who changed into a *moo* (giant lizard goddess) on her death. It was considered a place of the highest *mana* (spiritual power). Kamehameha III built himself a private retreat here, as well as a royal tomb for his mother, Queen Keopuolani, his sister Nahienaena, and her child (later moved to Wainee churchyard).

Lahaina

A long, thin strip of a town stretched along the waterfront, the attractive old whaling port of Lahaina still seems a nugget of 19th-century New England in paradise. Even though galleries and T-shirt shops replace the whaling era's grog shops and ships' chandlers, and a measure of rum at the Pioneer Inn now takes the form of a cocktail with a complimentary paper umbrella and half a fruit bowl floating on top, Front Street's clapboard buildings retain an old-fashioned, maritime air.

The 18th-century chieftain Kahekili held court in Lahaina, and Kamehameha I, in the early days of his reign, built the "Brick Palace," the first Western-style structure erected in the islands, down by the harbor. Set back from here, around the Reverend Baldwin's mission home, is the heart of old Lahaina, now a National Historic Landmark and well worth exploring on foot (see pages 130–131).

There is a helpful tourist information kiosk at the Wharf Cinema Center, 658 Front Street, where the free Lahaina Express bus service drops its passengers from Kaanapali. The kiosk is a handy place to make tour arrangments and to find out what bargains are available.

Traffic moves even more slowly than the pedestrians on Front Street, and parking in the town is a problem. There is a three-hour parking lot at the corner of Front and Prison Streets, and several of the shopping centers off Wainee Street (one block inland from Front Street) provide customer parking. The meters in the town center allow only one hour's parking.

The Carthaginian II *lies on a wharf opposite the Pioneer Inn*

Front Street, formerly the center of Lahaina's whaling industry. Today the main catch is tourists

▶▶ Baldwin Home Museum — 130B2

Front Street (tel: 808/661-3262)
Open: daily 10–4:30. Admission: moderate
This handsome green- and white-painted two-story house overlooks the harbor across the town square. The oldest existing building in Lahaina, the mission house was built in 1834. The Reverend Dwight Baldwin and his wife Charlotte moved here in 1838. Tours of the first floor reveal details of the life of a missionary physician in the 1800s. Besides period furnishings, there are handcrafted family heirlooms and the Reverend Baldwin's gruesome medical instruments, as well as his antique passport, which, without the benefit of a photograph, lists his features: "Forehead—High, Nose—Aquiline, Chin—Obtuse."

▶▶ Brig *Carthaginian II* — 130A2

Off Wharf Street (next to the Small Boat Harbor) (tel: 808/661-8527) Open: daily 10–4:30. Admission: moderate
The 93-foot steel-hulled *Carthaginian II* was built in the 1920s and is a replica of the fast, square-rigged brigs that brought the whalers and traders to Lahaina in the 19th century. It is now a whaling museum. Exhibits are augmented with audiovisual displays, including videos of whales in action and an original whaling boat that was recovered in Alaska and returned to Lahaina in 1973.

▶ Hale Pai — 122A3

Lahainaluna High School (2 miles north of Front Street)
Open: Mon–Sat 10–4. Admission: inexpensive
In 1831, the missionaries established the Lahainaluna Seminary up in the hills behind town. Here they installed a printing house, the Hale Pai, where they produced textbooks, religious tracts, dictionaries, and teaching aids in the newly devised Hawaiian alphabet.

The seminary, now a high school, and the printing house in its grounds are respectively the oldest educational establishment and oldest printing works in the country west of the Rockies. The Hale Pai printed the first newspaper and paper currency in Hawaii, and printing demonstrations are given using a replica of the original Ramage press. One of the best reasons for coming here is the view over the town.

ART COMES TO TOWN
Friday night in downtown Lahaina is "Art Night," when many of the town's 40 or so art galleries throw open their doors and invite visitors to come in and watch demonstrations, talk to local artists about their work, nibble snacks, and enjoy free entertainment. Marine art is big business in Lahaina, where whales and dolphins rule the canvas. This is home to Wyland, whose massive marine murals one critic described as "defacing buildings the length and breadth of North America."

The Lahaina–Kaanapali Sugar Cane Train

LUAU AND HULA
When it comes to finding a good *luau* on Maui, the Old Lahaina Luau, 1251 Front Street (tel: 808/667-1998) has a longstanding reputation for providing one of the most authentic Hawaiian feasts. The site is great—right on the beach front—numbers are limited and the music and dance are truly traditional Hawaiian. The Outrigger Wailea Resort (tel: 808/879-1922) has won awards for its *luau* and *hula* show with an ocean-front setting. The Hyatt Regency Maui (tel: 808/661-1234) in Kaanapali, and the Maui Marriott (tel: 808/661-5828) put on a more Polynesian-type experience.

▶ Hawaii Experience *130A3*

Domed Theater, 824 Front Street (tel: 808/661-8314)
Open: daily 10–10, shows every hour.
Admission: moderate
A whistle-stop tour of the best scenery Hawaii has to offer is provided courtesy of a giant three-story-high, 180-degree Omni-vision movie screen. During the 40-minute film, spectators "swim" with reef fish and humpback whales, brave close encounters with fiery fountains of volcanic lava, are dazzled by sunrise over the Haleakala crater, and swoop above Kauai's dramatic Waimea Canyon.

▶ Lahaina Jodo Mission *122A3*

12 Ala Moana Street
Open: grounds only, daily. Admission free
Near the northern end of Lahaina's Front Street, against a backdrop of the West Maui mountains, is the Buddhist Jodo Mission. Its compound contains the largest Amida Buddha statue outside Japan. The serene copper and bronze figure of the Amida, worshiped by the Pure Land Buddhists, stands 12½ feet tall, weighs around 3½ tons, and was brought here from Kyoto, Japan in 1968 to commemorate the arrival of the first Japanese immigrants in Hawaii 100 years before. (The pagoda and temple within the compound are closed to the public.)

▶▶▶ Lahaina–Kaanapali & Pacific Railroad *122A3*

Lahaina and Kaanapali depots inland of Honoapiilani Highway (free bus to central Lahaina)
Open: daily 8:30–4:30, schedules tel: 808/661-0080
Admission: one-way, moderate
A genuine 1890s locomotive known as the Sugar Cane Train plies the 6-mile (30-minute) route between Lahaina and Kaanapali. There are six round trips a day, and the conductor provides an entertaining history of the local sugar industry along the way.

▶▶▶ Molokini Excursions *122B3*

The marine preserve around the largely submerged, crescent-shaped Molokini Crater, 11 miles out from Maalaea harbor, is one of the world's best (and busiest) snorkeling spots. There is a stunning array of brilliantly colored reef fish in its warm, gin-clear waters, dolphins and sea turtles are frequently spotted, and from December to April the round trip out to the crater becomes an unofficial whale-watching cruise.

Most cruises leave from Maalaea harbor (off HI-30 at the southwest corner of West Maui) or the Lahaina Small Boat Harbor. Two of the nicest ways to go are aboard Maui Classic Charters' *Lavengro* (tel: 808/879-8188), an elegant 1926 schooner; and any of the Coon family's comfortable fleet of catamarans named *Trilogy* (tel: 808/661-4743). Snorkeling instruction and equipment, together with breakfast and lunch, are all part of the deal. Maui Classic Charters also operate morning and afternoon trips to the crater on the 53-foot, glass-bottomed catamaran *Four Winds*, which allows its passengers to admire the underwater scenery without getting wet (snorkelers are welcome, too).

►► Pioneer Inn 130A2

658 Wharf Street (tel: 808/661-3636)
Admission free

Built in 1901 by a Royal Canadian Mountie who journeyed all the way to Maui but did not get his man (instead he fell in love with a local woman and stayed), the Pioneer Inn is the oldest hotel on Maui. The timber-framed, Victorian-style inn was too late to welcome the whalers, but the walls of the lobby and bar are decorated with whaling memorabilia and antique photographs, as well as a copy of the original house rules ("Women is not allow in you room... If you burn you bed you going out"). The inn still takes guests, and there is a selection of restaurants and shops arranged around its central courtyard.

►► Wo Hing Temple 130A3

858 Front Street (tel: 808/661-5553)
Open: daily 10–4:30. Admission: donation

Guarded by a pair of carved jade *fu* dogs, this former temple is now a modest museum devoted to Chinese history and culture in the islands. It was built in 1912 by Chinese immigrants, but as the Chinese population in Maui declined so did the building, which was restored in 1983. Next door, in the old wooden cookhouse, among the pots, pans, woks, and baskets, there is a continuous showing of flickering, black-and-white films shot in downtown Lahaina by Thomas Edison in 1898 and 1906.

Pioneer Inn

DAY TRIPS FROM MAUI

Maui County covers the quiet neighboring islands of Lanai (see pages 146–151) and Molokai (see pages 110–121), both of which can be visited in a day from Maui. There are regular daily flights (15 minutes) from Kahului airport and ferries to Lanai from Lahaina. Charter companies offering day sails around Lanai include Navatek II (tel: 808/661-8787) and the excellent Trilogy Excursions' Discover Lanai tours (tel: 808/661-4743), which combine a day sail with a barbecue lunch on a private beach, snorkeling, scuba diving, and fishing, plus a bus tour of what was once known as the "Pineapple Isle."

Buddhist tranquility at Lahaina Jodo Mission

Around Old Lahaina

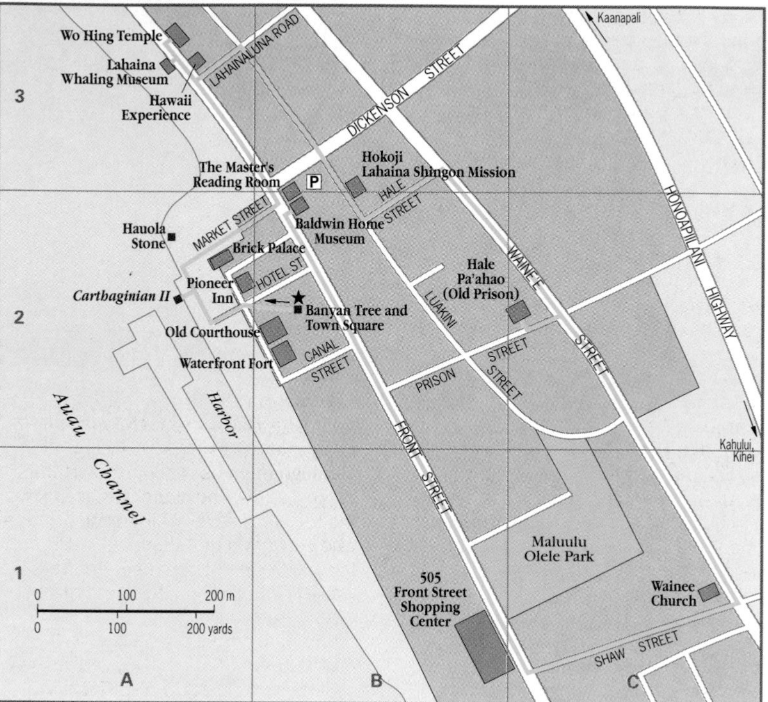

The historic heart of Lahaina is ideally suited to a leisurely sightseeing stroll because of its compact size. Preface the walk by having breakfast at the Pioneer Inn, which overlooks the harbor and the brig *Carthaginian II*. The entire stroll should take around an hour without stops for sightseeing.

To the south of the Pioneer Inn is the **town square**. It is dominated by a massive **banyan tree**, which was a mere 8-foot sapling when it was planted in April 1873 to celebrate a half-century of missionary work in Lahaina. Now its spreading limbs, supported on 12 major trunks, shade over two-thirds of an acre, making it the largest banyan tree on the islands. Behind the tree, the **Old Courthouse**, built in 1859, houses the Lahaina Arts Society gallery. In the far corner of the square, some coral blocks mark the site of an 1830s waterfront fort.

Still in the harbor area, have a look at the handsome square-rigged brig, the ***Carthaginian II***, which now tells the town's maritime and whaling history in a small on-board museum (see page 127). A little farther on from the brig is the site of the **Brick Palace**. Kamehameha I commissioned two ex-convicts from Australia to build a Western-style "Brick Palace" for Queen Kaahumanu here on the waterfront. The queen, however, preferred a traditional grass hut to the two-story brick building with its stuffy glazed windows. All that now remains of the palace is the excavated foundation. Nearby, below the seawall, the flat **Hauola Stone** was venerated in ancient times for its healing powers.

Go up Market Street into Front Street, turn left and walk two blocks to find the Chinese **Wo Hing Temple** (see page 129). During the 19th century, successful Chinese merchants in

Hawaii set up friendly societies, one of which built this small temple, now a cultural museum. From here, cross the street to Crazy Shirts, 865 Front Street. Tucked in the back of this shop is the **Lahaina Whaling Museum**, which has a small, free display of whaling artifacts, from log books to scrimshaw and harpoon guns.

Backtrack down Front Street to Lahainaluna Road; turn left for one block, then right onto quiet Luakini Street. Shaded by glossy breadfruit and mango trees, it is a welcome break from the bustling crowds in Front Street. Look for the **Hokoji Lahaina Shingon Mission**, a simple, green and yellow wooden mission building typical of many plantation-era Japanese temples. Take a left turn onto Hale Street, then right onto Wainee Street, passing the plumeria trees of the Episcopal Cemetery and the fanciful coral rock garden of No. 635, to Prison Street and the **Hale Paahao (Old Prison)**. This was built in 1854, and according to a contemporary report by one William Stetson, life was far from hard for the inmates of Lahiana's "stuck-in-irons-house." The single block of cells, constructed out of coral stone, is surrounded by a grassy yard, where male and female inmates "mingled promiscuously" and "any sedate individual could therefore lay back all day with a pipe in his mouth and enjoy himself...as well as though he was comfortably stowed away in a beer house."

The remains of the waterfront fort

Return to Wainee Street and walk as far as the **Wainee Church**. This is the site of Hawaii's oldest stone church, although the present edifice was built in the 1950s. The churchyard contains the tombs of several kings and queens who converted to Christianity; they include Queen Keopuolani, Princess Nahienaena, and the last king of Kauai, Kaumualii.

Turn right onto Shaw Street and return to Front Street, shop at the mall at **505 Front Street** or visit **Baldwin Home Museum** (see page 127).

Beneath the banyan tree

"DAMMING OF THE WATERS" PARK
In 1790, Kamehameha I scored a significant victory over his rival Kahekili in the Iao Valley. Though Kahekili himself was absent on Oahu, Kamehameha sailed across from Hawaii and engaged Kahekili's son, Kalanikupule, in battle. Armed with a Western cannon and assisted by two British seamen, Kamehameha's forces trounced the defending army and pushed it back into the mountains. The piles of bodies dammed the river, hence the name of Kepaniwai ("Damming of the Waters") Park, a mile or so downstream (see page 136).

Iao Needle is a short climb from the parking lot at the end of Iao Valley Road

West Maui

► Honolua–Mokuleia Bay and the North Coast *122A4*

HI-30, just beyond Mile Marker 32
Open site. Admission free

Northeast of Kapalua, HI-30 turns into a twisting corniche road that hugs the northern coast around to Nakalele Point (Mile Marker 38). There are panoramic views of the jagged black and red volcanic rocks crumbling into the ocean below, while Molokai looms large on the horizon across the Pailolo Channel.

Steep cliff paths lead down from the road to several secluded beaches. The sandy crescent of beach fronting the marine life conservation district of Honolua—Mokuleia Bay is rarely crowded, and it is an excellent place for snorkeling and bodysurfing.

►► Iao Valley State Park *122B3*

HI-32, 3 miles west of Wailuku (tel: 808/984-8109)
Open: daily 7–7. Admission free

The inaccessible green buttresses and misty valleys of the West Maui mountains encircle Puu Kukui, the summit of Maui's oldest volcano. This is the second wettest spot in Hawaii (after Kauai's Mount Waialeale), receiving an average 400 inches of rain a year. Over millions of years, erosion has chiseled away the softer rock that connected the Iao Needle to neighboring ridges, leaving the 1,200-foot-tall, free-standing volcanic plug wedged into a valley between steep, green cliffs.

Maui's north shore, around Honolua Bay, is a mecca for surfers

Iao Needle is the centerpiece of the state park, and there is a 133-step stairway winding up from the parking lot to a lookout platform. Below, other paths lead down to a boulder-strewn stream bed. (To avoid the crowds, visit the park in the early morning or after 4:30 PM.)

▶▶▶ Kaanapali–Kapalua *122A3*

Kaanapali, about 5 miles north of Lahaina, was the first planned resort development in the state and remains one of its most attractive vacation destinations. The long, sandy beach lining Kaanapali Bay stretches on either side of a volcanic outcrop known as Black Rock.

South of Black Rock, a 3-mile run of elegant, high-rise hotels and condominiums set in landscaped grounds offers hedonistic accommodations and fine restaurants. "Shop-'til-you-drop" vacationers have plenty of choice in the hotel boutiques and the classy Whalers Village shopping mall, which also offers two whaling museums (see below), while the temptations of downtown Lahaina are only 10 minutes away.

Outdoor activities include tennis, watersports, great snorkeling around Black Rock, and golf courses with views. Several nightclubs offer scope to night owls, and there are *luau* and family entertainment in the form of children's programs put on by hotels.

Between Kaanapali and Kapalua to the north is Napili Bay, where more moderately priced condominiums have gone up alongside a good swimming beach. Gracious living is restored within the 750-acre spread of the tasteful Kapalua Bay Resort, which has its own tennis courts, championship golf courses, and stores. Just north of Kapalua, D.T. Fleming Beach is definitely one of Maui's finest stretches of sandy shoreline.

For a riveting insight into the history of whaling in the Pacific region, do not miss the **Whalers Village Museum▶▶** (Whalers Village Mall, Kaanapali, tel: 808/661-5113. *Open:* daily 9:30 AM–10 PM. *Admission free*). The museum's informative signboards, displays of whalers' weapons, scrimshaw items, and a replica of a claustrophobic forecastle where a crew of between 12 and 20 men would be cooped up for months on end cover the subject in an accessible and lively way.

In the Hale Kohala, across from the museum, attention is focused on live whales. More models and photographs tell you in detail about these amazing creatures, and there is a film theater for video presentations. The gift shop does a brisk trade in whale books, model kits, jewelry, and art.

SHELL GAMES

Hawaii is one of the best places in the world to go shell hunting—with over 1,500 varieties with names like Episcopal miter, Hebrew cone, and horned helmet. The sandy shore of Maui are some of the best areas in the islands; the beaches from Maalaea Bay to Makena should provide a fertile hunting ground. Collect only shells that have been washed ashore. The coral reefs are delicate living formations and must be protected.

LIGHT AND SCENT

Did you know that the blubber of a single sperm whale could yield up to 2,000 gallons of high-quality oil? It was used in 19th-century lamps and for lubricating fine machinery. In addition to oil, sperm whales yielded spermaceti, a thick, white, waxy substance that was made into candles, and ambergris, which was used in perfumes to make the fragrance last longer.

Few mysteries run as deep as the enigmatic song of the humpback whale, and there are few sights as stirring as these magnificent creatures cavorting in their winter breeding and calving grounds off the coast of Maui. From November until April, Hawaii is one of the world's prime whale-watching spots.

WHALE-WATCHING
Hemmed in by Lanai and Molokai, the quiet, sheltered waters off the west coast of Maui are the best whale-watching territory in Hawaii. In winter, charter-boat operators offer daily whale-watching excursions, though plenty of whales are sighted from the shore off Kaanapali, Wailea and, best of all, Papawai Point overlooking Maalaea Bay. Sometimes a whale may come in as close as 100 yards from the beach. Other good spots around the Neighbor Islands for whale-watching include Kilauea Point and Poipu on Kauai; Hanauma Bay on Oahu; and the Big Island's Kona Coast.

Cetacean playground Humpbacks are not the only whales to be spotted in Hawaiian waters, since the islands also play host to the occasional sperm whale or killer whale, not to mention such year-round residents as pilot whales, and fellow members of the cetacean family, spinner, spotted, and bottlenose dolphins.

Cetaceans are warm-blooded, air-breathing marine mammals that nurse their young. The biggest is the 100-foot-long blue whale, while the smallest belong to the porpoise family. Humpbacks are the fifth largest of the cetaceans, a mature adult measuring between 40 and 50 feet and weighing around a ton per foot.

Feeding and moving Humpbacks, like blue and right whales, are baleen (toothless) whales (*Mysticetes*). Their mouths are lined with up to 600 rows of fringed baleen instead of teeth, and they feed by taking great mouthfuls of sea water—hundreds of gallons at a time, assisted by expandable vents in the throat. The water is then filtered past the rows of baleen, which capture plankton, small fish, and shrimplike krill. Humpbacks can consume almost a ton of food a day, but may live for almost six months without feeding.

The humpback's scientific name is *Megaptera novaeangliae*, meaning "great wing of New England," a reference to its enlarged pectoral fins. Each fin is between 15 and 16 feet long (the longest limb of any animal), and has a bone structure remarkably similar to that of a human hand. The whale uses its "pecs" to steer, but power is provided by the massive tail flukes. Although the humpback averages only 3–6 mph when on the move, its

A baby humpback whale in Maalaea Bay

caudal muscles, which control the tail, are so well developed that speeds of up to 20 mph can be achieved over short periods.

Whales need to breathe air, and the blow hole is placed on top of the head. When a whale "spouts," it ejects compresssed air from its lungs, which emerges in a fine mist. Whales' eyes are set low on either side of their heads, but their chief sensory mechanism is their ears. They have acute hearing and communicate using complex sequences of sounds known as "songs."

Migrations and breeding Hawaii's humpback whales are part of the North Pacific humpback population that spends the summer months feeding in the temperate waters off Alaska. At the onset of the arctic winter they journey south, some heading for California and Mexico or Japan, while around two-thirds aim for Hawaii.

Humpbacks come to Hawaii to breed and calve in the warm, shallow waters. The gestation period for a female is around 11 months, so having conceived one year the females return to calve the following winter. Whale calves are born tail first, measure between 12 and 14 feet, and weigh about a ton. The minute they are born the mother must nudge her calf to the surface to breathe. The calf must also be taught to swim, and mother and calf are usually attended by a protective second whale "escort" at first. Later they will travel as part of an extended family group, or pod.

Humpback numbers At the turn of the century, the world population of humpback whales was an estimated 100,000, about 15,000 of which belonged to the North Pacific. Commercial whaling had reduced the numbers to around 1,000 by the mid-1960s, but today that figure has increased to over 5,000, thanks to the international bans on whaling. Individual whales can be identified by the distinctive markings on their broad, flat tail flukes, which are as unique as a human fingerprint. Tracking individual whales has taught researchers a great deal about whale habits and migration patterns. Perhaps one day the experts may just unravel the mystery of whale song.

WHAT'S IN A NAME?
The humpback whale gets its name from the way it arches its back before diving. In whale-watcher jargon this is called a "round out." Other key behavior patterns are the slow and stately "head rise," when the top third of the body rises out of the water; the "pec slap," when the humpback rolls over sideways and slaps its pectoral fin on the surface of the water; "head slaps"; "tail slaps"; and the breathtaking "breach," when all or most of the body is propelled vertically out of the water.

Spouting adults

Whale-watching

Tram tours at the Maui Tropical Plantation

HAWAII NATURE CENTER
Located in Kepaniwai Park, the center offers guided hikes into the 2,000-acre Iao Valley forest preserve. The hikes, which last around 1½ hours, follow a rocky trail along the valley floor, and sensible footwear and rain gear are recommended. Children under 8 are not allowed. There are daily excursions Monday to Saturday, with additional hikes on Wednesdays. Call for schedules and reservations (tel: 808/244-6500).

▶ Kepaniwai Park 122B3

Iao Valley Road (2 miles west of Wailuku)
Open site. Admission free
Visitors explore a series of pavilions built in the different styles of Hawaii's main ethnic groups in this small cultural park, on the road to Iao Valley State Park. Lion-dog gates guard the Chinese pavilion, and there are Japanese gardens with dwarf trees, pagodas, and bridges around an airy Japanese bamboo house. The Portuguese corner is decorated with *azuelos* (hand-painted tiles), a white picket fence encircles a New England cottage, and the grass-roofed Polynesian hut has its own taro terrace.

▶ Maui Arts & Cultural Center 122B3

Maui Central Park, Kahului (tel: 808/242-7469)
Open: Gallery, Tue–Sun, call for hours. Admission free
On the outskirts of Kahului, a 3-minute drive from Wailuku, this attractive modern arts complex features a 1,200-seat theater, an outdoor amphitheater, and a gallery hosting frequently changing exhibitions. The box office doubles as a gift shop selling a small selection of reasonably priced artists' prints and cards. Telephone for details of the latest programs.

▶▶ Maui Tropical Plantation 122B3

HI-30, south of Wailuku (tel: 808/244-7643)
Open: daily 9–5. Admission free; tram tours, moderate
This tropical plantation is one of the most popular attractions on the island. Not surprisingly, it has a souvenir superstore piled high with all the usual T-shirts, pineapple-motif beach bags, and *aloha*-print fashions, along with an impressive line in more upmarket Hawaiian food items such as macadamia nut oil, exotic fruit relishes, honeys, and dried fruits, as well as fresh produce.

By day, tram tours (40 minutes) trundle around the 50 acres, with their areas of plumeria orchard, heliconias, and gingers, as well as pineapple and coffee, passion-fruit, papaya, and guava orchards. Guides describe the contribution sugar, fruits, and macadamia nuts make to the island's economy. A nursery sells exportable orchids, anthuriums, and hibiscus, and there are *lei*-makers on hand for demonstrations. Three times a week the plantation puts on a Hawaiian barbecue and dinner show.

►► Wailuku *122B3*

Guarding the access route to the sacred Iao Valley, the burial place of the highest Maui chieftains, Wailuku was an important site to the ancient Hawaiians. It became Maui's second town when Kamehameha I established the capital of the islands at Lahaina. When missionaries arrived here in 1832, they founded a school for girls to complement Lahaina's boys-only Lahainaluna Seminary. Wailuku later became a sugar town and is now Maui's administrative seat.

The Reverend Jonathan Green founded the mission station and girls' school in Wailuku on lands donated by Maui's governor, Hoapili, who made education compulsory for the island's children. Edward Bailey, the school's first principal, enlarged the building, now the **Bailey House Museum►►** (Iao Valley Road, Wailuku, tel: 808/244-3326. *Open:* daily 10–4. *Admission: inexpensive*).

An upstairs bedroom and sitting room have been fitted out with hefty Victorian furnishings, while on the first floor there are displays of Hawaiian artifacts, tools, crafts, and archeological finds, and an exhibition of Bailey's paintings, many of which were sold to fund the school. Bailey also raised money by milling flour and sugar, before going into the sugar industry full time when missionary funds were withdrawn in the 1850s. The museum gift shop sells a variety of Hawaiian crafts.

Below the Bailey House, on a slope above the main Iao Valley road, **Kaahumanu Church►** was named in honor of Kamehameha I's favorite wife, who was born on Maui and became an ardent convert to Christianity. The spotlessly clean 19th-century church, with its lofty wooden steeple, was founded on top of a *heiau* associated with Kahekili in what was no doubt a deliberate show of religious one-upmanship. In a corner of the churchyard there is an early Hawaiian Christian burial plot.

MISSIONS ON MAUI
Governor Hoapili played an important role in the success of the missions on Maui. Determined that his people should be educated, Hoapili made available land grants to set up mission schools in Lahaina and Wailuku. Though born Ulumaheihei, the future governor was renamed Hoapili or "Close Companion," for his friendship with Kamehameha I. After the king's death, Hoapili married Kamehameha's sacred wife, Keopuolani.

The Bailey House grew in several stages

Drive

The road to Hana

See map on pages 122–123.

Keanae Arboretum

The twisting road to Hana down the windward coast of East Maui is one of the island's, indeed Hawaii's, great excursions. It is also something of an endurance test, as on the last 30 miles or so of the route there are around 600 curves and 54 small bridges to negotiate. Allow three hours to drive from Kahului to Hana (54 miles) with a couple of stops, and another 30 minutes from Hana to reach the Oheo Gulch.

The first stretch of road on HI-36 through **Paia** (see page 142) is straightforward. The "Hana Highway" itself begins after Paia, when the road becomes HI-360, and the speed limit drops to a maximum 35 mph. About ¾ mile past Mile Marker 16 is the **Keanae Arboretum**, with 6 acres of towering trees, magnificent stands of bamboo, moss-covered tree trunks sprouting ferns, eucalyptus trees, palms, heliconias, hibiscus, and plumeria. At the top of the gardens, there is a series of terraced taro patches irrigated by a stream.

Continue as far as Mile Marker 19 and the **Wailua Valley State Wayside**

Lookout. Park the car and take the steps to the lookout with panoramic views out to sea across the farmlands and taro fields of the Wailua Valley, and inland to the Keanae Valley and mist-wreathed Koolau Gap, a breach in the rim of the Haleakala crater.

Just short of Hana, at Mile Marker 32, **Waianapanapa State Park** is a good place to stretch car-cramped legs, have a picnic, take a dip (beware of rough surf), or hike along the shore to a series of ancient caves. The wild and beautiful volcanic coastline has been sculpted by centuries of wind and waves into sea stacks and arches tufted with beach *naupaka* plants. There is a small black-sand beach, and a screwpine grove on the cliff.

Hana, the birthplace of Queen Kaahumanu, is a quiet, down-to-earth ranch and fishing town with one hotel (the Hotel Hana-Maui). In addition to its clutch of timber-framed houses, there is a 19th-century church, a couple of general stores, and a horse-back-riding center. The small museum of Hawaiiana and local history in the **Hana Cultural Center** is worth a stop (follow the signs) and is housed in a plantation-era cottage next door to the diminutive 1871 police station-cum-courthouse. This is also the place to pick up local information from the friendly staff.

Beyond Hana the road changes its name again (to HI-31), and gets more narrow and twisty and even more beautiful, winding along the cliffs and ravines and through a deep green tunnel of overhanging mango and guava trees en route to Kipahulu. Ten miles farther on from Hana, the **Oheo Gulch** is often referred to as the "Seven Sacred Pools"on maps. In fact, some 20 unsacred but impressive pools fed by the Oheo Stream drop down the last mile of the gulch in the shadow of Haleakala. The lowest of these are apt to turn into a series of municipal swimming pools full of hot, sticky tourists. The Pipiwai Trail (2 miles) cuts a rough track up through the rain forest to the base of the 400-foot Waimoku Falls (a two-hour round trip; sturdy shoes and mosquito repellent needed), or there is the short (½-mile, 20-minute) Kuloa Loop trail from the parking lot, along the coast and around to the gulch pools.

A mile beyond Oheo Gulch, look for the modest sign to Palapala Hoomau on the left and turn down the track to **Palapala Hoomau Congregational Church**. Flanked by drooping banyan trees, this tiny, pretty coral rock and wood church was built on the clifftop in 1857. It is the last resting place of famous aviator Charles A. Lindbergh (1902–1974), who is buried in the flower-filled country churchyard.

Pools at Oheo Gulch

The rare silversword plant (see panel opposite)

Sunrise from the summit of Haleakala is one of the great sights of Maui

East Maui

► Alexander & Baldwin Sugar Museum *122B3*

Puunene Mill, 3957 Hansen Road (tel: 808/871-8058)
Open: Mon–Sat 9:30–4:30. Admission: inexpensive

The cloying smell of molasses greets visitors to this small museum nestling in the shadow of the state's largest sugar factory. Displays in the old Superintendent's Residence tell the story of A&B, from its small beginnings as a 12-acre plantation founded by missionary children Samuel Alexander and Henry Baldwin in 1869, to one of Hawaii's "Big Five" companies. Detailed scale models, broad-ranging storyboards, and photographs illustrate plantation-era life, and there is an interactive sugar exhibit as well as a gift store selling Maui brown sugar.

►►► Haleakala National Park *123D2*

Haleakala Crater Road (HI-378), off HI-377 south of Makawao (tel: 808/572-9306)
Open: daily. Admission: inexpensive

The road up to the summit of Haleakala is festooned with signs warning drivers to look out for cattle, bicyclists (see panel opposite) and, as the treeline is surmounted, clouds. However hot it may be down on the beach, bring warm clothes for an ascent of the world's largest dormant volcano, as the rarified air at 10,000 feet can be extremely nippy. Above the sunny upcountry pastures, the upper reaches of Haleakala are subalpine desert. In winter, fog and freezing rain are not unusual, so call ahead for a weather report. Early morning is always the best time to visit because clouds obscure views later in the day.

Haleakala's vast crater is a geological masterpiece. In reality a giant depression formed by erosion, rather than a true crater made by volcanic explosion or the collapse of a

Cyclists with altitude

magma chamber, it plunges 3,000 feet down from the mountain rim and measures 7½ miles by 2½ miles. The surreal, multicolored landscape of volcanic ash and cinders, in dozens of different tones of red, brown, gray, and green, is dotted with cinder cone hillocks.

There are several viewpoints and a visitor center with interpretive displays and information by the Puu Ulaula Overlook. For serious hikers, there are 36 miles of trails that descend into the crater area, plus backcountry campsites. In summer, visitors to the crater rim can join the free ranger-guided walks, which last between 30 minutes and a couple of hours.

►► Kula *122C2*

Kula's botanical gardens (see below), surrounded by vegetable and flower farms, lie to the south of the Haleakala access road and make an interesting detour on a trip to the volcano. Another diversion is the 1894 **Holy Ghost Mission Church** on Lower Kula Road, built in three tiers and topped with a fancy tower and silver roofs. The pretty, octagonal interior is painted seashell pink and was decorated with Stations of the Cross by Portuguese immigrants who came to the island to ranch or farm.

The 8-acre **Enchanting Floral Gardens of Kula►** (HI-37, Mile Marker 10, tel: 808/878-2531. *Open:* daily 9–5. *Admission: inexpensive*), tucked behind a magnificent bougainvillea hedge, is a formal affair featuring more than 500 species of plants and flowers from around the world. Unusual exotics and tropical fruit trees, scented *pikake* (jasmine), and plumeria are planted around the flower beds. Bromeliads and vines clamber around arches that straddle the paths, and there are strategically placed gazebos at the best viewpoints.

The **Kula Botanical Gardens►►** (HI-377, tel: 808/878-1715. *Open:* daily 9–4. *Admission: inexpensive*) range over a 5-acre hillside site with outstanding views. The lava-rock terraces overflow with colorful bedding plants, shrubs, and exotics, and more than 1,700 different plants, from proteas to hydrangeas, flourish in the mild, damp climate at some 3,300 feet above sea level. There are strange little "pigtail" anthuriums with curling fingers, decorative red pineapples, scented honeysuckle, and banks of lilies and ferns. Look for oddities such as the "touchy-feely" velvet leaf from Madagascar, but do not touch anything in the toxic plant section, where a mature datura hangs over the *koi* pond.

FREEWHEELING IN PARADISE

For a 38-mile bike ride that tests the wrists not the legs, try coasting down Haleakala. Only about 400 yards of the switchback road down from the volcano summit to the coast require any pedaling, the rest is brake work. Operators such as Maui Downhill (tel: 808/871-2155), Maui Mountain Cruisers (tel: 808/871-6014), and Mountain Riders (tel: 808/242-9739) supply bikes, helmets, gloves, guides, escort vans, and a free hotel pickup service, plus onward tour options.

SILVERSWORDS

"Their cold frosted silver gleam made the hillside look like winter or moonlight," wrote Isabella Bird, who was a visitor to Hawaii in 1873. She was describing the rare Haleakala silversword plant (*Argyroxiphium sandwicense*), which the Hawaiians call *ahinahina* after Hina, the moon goddess. It grows only on Maui and the Big Island at elevations between 6,000 and 10,000 feet. The plant can live for up to 20 years, but blooms only once, producing a single tall spike with red-purple flowers, after which it dies.

Windsurfers off Wailea

UPCOUNTRY ARTS CENTER
A couple of miles north of Makawao on the Paia road is Kaluanui, a villa built in 1917 for sugar magnate Harry Baldwin. The house is now home to the Hui Noeau Visual Arts Center, and the first floor has been turned into a gallery shop and exhibition space for local and visiting artists.

Protea bloom

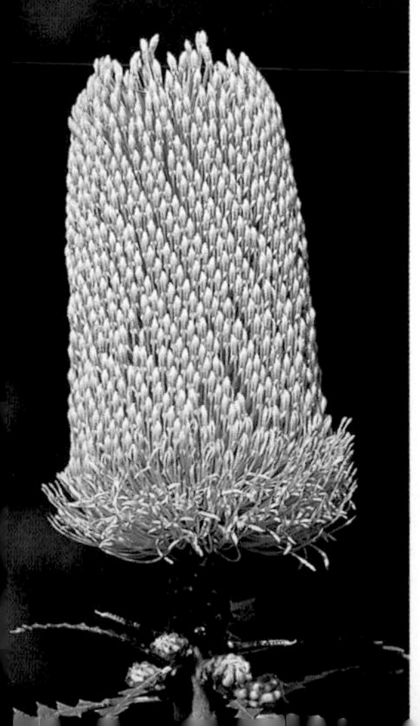

▶ Makawao *122C3*

Makawao's 19th-century antecedents are still visible in the Old-West-style, false-fronted stores leading downhill along Baldwin Avenue in the direction of Paia. But behind the freshly painted façades of this upcountry ranch town, old-time country stores have been hijacked by boutiques and designer household goods emporia selling everything from Provençal herb salad dressing to linen skirts and straw hats for that expensively contrived ranch-chic look.

Old-style Makawao still lingers in the no-nonsense (and "No Loitering," according to the sign) Komoda Store & Bakery, and Makawao Feed, Garden and Hardware Store, with its crate of day-old chicks on the floor and aisles overflowing with nuts and bolts, nails, and rat poison. And the town still goes back to its ranching roots for the annual Fourth of July rodeo.

▶▶ Paia *122C3*

On the road to Hana, Paia is a good place to have a meal: try Jacques Bistro, 89 Hana Highway (tel: 808/579-6255. *Open:* from 7:30 AM). Many of the false-fronted stores have been turned into boutiques and galleries selling arts and crafts, and antiques. One of the best is the excellent Maui Crafts Guild, 34 Hana Highway, at the entrance to town. This local artists' cooperative displays pottery, prints, wood and stone carvings, jewelry, and "fiber sculpture"—basketry woven from native plants (*Open:* daily 9–6).

West of town, Baldwin Beach has good bodysurfing and windsurfing. To the east, Hookipa Beach Park offers world-class windsurfing but you need experience to handle the conditions, and pro contests held there are worth a look.

▶ Sunrise Protea Farm *122C2*

Haleakala Crater Road (HI-378)
Open: daily 8–4. Admission free

Sunny days and cool nights are ideal for cultivating protea flowers, natives of South Africa and Australia. Proteas were first grown commercially on Maui in 1975, and Sunrise is one of the island's major producers, with more than a dozen varieties on show in a small walk-through garden. Bouquets and arrangements of fresh or dried flowers can be bought or shipped to the mainland U.S. from the shop.

▶▶ Tedeschi Vineyard 122C2

HI-37/31 (tel: 808/878-6058; www.tedeschiveyards.qpg.com)
Open: daily 9–5 (tours 9:30–2:30). Admission free

A lovely upcountry drive leads through rolling pastures and small settlements to the Tedeschi vineyards at the Ulupalakua Ranch on the southwestern slopes of Haleakala. During spring the roadside is adrift with the lilac-colored blossoms from dozens of jacaranda trees.

Perched at a cool elevation of 2,000 feet, the 22-acre Tedeschi vineyard was established in 1974. Its first vintage, however, was not a grape wine but Maui Blanc Pineapple Wine. Since then, three red wines, a white, a rosé, and two sparkling wines (all made with grapes) have appeared. The *méthode champenoise* Maui Brut-Blanc de Noirs has even been served at the White House. There are free tours of the winery and King's Cottage, where King David Kalakaua came to stay, as well as a wine shop and all-important tasting room.

Just down the road, the Ulupalakua Ranch Store sells snacks as well as genuine cattleman hats, bandanas, and Ulupalakua Ranch souvenirs.

▶ Wailea and Makena 122B2

The quiet, upmarket resort areas of Wailea and Makena lie to the south of the bustling Kihei shopping mall and condominium complex on a series of crescent-shaped beaches that stretch along the shore. It is so quiet here that migrating whales love it; and this is one of the best shoreline whale-watching spots on Maui.

Wailea has been nicknamed "Wimbledon West" for its tennis facilities, and it can also boast three championship golf courses as well as an upscale shopping mall. At the end of the coast road is Makena, with a further 36 holes of golf laid out by Robert Trent Jones Jr., and Makena Beach (in reality two adjoining beaches called Big Beach and Little Beach), a huge expanse of glittering sand with gorgeous views and clear waters.

THE SOUTHERN RANCHLANDS

For those who like their landscapes rugged and unpopulated, HI-31 runs into the open ranchlands above the south coast. Between the towering mountains and fractured black talons of rock clawing at the surf, the only signs of life amid the acres of billowing, flaxen grass are cattle and game birds. The first Western visitors to Maui landed at La Pérouse Bay, down on the scrubby southwest tip of the island. North of here, the red volcanic cone of Puu Olai rises to a height of 360 feet, and there are sea views off to Molokini, Kahoolawe, and Lanai.

The rolling hills of upcountry Ulupalakua

The upcountry ranchlands of Maui, the Waimea-Kamuela district of Hawaii's Big Island, and the West End of Molokai offer not only a change of scenery but a change of style. Perhaps it is some miraculous property of the upcountry air that has preserved an old Hawaiian paniolo *(cowboy) lifestyle that has altered little in 50 years or more.*

RIDING OUT ON THE RANGE

Makena Stables (tel: 808/879-0244) arranges rides, and visits to the Ulupalakua Ranch's Tedeschi Winery (see page 143). On the Big Island, Paniolo Riding Adventures (tel: 808/889-5354) head out across the Ponoholo Ranch in the Kohala Mountains. (For details of Molokai Ranch Trail Rides, see panel on page 118.)

Hawaiian paniolo *at the rodeo*

The upcountry ranchlands are Hawaii's *paniolo* country, where third- and fourth-generation cowboys still round up the herd on horseback and demonstrate their skills in the rodeo ring. Things have changed dramatically since those early days, but it seems not even the arrival of motorized "Japanese quarter horses" (all-terrain vehicles) is going to part the Hawaiian *paniolo* from his trusty "hoss".

A gift of cattle The British explorer Captain George Vancouver, who had sailed with Cook, introduced the first pair of cattle to the islands in 1793. They were a gift to Kamehameha I. The king loosed the beasts on Hawaii, and pronounced a *kapu* (taboo) on them so they could roam free and unmolested for 10 years. At the end of that time, herds of wild and unapproachable longhorn cattle were roving throughout the mountains and tearing up the native vegetation.

In 1803, Captain Richard Cleveland presented Kamehameha with a mare and her foal, and before long wild mustangs were also making themselves at home on the slopes of Mauna Kea. The chief ingredients for ranching were now in place, and there was a ready market for meat, hides, and tallow anchored in the increasingly busy ports of Lahaina and Honolulu.

A young New England adventurer, John Palmer Parker, and a former whaler, Irishman Jack Purdy, were charged with the task of bringing the king's herds under some sort of control. Together with Spanish and Mexican *vaqueros* (cattlemen) brought over from California, they taught the Hawaiians the ropes.

The *paniolo* The newcomers were known as *Espanols*, from the Spanish, or "*espaniolos*," which in turn became the pidgin Hawaiian *paniolo* for cowboy. Later they were joined by Portuguese immigrants from the Azores, who introduced the *braguinha*, or ukulele, this swiftly taking over from the Spanish guitar as the favorite accompaniment of the *paniolo* to "home-on-the-range" ditties.

The first organized move toward the establishment of Hawaii's great ranches came with Kamehameha III's Great Mahele land division in 1848. John Parker's *alii* wife, Kipikane, received 640 acres at Waimea, which under her husband's management increased with the purchase of additional pockets of land. Today, the vast 225,000-acre Parker spread is the fourth biggest (and the largest family-owned) ranch in the nation.

By the turn of the century, cattle ranching was Hawaii's third-biggest industry (after sugar and pineapples), and the *paniolo* were hard at work. One of the toughest jobs was loading live cattle for transportation to Honolulu. Maui's Ulupalakua Ranch would send a thousand head of steers across to Oahu every year, which entailed driving the cattle down to the shore at Makena and forcing the terrified animals into the surf. Here, they were loaded onto waiting longboats, tethered by their horns, and ferried out to the steamboat transport, where they were winched on board for the trip up the islands.

Hawaii's *paniolo* could play as hard as they worked. Not for nothing was the ranch town of Makawao once known as "Macho-wao." Back in 1908, Ikua Purdy, the Ulupalakua Ranch's head cowboy, stripped the five-times world champion roper, Angus MacPhee, of his title at the World's Steer Roping Championship held in Wyoming. Today's Hawaiian *paniolo* can still steal a march on any visiting cowboy at the rodeos held at the Parker and Molokai Ranch Arenas and Makawao's Oskie Rice Arena, named for a famous Maui ranch manager who helped found the Maui Roping Club in 1955.

Eyeing up the competition

RODEOS
The Oskie Rice Arena at Makawao is the centerpiece for the town's Fourth of July Rodeo Parade, as well as November's Maui County Rodeo Finals. The Fourth of July also sees the Parker Ranch Rodeo and Horse Races held at the Parker Ranch Arena in Waimea-Kamuela (tel: 808/885-7655); and August has the annual Molokai Ranch Rodeo (tel: 808/552-2791).

Breaking-in

Kalohi Channel
Auau Channel
Kealaikahiki Channel
Polihua Beach
Hale o Lono
Lapaiki
Kahua
Shipwreck Beach
Kaena Point
Kaena Heiau
Polihua Trail
Lapaiki
Kahua
Halulu
Kahokunui
Garden of the Gods
Keanapapa Point
1797ft
Mt Kanepuu
Lanai Pine Sporting Clays
Manunalai
Hauola
Keomuku Beach
Keomuku Village
Honopu
Koele
Hookio Battleground (1778)
Malamalama Church and Sugar Mill Ruins
Cavendish Golf Course
Lanai City
Munro Trail
Waiopa
Kahea Heiau
Halepalaoa Landing
Japanese Cemetery
Ana Puka Cave
3369ft
Mt Lanaihale
440
Lanai Airport
Palawai Basin
Luahiwa Petroglyphs
Lopa
Kaumalapau Harbor
Kapobo
Miki Basin
440
2073ft
Mt Puu Manu
Naha
Kaholo Pali
Lahaina, Maui
Ancient Village
Hulopoe Beach
Manele Bay
Kahekili's Leap
Palaoa Point
Kaunolu
Hulopoe Bay
Puupehe
Manele-Hulopoe Marine Life Conservation Area
0 5 km
0 5 miles
A B C
1 2 3

THE PRIVATE ISLAND Some 9 miles across the Auau Channel from Lahaina on Maui's resort-lined west coast, Lanai offers a radically different vacation experience. This small island was once the world's largest pineapple plantation and was virtually a tourist-free zone until the early 1990s.

When the bottom fell out of Hawaii's pineapple market in the 1980s, the Dole Food Co. Inc., which owns 98 percent of Lanai, turned to tourism in an effort to diversify and built not one but two superbly elegant resort hotels and equipped them with designer golf courses, fine restaurants, and every conceivable luxury. The Manele Bay Hotel, surrounded by glorious gardens, sits down by the ocean above a sandy bay, while the manor-house-style Lodge at Koele nestles on the slopes of Mount Lanaihale, 1,700 feet above sea level.

Lanai, at 18 miles by 13 miles, is the second smallest of the main Hawaiian islands, with a coastline ringed by cliffs and beaches. Along the east side of the island, a north–south ridge of mountains planted with Norfolk pines brings down some moisture, but Lanai is basically dry. Mormon missionaries introduced cattle ranching in the 1850s, and at the end of the 19th century unsuccessful attempts were made to grow sugar cane in the dusty red earth of the Palawai Basin. It was not until James Dole bought the island in 1922 (see page 151) that a successful crop of any kind was grown. That crop was pineapples, which became the mainstay of the island's economy.

▶▶▶ ISLAND HIGHLIGHTS

Hulopoe Beach *page 149*

Lanai City *page 149*

Shipwreck Beach *page 150*

Left: near the Garden of the Gods looking over to Molokai

Puupehe and the dramatic headland between Hulopoe and Manele Bays

KANEPUU DRYLAND FOREST
Off the Polihua Trail, just south of the Garden of the Gods, another jeep track heads west to Kanepuu. Here, the Nature Conservancy preserves 462 acres of rare dryland forest that contains 48 native Hawaiian species. Among the protected plants are *olopua*, native olive trees; *lama*, persimmon; *iliahi*, sandalwood; and several varieties of *nanu*, gardenia. The preserve is a restricted area, but interested visitors can contact The Nature Conservancy offices on Lanai (tel: 808/565-7430) for details of guided tours.

Lanai City, founded by James Dole in 1924, is home to 2,500 of the island's total population of 2,800. Their ethnic diversity—Filipino, Japanese, Korean, Puerto Rican, Caucasian, and Hawaiian—is a reminder of the island's plantation heritage. Lanai's population, which dwindled at the end of the plantation era, as young people left in droves to find work elsewhere, is on the rise again thanks to the emerging tourist industry.

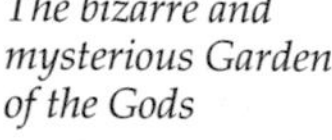

The bizarre and mysterious Garden of the Gods

LANAI'S TWIN RESORTS Beyond the 18th hole, landlubbers can take their pick from *hula* and horseback-riding classes, mountain biking, tennis, or hunting for pheasant, partridge, wild turkey, quail, mouflon sheep, and axis deer in season. On the water there are ocean-raft tours, whale-watching cruises (November–April), deep-sea fishing for *mahimahi* and *ono* (wahoo), and snorkeling and scuba diving. For the historically minded, there are petroglyphs and interesting archeological sites to explore, as well as Lanai's unique dryland forest, now under the protection of The Nature Conservancy (see panel).

Transportation on Lanai is limited, but then there are only a mere 30 miles of paved road. A hotel shuttle, which links Manele Bay and Koele via Lanai City, also serves the airport, and there are five daily round-trip boat crossings to Lahaina. You can also rent cars and four-wheel-drive vehicles to explore the dozens of jeep tracks that strike out across the island's 140 square miles of countryside to isolated beaches and abandoned fishing villages, or to traverse the mountainous and muddy 7-mile Munro Trail along the ridge that runs behind Lanai City and up Lanaihale, which is the island's highest peak.

▶▶ Garden of the Gods 146A2

Lying 6 miles to the northwest of Lanai City on the Polihua Trail, this dusty "garden" of volcanic pinnacles, giant boulders, and teetering rocks is an eerie place. Viewed in the middle of the day, it is not at its most impressive. Instead, the bizarre rock formations, said to house the spirits of Hawaiian warriors, are best seen at sunset (or sunrise), when the rays of shifting light accentuate the desert colors and cast long shadows.

▶▶▶ Hulopoe Beach 146B1

Road access from Manele Bay

This sandy crescent on Lanai's south shore is a favorite swimming and fishing beach. It is a marine conservation area, and has been voted one of the 10 best snorkel and dive sites in the world. Spinner dolphins are a common sight in the early morning, and whales appear offshore in the winter calving season.There are picnicking facilities and even a small campground.

▶ Kaunolu 146B1

Southwest coast; jeep trail from Kaumalapau Harbor

Kaunolu, a former fishing village, was abandoned in the 18th century. Now a National Historic Landmark, it is one of the finest collections of ancient Hawaiian ruins in the islands. Just up the coast at the sea cliff known as Kahekili's Leap, warriors would test their strength and courage by jumping out over a treacherous rock outcrop into the ocean 60 feet below.

▶▶▶ Lanai City 146B2

At the center of the island, in the lee of Lanaihale, the neat plantation town of Lanai City is built on a grid of broad streets lined with tin-roofed, timber-framed houses and flower-filled gardens. Around a spacious village green planted with Norfolk pines, there is a period playhouse, galleries, and a couple of Lanai-style mom-and-pop stores, their shelves laden with bottles of *kim chee*, *adobo* sauce, packs of instant *saimin* and *poi*, as well as more American food staples. There is a small museum in a plantation-era building next to the S. & T. diner.

To the north of the common, the Hotel Lanai was built by Dole in 1923 as a clubhouse to accommodate guests of the pineapple company. It now offers comfortable alternative accommodations to the two fancy resorts on the island and excellent meals.

To the south, at 8th Street and Gay, the police station boasts three little outhouse-like jail cells with padlocks on the doors, sufficient for coping with Lanai's virtually nonexistent criminal element.

LEGEND OF MAKAKEHAU
A trail leads up from Hulopoe Beach onto the rugged headland that divides Hulopoe from Manele Bay. Offshore is a huge black rock known as Puupehe ("Pehe's Hill"). Local legend tells of a fisherman, Makakehau, who had a beautiful wife called Pehe, whom he loved dearly and kept hidden away in a sea cave. One day when he was out collecting fresh water in the mountains, a storm blew up and surf submerged the cave, drowning Pehe. With the gods' help, Makakehau buried her on top of the rock, and then threw himself off to his death.

KEOMUKU VILLAGE RUINS
Keomuku, on the east coast, had a population of 2,000 around the turn of the century, but this former sugar town was abandoned for good in 1954. Today, there is little to see aside from a coconut grove and the 1903 Kalanakila O Ka Malamalama church. A couple of miles down the track, near the old wharf site of Halepalaoa, is an ancient *heiau* (temple) site.

Quiet Lanai City has transformed itself from an agricultural town into an exclusive resort

On the Munro Trail

JEEP RENTAL
Ordinary cars are available to rent on Lanai, but they really are a waste of money as the island has just 30 miles of paved road to explore. The only way to get off the beaten track by vehicle is to rent a Jeep, which is not cheap. The rudiments of four-wheel drive can be learned in a few minutes. Be sure to pack essentials such as water, sunscreen lotion, and picnic materials before setting out for the day. And don't wear white! That red dust gets everywhere.

►► Munro Trail 146B2

Trail from behind the Lodge at Koele
Open site. Admission free

This 7-mile jeep trail extends along the sharp ridge of mountains behind Lanai City and scales Lanaihale, the island's highest point at 3,366 feet. Viewed from the Palawai Basin, the island's mountainous backbone is feathered with matchstick-sized Norfolk pines planted by George Munro, a New Zealand naturalist and ranch manager who lived on Lanai from 1911 to 1935. The pines were designed to draw down the clouds and release moisture on the arid island, and the ridge is frequently cloaked in drizzle. Although this can render the trail a muddy morass, it makes a great if strenuous two-hour drive or day's hike. On a crisp, clear day the views from Lanaihale stretch over five islands—Maui, Molokai, Kahoolawe, Hawaii, and even distant Oahu.

►► Polihua Beach 146A3

North coast; Polihua Trail from Lanai City
Open site. Admission free

Windswept Polihua lies a dusty drive across the island to the north shore, and is famous for the sea turtles that come ashore to lay their eggs on the sandy beach here. Its name literally means "Bay of Eggs." Picnic and sunbathe by all means, but do not swim—strong currents make it very dangerous.

►►► Shipwreck Beach 146B3

Northeast coast (north from the road head)
Open site. Admission free

The aptly named Shipwreck Beach, known in Hawaiian as Kaiolohia, meaning "choppy" or "changing sea," is a beautiful and isolated 8-mile stretch of sandy beach and rocky outcrops, punctuated with the hulks of wrecked ships that have come to grief in the stormy Kalohi Channel. Although dangerous for swimming, it is a good place to beachcomb for driftwood and Japanese fishing floats. Just inland from the beach are rocks carved with ancient but well-preserved petroglyphs (rock carvings).

Shipwreck Beach

When Christopher Columbus introduced pineapples to Europe, the exotic delicacy was nicknamed the "King of Fruit." During the 16th and 17th centuries, colonists helped spread the pineapple throughout South America, India, and Asia. By the 18th century, pineapples were even grown in George Washington's hothouse at Mount Vernon.

Father of the pineapple Hawaii's pineapple industry was founded by Captain John Kidwell in the 1880s, but the true "Father of the Hawaiian Pineapple" was Boston-born James Drummond Dole. The 22-year-old horticulturist arrived in the islands in 1877, acquired a 61-acre plot of land on Oahu, and experimented with growing various types of fruit plants. Pineapples above all others thrived in Hawaii's mineral-rich soil.

Dole founded the Hawaiian Pineapple Co. in 1901, and by the 1930s Hawaii provided two-thirds of the world's canned and fresh pineapple. Dole's biggest plantation was on Lanai (which he bought in 1922), with some 16,000 acres under cultivation for the fruit until 1992, when the plantation finally closed.

Commercial pineapple-growing is backbreaking work. Encumbered with broad-brimmed sun hats, wearing canvas aprons and gloves to ward off cuts and scratches, and with faces covered with bandanas and goggles to keep out the dust, thousands of Asian immigrant laborers toiled in the hot, dusty fields, bent double from dawn to dusk. A skilled laborer could plant 1,000 plants daily (one-third of an acre). At harvest time he or she might be expected to pick a ton of fruit a day.

Tourism replaces pineapples Though many regret the demise of the Hawaiian pineapple industry in the face of low-priced competition from Asia, few who actually worked the fields are nostalgic. In Lanai there is cautious optimism that carefully managed tourism will provide a better standard of living for the next generation, and that the island's community spirit will survive intact.

"EXCELLENT FRUIT"
Pineapples are believed to have originated in Paraguay. Their scientific name, *Ananas comosus*, is derived from the Paraguayan *ananas* meaning "excellent fruit" in the Guarani Indian dialect, but the Spanish explorers called them *piña de Indias* for their resemblance to pine cones. Later the pineapple became a symbol of hospitality, and its unmistakable form was frequently used to decorate furniture during America's colonial period and even to adorn gateposts as a welcome for guests.

When pineapples were king

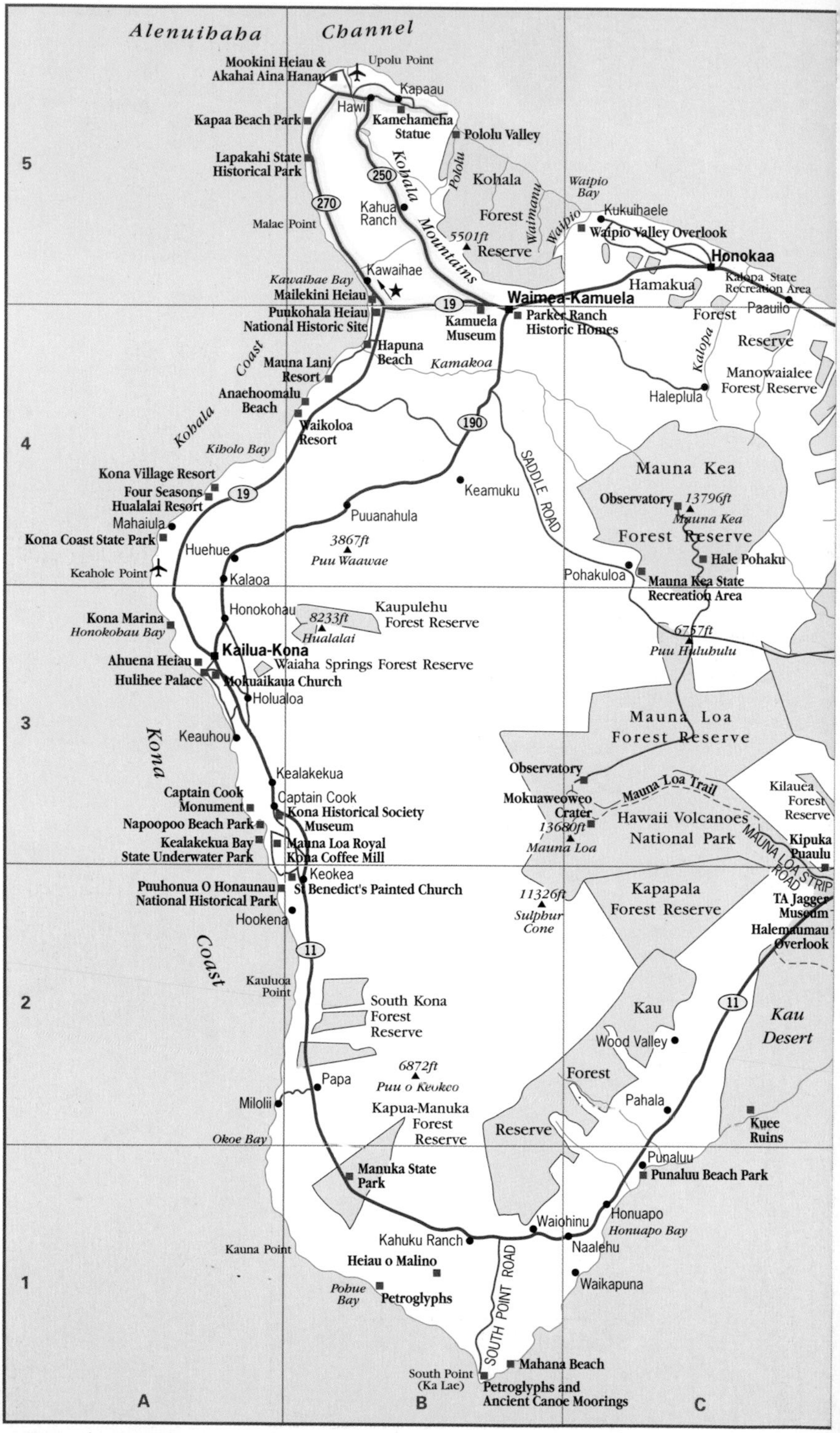

Alenuihaha Channel
Upolu Point
Mookini Heiau & Akahai Aina Hanau
Kapaau
Hawi
Kamehameha Statue
Kapaa Beach Park
Pololu Valley
Lapakahi State Historical Park
Pololu
Kohala Mountains
250
Kohala Forest Reserve
Waipio Bay
Waimanu
270
Kahua Ranch
Waipio
Kukuihaele
Malae Point
5501ft
Waipio Valley Overlook
Honokaa
Kawaihae
Kawaihae Bay
Hamakua
Kalopa State Recreation Area
Mailekini Heiau
Waimea-Kamuela
19
Paauilo
Puukohala Heiau National Historic Site
Kamuela Museum
Parker Ranch Historic Homes
Forest
Reserve
Hapuna Beach
Kamakoa
Kalopa
Mauna Lani Resort
Manowaialee Forest Reserve
Kohala Coast
Anaehoomalu Beach
Haleplula
Waikoloa Resort
190
Kiholo Bay
SADDLE ROAD
Mauna Kea
Kona Village Resort
Keamuku
Four Seasons Hualalai Resort
19
Observatory
13796ft
Mauna Kea
Forest Reserve
Mahaiula
Puuanahula
Kona Coast State Park
3867ft
Puu Waawae
Hale Pohaku
Huehue
Keahole Point
Kalaoa
Pohakuloa
Mauna Kea State Recreation Area
Honokohau
Kaupulehu Forest Reserve
8233ft
Hualalai
Kona Marina
Honokohau Bay
6757ft
Puu Huluhulu
Kailua-Kona
Ahuena Heiau
Waiaha Springs Forest Reserve
Hulihee Palace
Mokuaikaua Church
Holualoa
Mauna Loa Forest Reserve
Keauhou
Kona Coast
Kealakekua
Observatory
Captain Cook Monument
Captain Cook
Mauna Loa Trail
Kilauea Forest Reserve
Mokuaweoweo Crater
Napoopoo Beach Park
Kona Historical Society Museum
Hawaii Volcanoes National Park
13680ft
Mauna Loa
Kealakekua Bay State Underwater Park
Mauna Loa Royal Kona Coffee Mill
Kipuka Puaulu
MAUNA LOA STRIP ROAD
Keokea
Puuhonua O Honaunau National Historical Park
St Benedict's Painted Church
Kapapala Forest Reserve
11326ft
Sulphur Cone
TA Jagger Museum
Hookena
Halemaumau Overlook
11
Kauluoa Point
South Kona Forest Reserve
Kau
11
Kau Desert
Wood Valley
6872ft
Puu o Keokeo
Papa
Forest
Milolii
Kapua-Manuka Forest Reserve
Pahala
Reserve
Kuee Ruins
Okoe Bay
Punaluu
Manuka State Park
Punaluu Beach Park
Honuapo
Honuapo Bay
Waiohinu
Kahuku Ranch
Naalehu
Kauna Point
Heiau o Malino
Waikapuna
SOUTH POINT ROAD
Pohue Bay
Petroglyphs
Mahana Beach
South Point (Ka Lae)
Petroglyphs and Ancient Canoe Moorings

5
4
3
2
1
A
B
C

Hawaii

See drive pages 174-5

Ookala
Laupahoehoe
Hilo
Haakoa
Forest
Reserve
19
Kahuka
Hakalau
Akaka Falls State Park
Honomu
Pepeekeo Point
Maukaloa
Hawaii Tropical Botanical Garden
Onomea Bay
Kapue
Papaikou
Rainbow Falls
Hilo Bay
Liliuokalani Gardens
Hilo
Wailuku
Boiling Pots
Hilo Tropical Gardens
Hilo
Hilo International Airport
Forest
Lyman Mission House and Museum
Nani Mau Gardens
Mauna Loa Macadamia Nut Factory and Visitor Center
Reserve
Panaewa Rainforest Zoo
11
Haena
Upper Waiakea Forest Reserve
Waiakea Forest
Keaau
Kaloli Point
Oloa Forest Reserve
Anthurium Nurseries
130
Nanawale Forest Reserve
Cape Kumukahi
Lighthouse
Hawaii Volcanoes National Park
Pahoa
Lava Tree State Park
Akatsuka Orchid Gardens
Malama-Ki Forest Reserve
Isaac Hale Beach Park
Visitor Center
Winery
Puna Forest Reserve
Volcano
Kaueleau
Mackenzie State Park
Kilauea Crater 4090ft
Thurston Lava Tube
Keauohana Forest Reserve
Crater Rim Drive
Chain of Craters Road
Puu Oo
Kehena
Kalapana
Hawaii Volcanoes National Park
Hokuma Point
Halape Trail
Kupaahu
Wahaula Heiau
Puu Loa Petroglyphs
Apua Point

0 10 20 30 km
0 5 10 15 20 miles

D E

APPROXIMATE DRIVING TIMES FROM HILO

- Hapuna: 1 hour 45 minutes
- Kailua-Kona (via Waimea): 2 hours 15 minutes
- Volcanoes National Park: 45 minutes
- Waimea-Kamuela: 1 hour 15 minutes

APPROXIMATE DRIVING TIMES FROM KAILUA-KONA

- Hapuna: 45 minutes
- Kealakekua Bay: 45 minutes
- Volcanoes National Park: 2 hours 30 minutes
- Waimea-Kamuela: 1 hour

THE BIG ISLAND Hawaii, the biggest, youngest, and most southerly of the islands, is almost a world in miniature as it harbors all but two (Arctic and Saharan) of the 13 types of climatic region found on earth. Crammed into its relatively modest 76-mile by 93-mile outline are active volcanoes, desert scrub areas, rain forest, and rolling, green upcountry ranchlands. Dominated by massive Mauna Kea (13,796 feet) and Mauna Loa (13,680 feet), both rising more than 30,000 feet from the ocean floor, Hawaii is indeed the Big Island.

Sixty-five percent bigger than the rest of the *Hawaii nei* (Hawaiian island group) combined, and still growing, the Big Island is also rural, relaxed, and full of heart.

HISTORICAL BACKGROUND The first Polynesian immigrants may have landed at the Big Island's South Point as early as AD 500 and spread throughout the islands. Under the Tahitians the island witnessed the first human sacrifices, in the 13th century, and there are numerous ancient sites and petroglyphs that remain as a testament to Hawaii's importance over the centuries.

When Captain Cook died in Kealakekua Bay in 1779 (see pages 36–37), there were thought to be around 80,000 Hawaiians living on the Big Island under the rule of Kalaniopuu. On his death, he bequeathed guardianship of Kukailimoku, the family war god, to his nephew, Kamehameha. The young warrior built a great temple on the north Kohala coast, the Puukohala Heiau, dedicated to Kukailimoku, and united the islands into a single kingdom, which he called Hawaii after his island birthplace.

During Kamehameha I's reign, cattle and horses were introduced onto the Big Island and laid the foundations for large-scale ranching. The New England adventurer, John Palmer Parker, was appointed to manage the herds, and was allocated a small plot of land as a reward. He married Kamehameha's granddaughter and built up the vast Parker Ranch at Waimea, one of the largest in the U.S.

Surf's up on the Big Island of Hawaii

For winter sports enthusiasts the summit of Mauna Kea can provide some fun

Within a year of Kamehameha's death in 1819, the first missionaries arrived in "Owhyhee," and missions were soon established in Hilo, Kailua, and Waimea. From the mid-19th century, immigrant workers arrived to work Hawaii's sugar plantations, and the very first tourists began to make their way to the island. Mark Twain was bowled over by a night visit to Kilauea in 1866, where he saw lava flows that "looked like a colossal railroad map of the State of Massachusetts done in chain lightning on a midnight sky."

BIG ISLAND ROUNDUP Kilauea is currently the world's most active volcano, and is top draw at the Hawaii Volcanoes National Park. But this is by no means all that the Big Island has to offer. Each of the six ancient districts, linked by the Hawaiian Belt Road that encircles the island, has its own individual character and charms.

The island has two natural starting points (both with airports): Hilo, on the damp windward coast, and Kailua-Kona, focus of the Kona and Kohala coast resorts. Hilo is better placed for the volcano park, but despite its attractive bayfront position, it will never be a favored tourist destination. It rains too much here, a fact that also keeps the lush Puna district to the south rural and unspoiled.

The Belt Road around the island runs southwest from the volcano park through the sparsely populated Kau region to the Kona coast and coffee groves on the drier leeward shore. Kailua-Kona is a seaside town at the southern end of the barren lava fields that border the Kohala coast. Along the white-sand shoreline, the Big Island's top resorts have sculpted amazing gardens and golf courses from the black rock. To the north, the Kohala Mountains rise behind the ranch town of Waimea-Kamuela, and fall down to Hamakua, the green, rain-swept northeast. Sometimes known as the "Scottish Coast," Hamakua's valleys and cane fields have a backdrop of towering Mauna Kea, rain forest, and waterfalls.

It does take time to explore the Big Island, but its fans return again and again.

▶▶▶ ISLAND HIGHLIGHTS

Ahuena Heiau *pages168–169*

Hawaii Tropical Botanical Garden *page 176*

Hawaii Volcanoes National Park *pages 160–161*

Hulihee Palace *page 169*

Kona Village *Luau* *page 171*

Lyman Mission House and Museum *page 157*

Puuhonua o Honaunau National Historical Park *pages 165, 167*

Waimea–Kamuela *pages 172–173*

HELE-ON BUS

Hawaii's public transportation system, the Hele-On bus, is a real travel bargain. Buses cover nearly every corner of the island, stopping at most major attractions and resorts. There may be a long wait between buses, so plan carefully. They operate from Monday to Saturday (for information and times, tel: 808/961-8744).

A cast net fisherman in Hilo Bay

MARKET DAYS
On Wednesdays and Saturdays, Hilo's colorful Farmers Market spills out over the corner of Kamehameha Avenue and Mamo Street. Dozens of stalls are piled high with local produce, from glossy aubergines and peppers to Chinese greens and avocados, fat bunches of radishes, stacks of yams, sweet Maui onions, cherry tomatoes, baby bananas, papayas, guavas, and gourds galore, as well as gorgeous cut flowers. Extravagant sprays of orchids, parrot's-beak and lobster-claw heliconias, bird-of-paradise flowers, proteas, red ginger, and anthuriums grown in nurseries and back gardens all over the Hilo and Puna districts, erupt exuberantly out of massed plastic buckets.

Hilo and surroundings

The Big Island's county seat and chief seaport is Hilo, which skirts the rim of lovely Hilo Bay. Situated on the lush, rain-forested windward coast, it has the reputation of being the wettest city in the country. Try to visit in the morning when there is a better-than-average chance of hitting a dry spell.

Behind the parks, which replaced the waterfront area wiped out by a destructive *tsunami* (tidal wave) in 1960, downtown Hilo's remaining false-fronted shops and plantation-era buildings clamber up the hillside past missionary churches and the Lyman House Museum. The Big Island Visitors Bureau office on the corner of Haili and Keawe streets is the place to pick up a map showing historic sites and other local information (tel: 808/961-5797. *Open:* Mon–Fri 8–4:30).

►► Hilo Tropical Gardens *153D3*

1477 Kalanianaole Avenue (2 miles off HI-11)
Open: daily 9–5. Admission: inexpensive
Just south of town, these colorful tropical gardens have been open to view for 50 years. Narrow paths weave past fern trees and crotons, bushy azaleas, and orchids galore. There are canopies of passion fruit vines and plumeria, grottoes full of impatiens, bizarre ornamental pineapples that look like horticultural hand grenades, and an interesting section devoted to Hawaiian food and medicinal plants. Make liberal use of the free mosquito repellent posted by the entrance.

► Liliuokalani Gardens *153D3*

Banyan Drive
Open site. Admission free
The centerpiece of this park is the Japanese-style gardens laid out around a series of lava outcrops and small lagoons spanned by picturesque bridges. Dwarf palms and miniature stone pagodas dot the shore, and there are stands of bamboo and mango trees. At the top of the gardens, a bridge links Coconut Island (Moku Ola), a popular weekend picnic haunt, to the mainland.

►►► Lyman Mission House and Museum *153D3*

276 Haili Street (tel: 808/935-5021)
Open: Mon–Sat 9–5, Sun 1–4; guided tours of the Mission House, every half hour 9:30–11:30, every hour 1–4
Admission: inexpensive

The Reverend David Belden Lyman and his wife Sarah arrived in Hawaii in 1832, and became the mainstays of the Hilo mission for half a century. Their single-story mission home, thatched with *ti*-leaves, was built in 1839. Later, a second story was added to accommodate their eight children. Beautifully restored, the house has been furnished throughout with antiques, many of them Lyman family heirlooms, and re-creates the mid-19th-century mission lifestyle in fascinating detail.

Next door is the Lyman Museum, devoted to Hawaiiana. Chronological displays on the first floor cover every aspect of local history and culture, from native basketwork and royal regalia to the story of Captain Cook and Hawaii's immigrant past. Upstairs, the Earth Heritage Gallery gives the low-down on volcanoes, and in the seashell section, shell collectors can have a field day down among the bivalves, frilly murex shells, and conches amassed by Frederick Lyman.

► Mauna Loa Macadamia Nut Factory and Visitor Center *153D3*

5 miles south of Hilo on HI-11, then 3 miles east following signs (tel: 808/966-8618)
Open: daily 9–4. Admission free

The Big Island produces 90 percent of the world's crop of macadamia nuts and celebrates this fact with an annual Macadamia Nut Festival every August. One of the biggest players in the mac nut field is the Mauna Loa company, which processes some 32 million pounds of the delicious sweet, white nuts a year.

The road to the farm's Visitor Center passes right through the heart of the 2,500-acre, 225,000-tree Keaau Orchard. If one of the five or six annual harvestings is taking place, you can watch the action from viewing windows overlooking the processing plant. An on-site shop sells macadamia nuts in various guises, from the straight unsalted nuts to chocolate-covered macadamia nut cookies and macadamia nut-flavored coffees.

Liliuokalani Gardens

MERRIE MONARCH FESTIVAL

The weeklong Merrie Monarch Festival is held in Hilo each spring. This is the most prestigious *hula* festival in the islands, and draws *hula* troops from throughout the state as well as from overseas. There are two types of *hula* on show: the *kahiko*, or traditional interpretation of Hawaiian stories accompanied by drumming and chanting; and the *auana*, or modern style, in which competitors are judged on their elaborate costumes and adornment as well as for style and movement. The town is booked up months in advance for the festival. For further information tel: 808/935-9168.

Macadamia nuts

Tropical flora in the Nani Mau Gardens

►► Nani Mau Gardens *153D3*

421 Makalika Street (4 miles south of Hilo, off HI-11) (tel: 808/959-3541; web: www.nanimau.com) Open: daily 8–5. Admission: moderate

This stunning 20-acre spread of formal gardens is a must for plant lovers. The first section is divided up into groupings of related plants such as the Bromeliad Garden, the wonderfully scented Gardenia and Jasmine Garden, and a fruit orchard. An interesting small, modern museum examines the role of plants in nature, culture, and agriculture, and has a well-stocked reference library. From the glories of the Orchid Walkway, a path leads to the Makalapua Lookout for an overview of the 6-acre Annual Garden, with its colorful massed beds laid out around sweeping lawns.

►► Panaewa Rainforest Zoo *153D3*

Off Mamaki Street (4 miles south of Hilo via HI-11) (tel: 808/959-7224) Open: daily 9–4. Admission free

A great outing for children, this well laid out, 12-acre zoo is home to 150 animals from 50 species, including tigers, monkeys, and native birds. Rain shelters dotted about its grounds are well used, as the park has around 125 inches of precipitation a year, but the zoo is still a favorite picnic spot and there is plenty to enjoy.

► Rainbow Falls *153D3*

Follow signs off Waianuenue Avenue (1½ miles from Hilo) Open site. Admission free

Waianuenue Avenue leads up from the Hilo waterfront to the popular Rainbow Falls. *Waianuenue* means "Rainbow-Water," and as the 80-foot cascade plummets down a lava rock cliff, it sends up a fine mist of white spray frequently shot through with rainbows.

A path leads through the woods from the parking lot to a viewpoint overlooking the Boiling Pots, a series of pools linked by smaller falls. The smell of fermenting mangoes pervades the wood (the rotting fruits make the path slippery in season), while a massive banyan tree looks like an open invitation to the Swiss Family Robinson.

FISHY BUSINESS

Early risers looking for some local color should make tracks for the Suisan Fish Auction. This is held between 7:30 and 8:30 every morning except Sunday at the fish market by the mouth of the Wailoa River, next to the Liliuokalani Gardens. Local chefs and housewives inspect the morning's catch, and everyone discusses the price of fish.

The world's tallest sea mountain, 32,000 feet from the ocean floor, Mauna Kea reaches a height of 13,796 feet above sea level. A shield volcano shaped alternately by fire and ice, the "White Mountain" last erupted over 3,600 years ago; since then its peaks and troughs have been honed by glacial action.

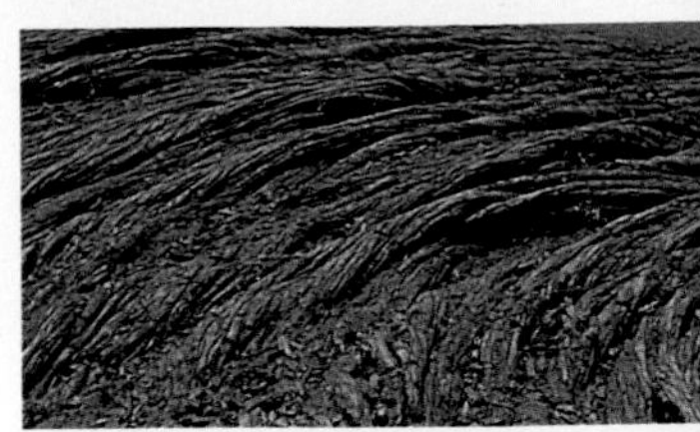

Tropical skiing From December to March or April, Mauna Kea's higher levels are often capped with virgin snow, so while it is a blistering 90 degrees on the beach, visitors with a taste for adventure can actually ski Mauna Kea with **Ski Guides Hawaii** (tel: 808/885-4188). Full-day ski packages include transportation and ski shuttles (there are no lifts), experienced guides (no marked trails either), and lunch. Equipment is also available to rent, and the best snow months are January and February.

Stargazing No other place on earth offers the same combination of altitude, clear air, absence of artificial light, and accessibility. As of 2000, 14 international observatories have been established here, along with the world's largest telescope for viewing both the northern and southern skies.

Observatory tours are available, but to get there it is better to join an excursion with Paradise Safaris, who operate from Kailua-Kona (tel: 808/322-2366), or with Mauna Kea Summit Tours (tel: 808/775-7121). They offer straightforward summit tours. Both companies issue warnings about the dangers of high altitude to sufferers of heart and respiratory conditions, and they will not take young children.

Saddle Road Access to Mauna Kea is via Saddle Road (HI-200), a poorly finished route that links Hilo to HI-190 just south of Waimea-Kamuela. Rental companies prohibit the use of their cars on Saddle Road. Drivers with four-wheel-drive vehicles interested in driving to the top should check weather conditions with the Visitor Center in advance (tel: 808/969-3218).

Observation point

Stargazers gather on Mauna Kea's summit

Molten pahoehoe lava

The South

▶▶▶ Hawaii Volcanoes National Park *153C/D2/3*

HI-11 near Volcano, 30 miles south of Hilo/95 miles east of Kailua-Kona (general information, including eruption update and weather report, tel: 808/985-6000; web: hvo.wr.usgs.gov)
Open: daily. Park, 24 hours; Visitor Center, 7:45–5; Museum, 8:30–5. Admission: inexpensive; tickets are valid for seven days

The sprawling 229,177-acre park comprises part of the state's two active volcanoes, Mauna Loa and Kilauea. It is the safest and most accessible place in the world to watch volcanic activity, and the park's various facilities include scenic drives, 150 miles of hiking trails, a visitor center, a museum, an observatory, campsites, and a hotel right on a crater rim.

Kilauea, the youngest and most active volcano in the Hawaiian Islands, is the central focus of the park. Measuring a mere 4,093 feet above sea level at its peak, Kilauea is small compared with neighboring Mauna Loa (13,677 feet). However, Kilauea's vast 2-mile by 2½-mile, 400-foot-deep summit caldera, caused by the collapse of a subterranean magma chamber, is as impressive as any, and the Puu Oo vent in the volcano's flank has been erupting continuously since 1983.

To orient yourself, pick up maps and information from the **Kilauea Visitor Center**, which also provides updates on volcanic activity and a short introductory film to the park shown every hour. Across from the center, a path cuts through to the Volcano House hotel and a crater-rim lookout with a panoramic view across the caldera to Madame Pele's firepit home, Halemaumau, a 500-foot-deep secondary crater that oozes wisps of sulfurous steam from fissures in its lava floor.

The 11-mile **Crater Rim Drive** is a must. It takes about an hour, but leave plenty of time for stops along the way. This loop drive encircles the caldera, passing through a great variety of terrains, and provides access to the 23-mile **Chain of Craters Road** that winds its way down to the coast. Here, lava flows from the active Puu Oo vent have added over 600 acres of new land since 1986.

MADAME PELE REIGNS
Madame Pele's presence in the Halemaumau Crater means that this region has always held a special spiritual significance for Hawaiians. Priests performed important religious rites here, and even today many visitors leave small gifts of coins, food, and flowers to placate the goddess. However, Madame Pele guards her firepit home jealously, and it is unlucky to remove so much as a pebble. Every day, park rangers receive packages of pilfered lava fragments accompanied by tales of the bad luck they have brought upon the senders.

The Thurston Lava Tube is not for anyone who is claustrophobic

Lava from Kilauea's Puu Oo vent builds a new coastline

Heading counterclockwise around the caldera, you come to areas of odoriferous sulfur banks and hissing steam vents, where groundwater seeps through cracks in the earth and vaporizes in temperatures that can reach 212–300°F just a few feet beneath the surface.

The **Thomas A. Jaggar Museum**, named for the founder of the Hawaiian Volcano Observatory, covers vulcanism in general but with particular emphasis on Hawaii. Dramatic action videos show live footage of volcanic eruptions, while working seismographs measure minute earth movements.

Leaving the *lehua* scrublands behind, the road runs across the southwest rift zone's blackened lava flows stretching like a sea of cracked and crumpled tarmac away from the crater rim. Here, the **Halemaumau Overlook**, just a few minutes' walk from the road, is worth a stop.

Other popular side trips include the eerie **Devastation Trail**, a boardwalk across pumice-cinder dunes scattered with the bleached wood bones of a former forest. Also the **Thurston Lava Tube**, a 450 foot-long tunnel created as molten lava continued to flow beneath a cooled and set crust, all but buried in the mossy, green *hapuu* (tree-fern) forest on the windward side of the caldera.

Giant **Mauna Loa** ("Long Mountain"), quiet since 1984, is a textbook example of a shield volcano. From the ocean floor to its 3-mile by 1½-mile, 600-foot-deep summit caldera, Mauna Loa's massive barrow-shaped form measures 10,000 cubic miles. Few visitors actually tackle Mauna Loa, which towers almost 2 miles higher than Kilauea. Its summit lies 33 miles northwest of the park headquarters, and a two-day hike from the top of the Mauna Loa Strip Road. However one excellent detour from the Strip Road is **Kipuka Puaulu**, an island of mature forest amid the lava flows that acts as a bird reserve.

VOLCANOES NATIONAL PARK TRAILS

Those exploring the park on foot have several options. The challenging four-day Mauna Loa Trail, two-day Halape Trail down to the coast, and full-day Napau Crater Trail with fine views of the Puu Oo vent, are for serious hikers. But the Crater Rim Trail is a relatively straightforward seven hours, and it can be shortened by taking in parts of the Halemaumau or Byron Ledge trails across the central lava fields of the Kilauea crater, or the Kilauea Iki Trail, which descends through lush jungle to a young secondary crater.

EN ROUTE STOPS
Just east of South Point Road, a handful of small villages offers a convenient break in the 100-mile journey between Kailua-Kona and Volcano. Half-pint-sized Naalehu, the southernmost community in the U.S., boasts the Mark Twain Monkeypod Tree, which shoots from the roots of a long-toppled tree planted by the author in 1866. Also at Naalehu, the Punaluu Bake Shop serves its own recipe sweet bread, sandwiches, snacks and cold drinks. Punaluu itself has a beach park, and a rocky beach with a picnic pavilion overlooking Ninole Cove.

Volcano Golf Course, in sight of the Kilauea Caldera

▶ Isaac Hale Beach Park 153E3

HI-137, south Puna
Open site. Admission free
Highway 137 divides just beyond Lava Tree State Park (see below), and the right fork to the Isaac Hale Beach Park makes a pretty drive to the coast. For the last few miles the single-track country road runs through a dense tunnel of mango trees and, in season, the air is heavy with the scent of squashed and fermented fruit.

The waterfront park does not have much of a beach, but the rocky shore is a popular weekend picnic spot. Local families come here to fish, surf, and launch boats from the ramp. To the north (off HI-137), there is a road out to Cape Kumukahi, the easternmost cape in the state, with an old lighthouse that narrowly avoided the lava flows of Kilauea's 1960 eruption.

▶▶ Lava Tree State Park 153E3

HI-132, 2½ miles east of HI-130 at Pahoa
Open site. Admission free
Once upon a time, deep in the rainforest jungle, a lava river flowed, engulfing all in its wake and turning trees to stone. It sounds like a fairy tale, but a river of molten lava from Kilauea did pass this way in 1790 and engulfed an *ohia* grove. Moisture contained within the tree trunks was sufficient to set a solid lava coating, leaving casts of the trees behind when the lava flow receded. Dozens of lava stumps and tubes are now dotted around amongst the ferns and new *ohia* forest. Along the 20-minute trail, look for wild orchids in the woodland clearings.

▶ South Point 152B1

Almost halfway between Volcano and Kailua-Kona, South Point Road strikes off HI-11 at Mile Marker 69 and travels down to South Point, the southernmost point in

the U.S. The Hawaiians call it Ka Lae, and it is thought that this is where the first Polynesians came ashore. Archaeological remains include petroglyphs (see page 170) and canoe moorings set in solid rock.

Local fishermen take advantage of the excellent fishing off the coast by mooring their boats at the base of the sheer cliff, then reaching them on ladders. A 3-mile hike to the north leads to green-sand Papakolea Beach, created by the collapse of an olivine cinder cone.

►► Volcano *153D2*

Just east of the volcano park, bypassed by HI-11, the little village of Volcano offers a couple of stores, a pleasant inn (Kilauea Lodge), and several friendly bed-and-breakfast establishments tucked discreetly behind hedges of hydrangeas and tree ferns in the cool, damp raintorest. In addition to the national park, there are a couple of minor local attractions and the Volcano Golf & Country Club (tel: 808/967-7331), where players can enjoy 18 holes of golf with volcano views.

In operation since 1974, **Akatsuka Orchid Gardens►** (HI-11 at Mile Marker 22.5. *Open:* daily 8:30–5. *Admission free*) have one of the largest orchid collections in Hawaii. The greenhouse garden contains a profusion of rare and colorful blooms, some fragrant, some bizarre. There are also dozens of waxy anthuriums, fiery red ginger flowers and massed bougainvillea in several shades. Cut flowers and plants are available for sale and can be shipped direct to the mainland.

The southernmost winery in the U.S., the **Volcano Winery** (tel: 808/967-7479; web: www.volcanowinery.com) (Golf Course Road, Volcano, off HI-11. *Open:* daily 10–5:30. *Admission free*) specializes in a brace of white wines from the relatively new Symphony grape variety, and there is also a selection of exotic wines flavored with tropical fruits such as guava and passion fruit, as well as a grape-free honey wine. Production is around 1,500 cases a month, and most of it is sold within the Islands. Tastings are offered in the gift shop, which sells souvenirs with a vinous theme.

Black volcanic sand on Mahana Beach

POLLINATION TRICKS

Strange but true, the yellow and brown "dancing doll" orchid (*Oncidium*) relies on an elaborate hoax to ensure its pollination. It attracts the attention of naive young centris bees by masquerading as an enemy insect. The bees challenge the "intruder" bloom with head butts and wind up carrying the pollen on their brows. The bees will then pollinate several plants.

Petrified lava trees near Pahoa

Captain Cook monument at Kealakekua Bay

The Kona Coast

►► Kealakekua Bay 152A3

Napoopoo Road, off HI-11 at Captain Cook (12 miles south of Kailua-Kona), or HI-160 north from Honaunau Open site. Admission free

The laid-back country town of Kealakekua straddles the Belt Road (HI-11) high above broad Kealakekua Bay. At the southern end of town, near the village of Captain Cook, signposts indicate the twisting 4-mile road that leads down to the shore past gardens dripping with fruit and tropical flowers, roadside stalls selling bargain-priced mangoes and papayas, coffee groves, and the massed yellow blooms of a commercial plumeria orchard.

When Captain Cook sailed into Kealakekua Bay on January 17, 1779, almost a year since he had first set foot in the Hawaiian Islands at Kauai, the British explorer was greeted as an incarnation of Lono, the peaceable Hawaiian god of agriculture and fertility. Cook and his ships, HMS *Resolution* and HMS *Discovery*, stayed in Kealakekua for three weeks enjoying Hawaiian hospitality and entertaining the chieftain Kalaniopuu and his entourage in return.

A week after the ships set sail again, Cook was forced to return when the *Resolution*'s mast was snapped in a squall. This merely served to confirm the Hawaiians' growing doubts about the visitors' godliness, and, during a dispute over a stolen boat, Cook was killed in a skirmish on the north shore of the bay.

Because of its clear water and variety of marine life, the bay is now protected as a Marine Life Conservation District, one of the state's underwater parks. It is one of the few places in Hawaii where spinner dolphins swim close to the shore (they use the protected waters for resting and breeding). Kealakekua's reefs offer superb snorkeling and diving with excellent visibility. Snorkeling trips are available from Fairwind, Captain Zodiac and others.

► Kona Historical Society Museum 152A3

HI-11 (Mile Marker 112.5), Captain Cook (tel: 808/323-3222; web: www.ilhawaii.net/~khs)

Open: Mon–Fri 9–3. Admission: inexpensive

Housed in the old Greenwell Store at Captain Cook, this local history museum displays a modest collection of period photographs, antiques, and memorabilia, much of it related to the Greenwell family. Businessman and rancher Henry Greenwell built the store next door to the family home (now in ruins) in the mid-19th century from volcanic rock and lime mortar made from crushed coral. It served as a travelers' watering post, dry goods store, and post office, and the Greenwells were among the first to export Kona coffee to Europe in the 1870s.

► Napoopoo Beach Park 152A3

Kealakekua Bay

There is good swimming and snorkeling from this rocky stretch of shore, which borders onto Kealakekua Bay. A small park contains changing rooms.

Near the park, the stone platform of Hikiau Heiau was an important ancient Hawaiian shrine dedicated to the god Lono. Captain Cook's auspicious appearance at this sacred site during the wintertime Makahiki festival

CAPTAIN COOK MONUMENT

On the inaccessible north shore of Kealakekua Bay, the Captain Cook Monument commemorates "the great circumnavigator" near the spot where he fell. The white marble obelisk, erected in 1874 by his fellow countrymen, can be reached by boat. The little jetty was donated by the Commonwealth of Australia in recognition of "the discoverer of Australia and these islands." There is also a path down the cliffs, but it is very overgrown and the hike back to the top is tough.

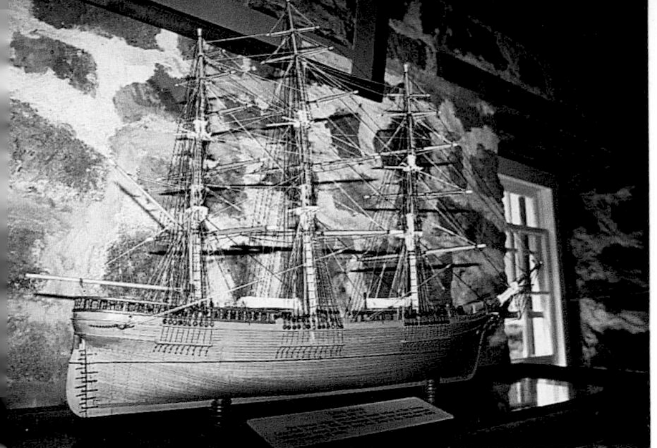

Model ship at the Kona Historical Society

celebrations (see page 35) guaranteed him and his men a warm welcome.

A plaque records the burial of seaman William Whatman, performed by Captain Cook here on January 28, 1779. This funeral was the first recorded Christian service to be held in the islands.

►►► Puuhonua O Honaunau National Historical Park *152A2*

HI-160 (off HI-11), 22 miles south of Kailua-Kona (tel: 808/328-2288; web: www.nps.gov/puho)
Open: Mon–Thu 6 AM–8 PM, Fri–Sun 6 AM–11 PM; Visitor Center: daily 7:30–5:30. Admission: inexpensive

Up until 1819, every aspect of Hawaiian life was regulated by *kapu*, a system of taboos designed to protect society and natural resources (see page 33). The punishment for breaking any *kapu* was death, and the only possibility of absolution for a *kapu*-breaker was to reach a *puuhonua*, or place of refuge. In the mass destruction of religious sites that followed the abolition of the *kapu* system, the Puuhonua O Honaunau ("Place of Refuge at Honaunau") escaped by

Continued on page 167

NAUPAKA

The indigenous beach *naupaka*, with its strange half-formed white flower, is a common sight along Hawaii's shores. Another type of *naupaka* grows in the mountains, and when the two half-flowers are placed together they make a whole. As the story goes, there were two lovers whom the goddess Pele wished to part. When she failed to win the young man's love, she hurled fiery lava after him, but the youth was rescued by Pele's sisters and turned into mountain *naupaka*. Pele then chased the girl into the sea until again the sisters intervened, transforming her into beach *naupaka*.

The ancient Hikiau Heiau at Napoopoo

Throughout the world, the name Kona has become synonymous with coffee. Above the sunny South Kona coast more than 600 coffee farms crowd into a narrow belt stretching along the leeward slopes of the Mauna Loa and Hualalai mountains. Every year they produce over 2 million pounds of the world's finest coffee.

PLANTATIONS IN ACTION
Numerous coffee farms along the Belt Road (HI-11) offer tastings and farm and mill tours. Visitors are welcome to drop in on the Langenstein Farm (Mile Marker 104.5), where Kona coffee is grown, picked, milled, and roasted on the property. Another good place to see a working plantation is family-owned Bay View Farm, near St. Benedict's Painted Church (off HI-160; see page 167).

King of coffee Kona's coffee farms flourish in elevations between 800 and 2,000 feet above sea level, where the combination of rich volcanic soil, wind shelter, rainfall, and all-important cloud shade in the hot afternoon produces ideal conditions for coffee-growing.

The first coffee bushes were introduced to the islands in 1828. Hawaii is the only place in the U.S. where coffee can be grown commercially, and the Big Island is by far the most renowned producer. Connoisseurs particularly prize Kona coffee's delicious aroma and mellow, full-bodied flavor.

Harvesting of the bright-red coffee berries, known as "cherries," takes place in the autumn and winter, generally between August and February. The handpicked cherries are then milled to extract the coffee beans, which are sun-dried on racks, then sorted, roasted, and packaged for the market.

An average plant produces 5 pounds of cherries a year, which converts to about a pound of processed beans. The highest-grade coffees are made from pea berries, single beans from the cherry, which normally produces two.

Vintage chocolate Another U.S. commercial first for the Big Island is Hawaiian Vintage Chocolate, the nation's only chocolate producer. In 1986, Jim Walsh planted 18,000 cocoa trees and his first "vintage" went on sale in 1992. Since then, Hawaii's top chefs, as well as restaurateurs from as far away as New York, have been clamoring for his top-quality product, made from fragrant and flavorful criollo cocoa.

Bags of flavor from the Kona Coast

Continued from page 165

virtue of its importance. A former royal village as well as a refuge, it was one of the most sacred sites in Hawaii.

Reconstructions of traditional timber-framed buildings have been built in the former royal palace grounds. These are still divided from the *puuhonua* by a tremendous 1,000-foot-long, 10-foot-high, and 17-foot-thick L-shaped drystone wall. At its northern end, the thatched Hale O Keawe mausoleum-temple, which was rebuilt in 1968 on mid-17th-century foundations, is guarded by ferocious *kii* idols. Raised platforms around the enclosure, known as *lele*, were used for offerings to placate the gods. Take plenty of time to explore the park. Picnicking is permitted and the grounds stay open until late.

► Royal Kona Coffee Mill *152A3*

Mamalahoa Highway, near Honaunau School (tel: 808/328-2511). Open: daily 9–5. Admission free

Kona's coffee country delivers a mean cup of coffee. Visitors can sample a selection of coffees and learn how it is grown and processed. Coffee blends run the gamut, from French, Viennese, or espresso-style roasts to exotic concoctions flavored with vanilla, chocolate, macadamia nut, or cinnamon. There is a short video presentation and a store crammed full of tasty products, from chocolate-dipped coffee beans to macadamia nut brittle.

►► St. Benedict's Painted Church *152B2*

Signposted off HI-160, east of Puuhonua O Honaunau (tel: 808/328-2227) Open: daily. Admission free

This small wooden church built in 1928 makes a popular detour above the Puuhonua O Honaunau and Kealakekua Bay. The interior has been decorated from head to toe: biblical scenes and grandiose *trompe-l'oeil* vistas cover the walls, while Hawaiian-language quotations from the scriptures wind around the pillars.

SANCTUARY

Both land and sea routes to the *puuhonua* were fraught with dangers, but if a *kapu*-breaker made it to the refuge, he or she could return home safely after a ceremony of absolution. Sanctuary was also offered to those too young, old, or disabled to fight in times of war. Defeated warriors could seek sanctuary as well; when the fight was over they then owed allegiance to the victor.

HALE O KEAWE

The *heiau* (temple) of Hale O Keawe in the *puuhonua* was built around 1650 in honor of Chief Keawe, whose bones were later stored there, carefully wrapped in cloth. Hawaiians believe that *mana*, or spiritual power, remains in the bones after death, so Hale o Keawe became a place of spiritual force. Over the years, the remains of 23 other chieftains, forebears of Kamehameha I, were also interred there, but all the bones were removed to a secret hiding place in 1829.

Most of St. Benedict's interior decoration is the work of Father Everest Gielen, the Belgian priest who built the church

KAILUA PIER
Kailua Pier is always bustling. It is a great place for a stroll, or to just sit and watch the pleasure boats and fishing vessels coming and going, outrigger crews practicing their paddle work, and kids cavorting on the murky beach after school. Kailua Bay Charter Company (tel: 808/324-1749) and *Nautilus II* (tel: 808/326-2003) leave from the pier daily for one-hour reef jaunts. There are also snorkel cruises with Body Glove (tel: 808/326-7122) or Captain Zodiac (tel: 808/329-3199), among others; and submarine adventures with *Atlantis* (tel: 808/329-6626).

Kailua–Kona

Located midway down the Big Island's drier, sunnier leeward side, Kailua sits on the boundary between the Kona coast to the south and the Kohala coast to the north. It was a Hawaiian gathering place for centuries, and in the early 19th century became the capital of the Hawaiian kingdom for the last few years of Kamehameha I's reign. This was also the spot where the first missionaries put ashore in the islands in 1820.

Kailua is sandwiched between the luxury resorts of the south Kohala coast and a long strip of condominiums and hotels stretching down to Keauhou. All the main sights and stores are found on Alii Drive, which parallels the shore. Here, the touristy Kona Inn Shopping Village is a good place to pick up local information. The Big Island Visitors Bureau also has an office in the Kona Plaza Shopping Arcade, next to Mokuaikaua Church (tel: 808/329-7787. *Open:* Mon–Fri 8–12, 1–4:30).

▶▶▶ Ahuena Heiau 152A3

In the grounds of King Kamehameha's Kona Beach Hotel, Palani Road
Open site. Admission free

In 1812, his kingdom secured, the aging Kamehameha I returned to his home island of Hawaii and established the royal court at Kamakahonu ("Eye of the Turtle"), an oceanfront site just north of the present-day Kailua Pier. Here, he rebuilt an ancient *heiau*, which had once been a sacrificial site, rededicated it to peace-loving Lono, and lived out his days in a traditional compound of thatched buildings, several of which have been reconstructed overlooking the bay.

Dominating the Hale Pahu ("House of the Drum") and Hale Mana, where the king prayed and consulted with his ministers, is a tall Anuu, or oracle tower, used by the high priest to commune with the gods and proclaim their will.

Offerings at the reconstructed Ahuena Heiau temple complex

Placed around the compound are *lele* (raised platforms) used for offerings, and protective *kii akua* (carved temple images). When Kamehameha died in 1819, his body was prepared for burial at the *heiau* before being taken to a secret burial place.

The spire of Mokuaikaua Church rises behind the waterfront and Hulihee Palace

▶▶▶ Hulihee Palace 152A3

5718 Alii Drive (tel: 808/329-1877)
Open: Mon–Fri 9–4, Sat–Sun 10–4
Admission: inexpensive

The Iolani Palace in Honolulu claims to be the only true palace in the U.S., but as far as the locals are concerned this modest residence also qualifies. Built for Governor John Adams Kuakini in 1838, the fine seafront house became a favored royal summer retreat and contains plenty of regal memorabilia.

Governor Kuakini stood 6 foot 6 inches tall and the Hulihee's imposing *koa*-wood doors were built to accommodate his height. The 3-foot-thick walls keep the high-ceilinged rooms cool in summer, and the splendid furnishings include a four-poster bed adorned with carved crowns and a custom-built chair made for the 6-foot 4-inch Princess Ruth Keelikolani.

The palace gardens lead down to a tiny beach with good snorkeling. On weekday afternoons, visitors may be treated to an impromptu show if a *hula halau* (*hula* school) is practicing in the garden.

▶▶ Mokuaikaua Church 152A3

Alii Drive (tel: 808/329-1589)
Open daily. Admission free

Edged by colorful plumeria and hibiscus blossoms, the church is set back from the road opposite the Hulihee Palace. The very first Christian church in the Hawaiian Islands was established on this site in 1820, and several simple thatched buildings followed before the present lava-rock structure was completed in 1837.

Native *ohia* and *kou* woods were used for the interior, and the body of the church is ringed by a wooden gallery. Behind a *koa*-wood screen at the rear is a small historical display with views of Kailua—Kona and its group of thatched huts as it was *circa* 1845, plus a model of the brig *Thaddeus* that brought the first New England missionaries to the islands.

KING KAMEHAMEHA'S KONA BEACH HOTEL
En route to the Ahuena Heiau, take time to inspect the various exhibits on display in the lobby of King Kamehameha's Kona Beach Hotel. In among the artifacts and portraits of Hawaiian royalty, full size mounts of World Record Pacific Blue Marlin leap out from between the trophies and assorted memorabilia relating to the annual Hawaiian International Billfish Tournament, and there is also a collection of Hawaiian musical instruments.

The ancient Hawaiians did not have a written language, but they recorded detailed messages using petroglyphs, symbolic carvings etched in smooth rock. Called kii puako *("stone images"), many thousands are scattered throughout the islands, but the greatest concentration is found on Hawaii, in the Hawaiian Volcanoes National Park.*

WATCH YOUR FEET
When visiting petroglyph areas, take care not to step on the dozens of ancient carvings. It is also forbidden to take rubbings of the images except at specially designated areas such as at the Puako Petroglyph Preserve in the Mauna Lani resort.

Early morning or evening is the best time to see petroglyphs and to take photographs, as the sharply angled light accentuates the features.

Rock carvings The word "petroglyph" comes from the Greek *petros* for "rock," and *glyphe* "to carve." Though often described as rock art, petroglyphs were more important than mere decoration, since they were used to record special festivities, religious beliefs, and ancestor genealogies. Other images described day-to-day activities such as hunting, fishing, and journeys, and important events including pregnancy, birth, and death.

On the Hawaiian Islands, petroglyphs occur most commonly on smooth expanses of *pahoehoe* lava or on cliff faces and inside caves. Most were made with a sharp rock acting as a chisel and struck repeatedly with a heavy hammer stone, or by rubbing a blunt stone against the lava surface to break the natural glaze.

Ancient petroglyphs

Petroglyph sites There is a good chance that sites where ancient Hawaiians gathered, or which were the focus of their journeys, will yield up petroglyphs. The historic 175-mile Ala Kahakai Trail from the northern tip of the Big Island at Upolu Point to the Volcano area passes through the bleak lava flows spreading down to the Kohala coast. Here, tucked in among the resorts and golf courses, are two important sites.

At the petroglyph field near the King's Shops mall at the Waikoloa Beach Resort there are more than 9,000 carved images, some dating from as early as the 10th century. In the grounds of the Mauna Lani resort, interpretive signboards guide visitors around 3,000-plus stickmen, shapes, and symbols at the Puako Petroglyph Preserve. But by far the greatest concentration of petroglyphs is found at the Puu Loa site in the Hawaii Volcanoes National Park, where a 2-mile trail takes in some 15,000 carvings dating from many different ages, with the greatest concentration of them at the Hill of Long Life.

Kohala Coast and the North

►► Anaehoomalu Beach 152B4

Waikoloa Beach Resort, off HI-19
(24 miles north of Kailua-Kona)
Open site. Admission free

The sandy sweep of coconut palm-fringed Anaehoomalu, bordering the Waikoloa resort complex, is an excellent family beach with calm water and good snorkeling. Helpful signboards list the various marine species that swim about in the bay, and there are rock pools to poke around in, too. Windsurfing equipment and sail boats can be rented here, and full rest-room and changing facilities are provided.

Visitors are welcome to explore several historic sites in the area. A series of ancient Hawaiian fishponds border the beach, while there are dozens of mysterious petroglyphs spread over a lava area near the Waikoloa Beach Resort's King's Shops mall (see page 170).

►►► Hapuna Beach 152B4

Off HI-19 (31 miles north of Kailua-Kona)
Open site. Admission free

This is one of the Big Island's finest beaches (and so it is often crowded), with a broad crescent of dazzling soft white sand backed by *Kiawe* trees. It is also a renowned body-surfing spot when the waves are on form. At other times, the exceptionally clear water makes for interesting snorkeling around a rocky outcrop near the center of the beach, but watch out for boogie-boarders. The beach park facilities include a snack concession, barbecue grills, picnic tables, and showers.

►►► Kona Village *Luau* 152A4

Kona Village Resort, off HI-19 (15 miles north of Kailua-Kona)
Open: Friday only; reservations, tel: 808/325-5555
Admission: expensive

The Kona Village Resort hosts one of the state's best *luau* (see pages 16–17). Make reservations in advance, and arrive in plenty of time to explore the grounds with their Polynesian-style accommodations. Visitors can check out the petroglyphs, or take a stroll on the beach and generally work up a serious appetite for the feasting ahead. Do not miss the moment when the steaming *imu* (underground oven) is unwrapped. It is pure theater!

KONA MARINA
Want to charter a boat, arrange sail, snorkel, and dive adventures, or organize a day's or half-day's deep-sea sport fishing? Then drop by the Honokohau Marina, just north of Kailua-Kona on the road to the airport, where all these activities can be arranged. The complex is a popular anchorage for yachts and also contains the Harbor House bar-restaurant and fishing supply shops.

Body-boarding at Hapuna

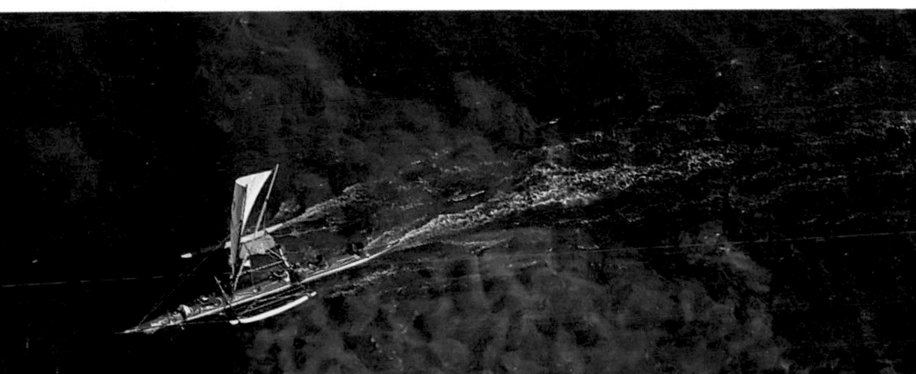

Sailing on Anaehoomalu Bay

PARKER RANCH STORE
Next door to the Parker Ranch Visitor Center, would-be cowboys and girls can get fitted out *paniolo*-style from a selection of western clothes on sale in the Parker Ranch Store. Western-style shirts, hats, boots, and belts come in all shapes and sizes, and there is the complete young person's gunfighter outfit in chic but impractical (unwashable) suede.

JOHN PALMER PARKER
Parker first came to Hawaii in 1809 aboard a whaling ship from Massachusetts. Glad to escape the ship's stench, he spent some time in the islands, and he befriended Kamehameha I before going back to sea. He returned to Hawaii for good in 1814, and worked for the king rounding up wild cattle (see pages 144–145) before ranching on lands leased from the crown. Parker was over 50 before he owned a single acre in his own right.

►►► Waimea–Kamuela *152B4*

Usually known as Kamuela (Hawaiian for "Samuel") to distinguish it from the town of Waimea on Kauai, this pleasant upcountry town is "Parker Ranch Central." A Western-style town, it lies at the heart of Hawaii's *paniolo* (cowboy) country, surrounded by lush pastures, rolling ranchlands, and patches of forest. Its location in the foothills of the Kohala Mountains at a cool and comfortable 2,500 feet above sea level makes it a delightful escape from the broiling coast, and there are several worthwhile attractions as well as the landscape.

The history of ranching on the Big Island is really the story of the Parker Ranch and is told in the **Parker Ranch Visitor Center►►►** (Parker Ranch Shopping Center, HI-190, tel: 808/885-7655. *Open:* daily 9–5. *Admission: moderate*; joint tickets with Parker Ranch Historic Homes, see below). From a 2-acre parcel of land allocated to John Palmer Parker for the sum of $10 in 1847, the Palmer spread has grown to 225,000 acres and is now one of the largest ranches in the U.S., stretching from the mountains to the ocean.

Artifacts, photographs, and a short film explain both family and Big Island history. Informative signboards impart all sorts of anecdotes and descriptions of life on the ranch, and there is even a reconstructed back-country *paniolo* hut made of weathered *koa*-wood shingles.

There are two very different family houses at the **Parker Ranch Historic Homes►►** (HI-190, half a mile south of town, tel: 808/885-5433. *Open:* daily 10–5. *Admission: moderate*; joint tickets with Parker Ranch Visitor Center), each offering an intriguing slice of Parker family history. On the one hand is a reconstruction of John Palmer Parker's humble New England-style wooden saltbox house, Mana Hale; on the other is gracious Puuopelu ("Rolling Hills"), the home of his son and heirs.

Visits begin at Puuopelu, founded by John Parker II in the mid-19th century. The single-story exterior is deceptively modest, for the spacious interior has inherited a theatrical elegance from its last owner, the actor-singer Richard Smart, a sixth-generation Parker who died in 1992. French and Italian furnishings and Asian porcelain set the stage for his art collection, which includes works by Degas, Renoir, and Dufy.

Parker Ranch, Mana Hale

When John Palmer Parker Sr. died, he left the ranch to his son John II and grandson Samuel, who were total opposites. While John moved from the original Mana Hale homestead to Puuopelu and undertook the serious business of ranching, Sam stayed on at Mana Hale and had a thoroughly good time. Sam Parker was a friend of King David Kalakaua, and had a reputation for being a lavish and hospitable host. His cozy, four-room *koa*-wood cabin is now adorned with 19th-century photographs of the ranch-owner with his family and cronies (including the king), framed royal warrants bestowing legions of honors and titles, and family papers as well as solid, old-fashioned furniture.

John Palmer Parker's great-great-granddaughter, Harriet Solomon, and her husband Albert have been amassing artifacts and antiques for over 60 years, and the fruits of their labors have taken over most of the first floor of their home. The resulting **Kamuela Museum▶▶** (2 miles west of Kamuela on HI-19 at HI-250, tel: 808/885-4724. *Open:* daily 8–5. *Admission: inexpensive*) is wonderfully eclectic and somewhat eccentric.

One of the larger specimens in the display at Kamuela Museum

After stepping carefully past the giant stuffed bear that guards the reception hall, you may feel as if you have been let loose in an Aladdin's cave where dinosaur bones and ancient Hawaiian strangling cords jostle for attention with a gate key from the Iolani Palace and a pen filled with volcanic ash from Mount St. Helen's. There are Hawaiian hammer stones for smashing holes in war canoes, an 18th-century silver muffineer for sprinkling sugar on muffins, and then there is the tale of the Japanese pilot's sister who tracked down the machine gun salvaged from her kamikaze brother's plane.

Mexican sun screen

Drive

North Kohala

See map on pages 152–153.

A terrific trip, this 75-mile drive encompasses ancient Hawaiian sites, a beautiful north coast valley, and a memorable upcountry excursion. You might stop in Waimea-Kamuela (see pages 172–173), and if you really want to get a feel for the Big Island's *paniolo* country, call Paniolo Riding Adventures (tel: 808/889-5354) in advance, and book a couple of hours' horseback-riding on an 11,000-acre mountain ranch.

Start at the intersection of HI-19 and HI-270, 10 miles west of Waimea-Kamuela, and take HI-270 north for ½ mile to the **Puukohola Heiau** (tel: 808/882-7218; web: www.nps.gov/puhe) (*Open:* daily 7:30–4. *Admission:* inexpensive). In response to a prophecy that he would rule the islands if he constructed a mighty *luakini heiau* (sacrificial temple) dedicated to Kukailimoku, his ancestral war god, Kamehameha I had this huge lava stone platform built within a year. The inaugural sacrificial victim was his cousin and rival, Keoua. Continue north on HI-270 for 13 miles.

The **Lapakahi State Historical Park** (tel: 808/889-5566) (*Open:* daily 8–4. *Admission free*) is set among rocks and boulders, sun-bleached grasses, and twisted-trunk *kiawe* trees on the seashore. This old Hawaiian fishing village dates back around 600 years, and a self-guided tour leads around house sites and shrines, and past boulders that were used for salt-drying or covered in little holes to make *konane* "boards" for playing a Hawaiian version of Chinese checkers.

Another 6 miles north on the HI-270, there is a left turn for Upolu Airport and something of an off-road detour (check whether your car rental company permits their vehicles on this road.) At the entrance to the airfield turn left again and follow a graded dirt track for 2 miles along this rugged and remote stretch of coast, buffeted by wind and surf, until you come to the **Mookini Heiau**, one of the most complete and imposing of the ancient Hawaiian sites. Founded in the 13th century, it is believed to be one of the first *luakini* (sacrificial sites) in the islands.

The stone-walled compound of **Akahi Aina Hanau** nearby was specifically chosen for its isolation when Kekuiapoiwa, Kamehameha's mother,

Beachfront Lapakahi

Puukohala Heiau

gave birth to her child in secret in the mid-1700s. Prophecies of the child's future power and success put his life in danger from his own father, and the child grew up in hiding in the Waipio Valley beyond the reach of the court. He was later named Kamehameha, the "Lonely One." Return to HI-270.

As the road continues north it enters the luxuriant north shore rainbelt, and there is an explosion of greenery, fruit trees, and flowering plants along the roadside. Drive through the quiet plantation town of Hawi to the village of Kapaau (3½ miles), where the original of the famous **Kamehameha Statue** in Honolulu stands outside Kapaau's Kohala District Courthouse. Cast in Italy in 1880, the bronze statue was lost at sea on its way to the islands, and was then rediscovered in the Falkland Islands years later, after a second cast had already been installed in Honolulu.

From Kapaau, continue east to Pololu Point at the end of the road (5½ miles). There is a marvelous view from the lookout across the **Pololu Valley**, which cuts back into the interior from the north-coast sea cliffs. A steep (often muddy) trail leads down through guava and ironwood trees to the shore.

Retrace the road to Hawi and, just beyond Mile Marker 23, turn left onto HI-250. This wonderful upcountry route through the horse and cattle pastures of the **North Kohala Mountains** is a highlight of the drive. The rolling green landscape, full of peaks and knolls, patches of ironwood forest and not infrequent rainbows, becomes positively alpine as the road reaches its 3,564-foot crest before descending toward Waimea-Kamuela. From the intersection of HI-250 and HI-19 it is 10 miles back to where you started.

Pololu Valley pali

Enigmatic stone stacks on the shore

SCENIC DETOUR
There is a pretty detour off the main Belt Road (HI-19) up the Hamakua Coast north of Hilo. Approximately 7 miles north of Hilo, just beyond a pedestrian overpass, look for a blue sign on the right marked "Scenic Route 4 miles long." Exit from HI-19 here and follow the coastal loop road as it winds over a series of streams and through lush tropical jungle, past the Old Yellow Church and Hawaii Tropical Botanical Garden until it rejoins HI-19.

Hamakua Coast

►► Akaka Falls State Park *153D4*

13 miles north of Hilo on HI-19, then 5 miles west on HI-220, Akaka Falls Road
Open: daily. Admission free

Tucked into the rain forest behind the coast, the Akaka's combination of gorgeous tropical plants and splashing waterfalls exemplifies picture-postcard Hawaii. A circular trail (20 minutes) plunges down into a valley planted with philodendrons, heliconias and torch gingers, orchids, and great stands of bamboo. From the 100-foot Kahuna Falls, the path winds on to Akaka, a white-water cascade that thunders more than 420 feet down the rock face to a cauldron of black volcanic rock below. It is particularly impressive after heavy rains (bring mosquito repellent). The village of Akaka Falls, with an assortment of shops, places to eat and a flea market, is just below the park, its torpor somehow undisturbed by the streams of tourists.

►►► Hawaii Tropical Botanical Garden *153D4*

Off HI-19, 8 miles north of Hilo
(tel: 808/964-5233; web: www.htbg.com)
Open: daily 9–4:30. Admission: moderate

These magnificent tropical gardens carpet 45 acres of a lush valley stretching back from the ocean's edge at Onomea Bay. Within the rain forest, native birds and brightly plumed South American macaws add a flash of color. More than 2,000 different plant species contribute to the eye-catching array of heliconias, bromeliads, mango trees, coconut groves, and tropical fruits. Special features include medicinal plants, a water-lily lake, and Japanese *koi* ponds.

Visitors park at the reception center in the converted yellow church building on the Scenic Route (see panel); transportation is provided to the gardens. Bring mosquito repellent; umbrellas are provided on rainy days.

► Honokaa *152C5*

At one time the old plantation town of Honokaa looked like a spent force, but efforts to pull Mamane Street, the main street, back into shape are paying off. Behind Western-style raised sidewalks, old-fashioned, false-fronted shops have been occupied by small businesses. Browsers can while away a half-hour or so in a handful of curio shops, and the Bad Ass Macadamia Nut Company (which also produces coffee) welcomes visitors to its local candy factory.

Giant bamboo in the Hawaii Tropical Botanical Gardens

▶▶ Waipio Valley 152C5

HI-240, 10 miles northwest of Honokaa
Open site. Tours, Mon–Sat 8 or 9–4 (reservations advised). Admission free. Tours: expensive

The verdant and fertile Waipio ("Curving Water") Valley, inhabited for over 1,000 years, is a classic ancient Hawaiian *ahupuaa*, a triangular wedge of land that contained all the elements needed to sustain viable communities—arable land, timber forest, fresh water from the mountains, and fish from the sea.

From a mile-wide black-sand beach, the valley floor stretches back 6 miles into the 2,000-foot-high *pali* (cliffs), between towering green walls streaked with waterfalls. Once the most cultivated valley on the island, it was home to several thousand Hawaiian villagers who planted taro patches, yams, bananas, breadfruit, and coconut groves here. There was an abundance of wild game and good fishing, and fishponds were constructed to farm *opae* (shrimp) and mullet. Today, only a very few families remain, still cultivating taro and tending gardens lush with mangoes and guavas. Few traces of the original settlement site are visible.

There is a valley lookout just north of Kukuihaele, at the head of a twisting road (suitable for four-wheel drives only) to the valley floor. Waipio Valley Shuttle (tel: 808/775-7121) gives minibus tours down to the valley, and there are mule-drawn wagon rides with Waipio Valley Wagon Tours (tel: 808/775-9518); both tours last 1½ hours. It is also possible to hike down the steep trail (about 25 minutes), but the journey back is tough.

TRAIL TO WAIMANU VALLEY

One of the finest hikes in the islands is the 12-mile round-trip trek from Waipio to the neighboring uninhabited Waimanu Valley. It crosses the floor of the Waipio Valley and then there is an arduous climb up the 1,200-foot cliffs on a winding, switchback path, which continues up and down numerous ravines to Waimanu. There are fabulous views and wild, "Jurassic Park" landscape, but only experienced and well-equipped hikers should attempt the trek.

The remote Waipio Valley can only be reached by a steep road down from Kukuihaele

Hawaii offers some of the best deep-sea sport fishing in the world, and nothing can compete with the Big Island's Kona coast for magnificent Pacific blue marlin. Kailua-Kona is host to the prestigious annual Hawaiian International Billfish Tournament, the father of amateur sport-fishing competitions in the Pacific, attracting anglers from far and wide every summer.

NEIGHBOR ISLANDS' SPORT FISHING
Kona may boast the biggest tournament fishing, but all the islands offer sport fishing, mainly off their leeward shores. The rich fishing grounds off Oahu's Waianae Coast have been popular with the Hawaiians for centuries; charter boats are available from Waianae and from Honolulu's Kewalo Basin. Kauai's charter fleet puts out year-round from Nawiliwili and reels in spectacular yellowfin in spring. Penguin Banks, off Molokai's West End, is legendary; and from Maui, boats head out from Lahaina and Maalaea small boat harbors.

Ideal conditions The Kona coast has two of the prime ingredients for great deep-sea fishing: it has the calm seas that are generally found on the sheltered leeward sides of the islands; and there is easy access to deep water—anglers can reach deep-water fishing grounds of 100–1,000 fathoms a relatively short distance offshore. Hawaii's main sport-fishing season lasts from spring through autumn, hitting a peak at the July/August tournament time. Hawaii is the only place in the world where Pacific blue marlin are caught every day of the year.

A wealth of fish Pacific blue marlin, called *au* by the Hawaiians, is the king of catches, with record-breaking billfish weighing in at over 1,000 pounds, but several other game fish are also up for grabs in local waters. Yellowfin tuna (*ahi*) weigh between 2 and 200 pounds. Dolphin fish (*mahimahi*), not to be confused with true dolphins, which are mammals rather than fish, can weigh up to 70 pounds. There are also swordfish, skipjack tuna (*aku*), giant trevally (*ulua*), the wahoo (*ono*) and several other species.

Boats and tackle Nearly 80 professional deep-sea fishing charter boats operate out of the Big Island's Honokohau Marina, north of Kailua-Kona. They offer full-day (eight-hour) and half-day (four-hour) charters for individuals, or "share boats" for an average of four to six anglers. Tackle is provided. The catch is generally left for the crew, but any potentially record-breaking fish may be taken to Kailua Pier for a weighing-in at the historic tournament fish scale, which will record weights of up to one ton!

Small ahi *are great sport on light tackle*

Travel Facts

Arriving

By air

The major gateways to Hawaii include the following:

• Oahu
Hawaii's major airport is **Honolulu International** (tel: 808/836-6411), about a five-hour flight from west coast cities and a 20-minute drive from Waikiki. If you're flying from Honolulu to another island, you'll need to locate the interisland terminal for Aloha Airlines and Hawaiian Airlines (or the one for Island Air) to the left of the main terminal as you come out of the exit. There is a free WikiWiki Shuttle bus to take you to and from the interisland terminals; however, it is an easy five-minute walk between the main terminal and the interisland terminals.

• Maui
Maui's efficient **Kahului Airport** (tel: 808/872-3803), in Maui's central town of Kahului, has a new modern terminal. Maui's other airport, the **Kapalua–West Maui Airport** (call Island Air), capably handles the traffic it gets. For visitors to West Maui, landing at the Kapalua facility is the easiest way to arrive. It saves about an hour's drive from the Kahului airport. The tiny town of **Hana** in East Maui also has an airstrip (tel: 808/248-8208), but it is only serviced by one commuter airline (Island Air) and charter carriers.

Frequent interisland flights are available on several local carriers

• Kauai
On Kauai, visitors have a choice between the recently expanded **Lihue Airport** (tel: 808/246-1400) on the east side of the island, and **Princeville Airport** (tel: 808/826-3040) near the north shore.

• The Big Island of Hawaii
Those flying to the Big Island generally land at one of two fields. Kona's **Keahole-Kona International Airport** (tel: 808/329-2484), on the west side, best serves Kailua-Kona, Keauhou, and the Kohala Coast. **Hilo International Airport** (tel: 808/933-4782), formerly General Lyman Field, is also a large, new airport but is more appropriate for those going to the east side. Waimea Airport serves commuter aircraft.

• Lanai and Molokai
Lanai (tel: 808/565-6757) and **Molokai** (tel: 808/567-6140) airports are centrally located on those islands. Both are small rural airports that can handle only a limited number of flights and planes per day.

Carriers Carriers serving the Honolulu International Airport include **Aloha** (tel: 800/367-5250); **American** (tel: 800/433-7300); **Continental** (tel: 800/231-0856); **Delta** (tel: 800/221-1212);

Hawaiian (tel: 800/221-1212); **Northwest** (tel: 800/225-2525); **TWA** (tel: 800/221-2000); and **United** (tel: 800/241-6522). Many flights originate in Los Angeles and San Francisco, but it is also possible to fly direct from Dallas, Chicago, St. Louis, New York, Seattle, Minneapolis, San Diego, and other gateways. United Airlines—which handles some 50 percent of the airline traffic to Hawaii—flies directly into the Big Island's Keahole Airport, Maui's Kahului Airport, and Kauai's Lihue Airport.

By sea

Aside from working a passage to the islands on a cargo ship or crewing for an ocean-going yacht, the only way to get to Hawaii by sea is with a cruise ship, and such cruises are now booming. The San Francisco-based **Royal Cruise Line** (tel: 415/956-7200) operates winter cruises lasting between eight and 16 days that visit the islands of Maui, Kauai, and Hawaii. **Cunard** (tel: 800/221-4770) and **Holland America** (tel: 800/426-0327) include stops in Hawaii on their longer Pacific cruises. Another cruise line that visits the Hawaiian Islands is

An aloha *welcome*

the **Royal Caribbean Cruise Line** (tel: 800/327-6700). Within the islands, American Hawaii Cruises operates loop cruises lasting seven days and calling at several islands within the group (see **By boat**, page 184).

Customs

The State Department of Agriculture (tel: 808/973-9560) maintains strict regulations on the import of live plants and animals to Hawaii by visitors. Dogs and cats may be required to undergo a 120-day quarantine period. For more information, contact the **Plant Quarantine Branch** (tel: 808/586-0844) or **Animal Quarantine Station** (tel: 808/483-7151).

Help with directions

Essential facts

Climate and when to go

The main Hawaiian Islands all lie within the tropics, which means temperature variations are slight from season to season. The charts below show some of the variations between islands. Average summer (May–September) temperatures range from 73°F to 88°F. In winter (October–April), expect an average of 65°F to 83°F and snow on the 13,000-foot peaks of the Big Island.

Even in the height of summer, the islands are generally fanned by cooling northeastern trade winds. Occasionally the wind direction shifts to the south, bringing muggy "Kona conditions" and the possibility of tropical storms.

Hawaii's wet season lasts from December to February, though rain showers on the sheltered leeward coasts tend to be fairly short-lived. Throughout the year, the islands' windward coasts (north and east) are wetter and greener than those on the south and west.

There is sunbathing weather in Hawaii year-round, especially on the sunnier, drier leeward sides of the islands, where most of the major resort areas are situated. Golf is played all year, too.

Conditions for diving and snorkeling are best in the summer when the ocean is calm and the water clear, while surfers are likely to find the biggest waves in winter. Winter is also the whale-watching season, when humpback whales from Alaska venture south to breed and calve in Hawaiian waters between November and March.

Public holidays

Hawaii observes all the major public holidays, plus it has a few special ones of its own:

- **New Year's Day** January 1
- **Martin Luther King Day** 3rd Monday in January
- **President's Day** 3rd Monday in February
- **Prince Kuhio Day (Hawaii)** March 26
- **Lei Day (Hawaii)** May 1
- **Memorial Day** Last Monday in May
- **Kamehameha Day (Hawaii)** June 11
- **Independence Day** July 4
- **Admission Day (Hawaii)** 3rd Friday in August
- **Labor Day** 1st Monday in September
- **Veterans' Day** November 11
- **Thanksgiving Day** 4th Thursday in November
- **Christmas Day** December 25

Time differences

Hawaii observes Hawaiian Standard Time, which is two hours behind Pacific Standard Time and five hours behind Eastern Standard Time. However, Hawaii does not observe daylight saving time, so you should add an extra hour to the time differences between April and October.

Money matters

All the major credit cards (American Express, Carte Blanche, Diners Club, Discover, MasterCard, and Visa) are widely accepted throughout the state. But if you plan to visit the more remote parts of the islands, it is a good idea to carry a certain amount of cash for purchases in small, upcountry towns as well as for out-of-the-way bed-and-breakfast establishments.

Local taxes

A 4 percent sales tax is added on to most sales, including foodstuffs sold

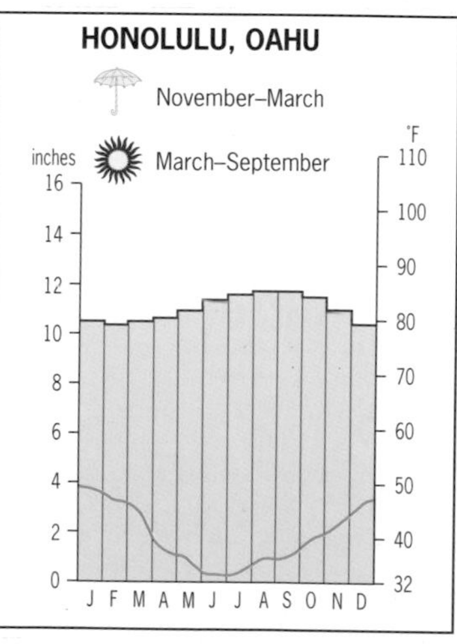

Regatta racing off Waikiki, Oahu

in supermarkets. Other taxes are also added to car-rental bills and accommodations charges.

Souvenirs to bring home

The most popular souvenir of Hawaii is probably the Aloha shirt, on sale everywhere.

High-quality genuine Hawaiian-made articles of the arts and crafts variety are available throughout the islands. Museum gift shops are often a good place to look for items such as *kukui*-nut jewelry, quilting kits, and *koa*-wood carvings. The Mission Houses Museum also has inexpensive prints which have been produced from period plates on the original mission press.

Food from afar always makes a good souvenir. Macadamia nuts are a Hawaiian specialty and come in many guises, both sweet and savory. Jams, jellies, and preserves made from exotic fruits such as guavas, pineapples, and mangoes are another suggestion, while coffee grown on the Big Island's Kona Coast is light to pack, and its aroma will bring back many memories.

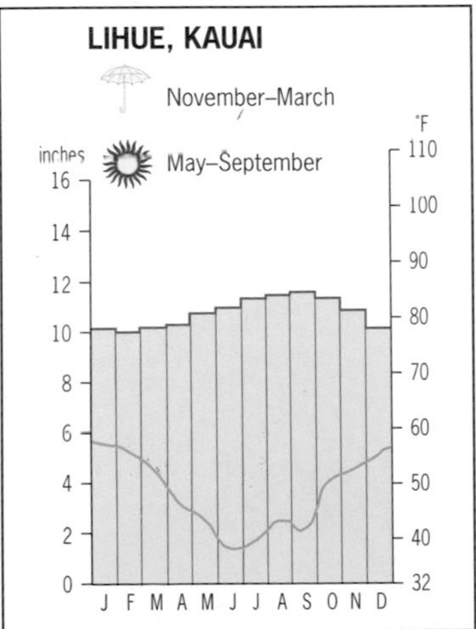

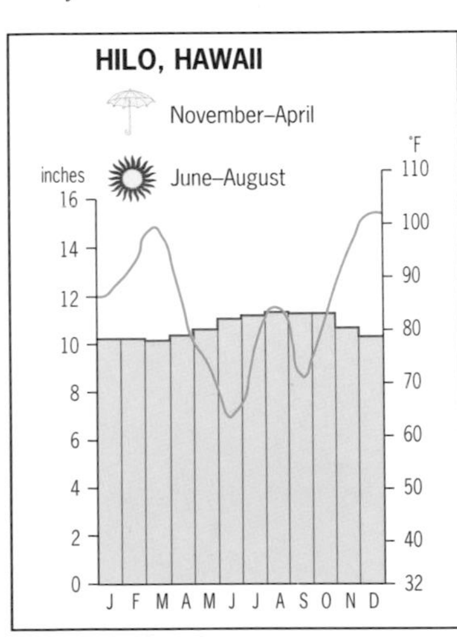

Getting around

By air

Island-hopping by air is a way of life in Hawaii. It is quick and easy, and most flights take only between 20 and 30 minutes.

Hawaiian Airlines (U.S. mainland, tel: 1-800/367-5320) and **Aloha Air** (U.S. mainland, tel: 1-800/367-5250) each offer more than 200 jet services daily to and from all the main islands.

Molokai Air Shuttle (tel: 808/567-6847) has daily flights from Oahu to Kaunakakai and Kalaupapa on Molokai.

Aloha Airlines subsidiary **Island Air** (tel: 808/484-2222) serves smaller commuter airports such as Kapalua on Maui and Kauai's Princeville, as well as Molokai and Lanai.

Oahu
- **Main airport:** Honolulu International.
- **Hawaiian Airlines** (tel: 808/838-1555).
- **Aloha Airlines** (tel: 808/484-1111).

Kauai
- **Main airport:** Lihue.
- **Commuter airport:** Princeville.
- **Hawaiian Airlines** (tel: 808/245-1813).
- **Aloha Airlines** (tel: 808/245-3691).

Molokai
- **Main airport:** Hoolehua (Kaunakakai).
- **Commuter airport:** Kalaupapa.
- **Hawaiian Airlines** (tel: 808/553-3644).
- **Island Air** (tel: 808/567-6155).

Maui
- **Main airport:** Kahului.
- **Commuter airports:** Hana (East Maui) and Kapalua (West Maui).
- **Hawaiian Airlines** (tel: 808/871-6132).
- **Aloha Airlines** (tel: 808/244-9071).

Lanai
- **Main airport:** Lanai City.
- **Hawaiian Airlines** (tel: 808/565-7281).
- **Island Air** (tel: 808/565-6744).

Hawaii
- **Main airports:** Hilo International and Keahole-Kona International (Kailua-Kona).
- **Commuter airport:** Waimea-Kohala.
- **Hawaiian Airlines** (tel: 808/326-5615).
- **Aloha Airlines** (tel: 808/935-5771).

By boat

The rough seas of the open ocean around the islands are not conducive to ferry traffic. However, a boat service plies the relatively sheltered waters between Lahaina on the West Maui coast and the island of Lanai.

Cruise ships are better suited to the conditions. **American Hawaii Cruises** (tel: 1-800/765-7000 or, on the mainland, 1-800/944-5988) offers regular seven-day loop cruises out of Honolulu that visit four ports in Maui, Hawaii, and Kauai.

Car rental

The best way to explore the islands is by car. Charges for rental cars in Hawaii match or are lower than those available on the mainland. Fly-drive deals, and some hotel packages that

Atlantis *submarine shuttle boat off Diamond Head*

combine accommodations with car rental, offer good value.

All the major rental agencies are represented on the larger islands; on Molokai the choice is limited to Budget and Dollar, and on Lanai only Dollar operates.

To rent a car in advance, contact:

- **Alamo** (tel: 1-800/327-9633).
- **Avis** (tel: 1-800/321-3712).
- **Budget** (tel: 1-800/527-0700).
- **Dollar** (tel: 1-800/800-4000).
- **Hertz** (tel: 1-800/654-3011).
- **National** (tel: 1-800/2327-7368).

Documentation Drivers must be over 25 and have held a full, valid license for a minimum of one year. Some form of collision damage insurance is required when renting a vehicle, and visitors should read the insurance stipulations very carefully. If you do not have a major credit card, a sizable cash deposit may be required.

Rules, regulations, and road conditions The maximum speed limit is 55 mph unless otherwise stated. Speed limits in urban areas vary between 20 and 40 mph, and they are also kept deliberately low in some country areas even when the road conditions are good. The local police set speed traps on long, straight stretches of road.

Throughout the state, the main highway system is well maintained and as efficient as the constraints of local geography will allow. However, the roads are largely two-lane, and local drivers like to take their time, so leave plenty of leeway when planning a trip.

There are certain stretches of road in the Hawaiian Islands that are off-limits to drivers of rental cars. Whatever the local map says, check and follow the details on the map supplied by the rental compay before setting out on an island drive. For instance, a section of the marked "road" shown on some maps west of Hana on Maui's south coast is actually a rocky and narrow dirt track out of bounds to drivers of rental cars, and any accidents or damages incurred in such an area are not covered by the rental companies' insurance policies.

Public transportation

Local bus services provided by Oahu's The Bus and the Big Island's Hele-On bus are cheap, efficient, and offer a comprehensive network of routes covering most of the two islands' important towns, attractions, and resort destinations.

The other islands are less well served. Kauai has a peak-hour service, the Iniki Bus, which runs up the east coast from Lihue, and west to Waimea. Maui has airport and local resort shuttles, but no integrated island-wide transportation system. Neither Molokai nor Lanai has any public transportation at all. (See individual island entries for further details.)

Tours

Tour companies abound in Hawaii, and transportation comes in all shapes and sizes, ranging from air-conditioned coaches or minibuses to glass-bottomed boats, helicopters, and even bicycles. Hotels and activity desks in main resort areas are a good place to check out the options available.

For the most extensive range of **full- or half-day bus tours**, try **Polynesian Adventure Tours** (tel: 808/833-3000). Based in Oahu, the company has local island branches in Kauai, Maui, and Hawaii and also organizes day trips to the Neighbor Islands.

Sightseeing, snorkel, and dive cruises are a specialty of Maui, Lanai, and the Big Island. On Kauai, boat trips offer stunning views of the Na Pali coast. And in winter, do not miss the opportunity to go whale-watching.

The best islands for **helicopter tours** are Kauai, Maui and Hawaii. There is eye-popping scenery along Kauai's Na Pali coast and Waimea Canyon; Maui boasts the world's largest dormant volcano, Haleakala; and the Big Island's volcanoes offer both fire and ice.

Local bicycle operators on Maui and Hawaii have perfected the almost effortless **bicycle tour.** They specialize in downhill excursions, delivering safety-kitted clients and mountain bikes to upcountry locations, then shepherding them back down.

Floral phone booths in Honolulu

Communications

Media

The state's top-selling daily papers are *The Honolulu Advertiser* and *The Honolulu Star Bulletin*. Mainland U.S. papers are available on newsstands; the best selection of current domestic and international magazines is available at bookstores such as Borders, Barnes & Noble, and the like.

Free tourist publications are everywhere and jam-packed with discount vouchers for attractions, activities, and restaurants. *This Week* has individual Oahu, Maui, Kauai, and Hawaii editions covering local events, attractions, entertainment, and dining, plus maps, tour suggestions, and short local-interest features.

Post

Post offices, found in all major towns, are generally open Monday–Friday 8:30–5, and Saturday 8–noon. Stamps can also be bought in hotels.

Telephones and faxes

Public pay phones are found on many streets and public areas, and also in restaurants, bars, and hotel lobbies. The area code for the state of Hawaii is 808. It is not needed if you are dialing a local number on the same island, but use it when making interisland calls or calls to Hawaii from outside the state.

Telephone calls made from hotel rooms are generally subject to a service charge, which can add considerably to the basic cost. Some hotels levy a small daily room charge that covers any local calls.

It is cheaper to make calls in the evening and on weekends. Interisland calls are considered long distance.

Most hotels offer fax service; charges are determined according to the length of the document. Incoming faxes are cheaper, if not free.

Language

English and Hawaiian are the two official state languages, though you are unlikely to hear much Hawaiian being spoken, except perhaps at a traditional church service or a local festival. It is a soft rolling language, both interesting and refreshing to the ear. Pidgin (see page 28) is much used by the *kamaaina* (locals), who may or may not welcome attempts by *malihini* (newcomers) to mimic them. Japanese is widely spoken, and it is not unusual to hear Vietnamese and Chinese being spoken downtown, or Tagalog in rural areas.

Mail boxes on parade

Emergencies

Crime

Hawaii is the land of *aloha*, but like anywhere else in the world it is not crime-free. The greatest problem for tourists is petty theft. Car break-ins are fairly common, so be on your guard. Cars parked at attractions and beaches are often targets, so remove all valuables before locking up.

It pays to take a few elementary and commonsense precautions:

- always carry money and valuables in an inside pocket or in a bag with a secure strap
- never carry your money and travel documents in the same wallet or bag
- never leave valuables visible in a parked car or unattended on a beach
- do not flaunt valuable jewelry
- pay particular attention to expensive cameras and video cameras

Violent crime directed at tourists is relatively rare, but Waikiki has had its problems. After dark, there is a fair amount of street prostitution here. Avoid unlit streets and alleyways, and do not walk alone.

Despite the determined efforts of the state authorities to stamp out local marijuana-growing, visitors, especially the young, may be approached by drug dealers hawking *pakalolo* (pot). Buying and smoking are illegal.

Emergency telephone numbers

- **Dial: 911** for police, ambulance, or fire service.

Lost property

Report lost or stolen traveler's checks and credit cards to the police as well as to a bank displaying the logo of the issuing company, or direct to the credit card company's emergency telephone number.

If items have been left on a plane or bus, report the loss to the airline company or bus operator as soon as possible. If the item has been found, it will be held at the appropriate lost and found property office for collection.

Any lost or stolen valuables covered by insurance should be reported to the police and a copy of the report obtained for insurance purposes.

State sheriff

Medical treatment

Hotel reception desks will be able to help with a list of local doctors, or look under "Physicians" in the telephone directory, where you will also be able to find dentists and hospitals listed.

In a real emergency, call 911.

Lifeguard towers are found at many popular beaches

Other information

Camping

The majority of Hawaii's camping facilities are operated by the federal, state, and county park services, and camping permits are required.

Visitors planning a camping vacation, or even a couple of nights under canvas in a state or national park, should contact the local offices listed below for full details on the camping facilities available and to obtain the necessary permits.

State parks do not charge a fee for camping permits, but there is a charge for tent camping at some county parks. In general, the length of a stay is limited; the maximum period allowed is between three and seven days.

In addition to campgrounds, both Maui's Haleakala National Park and the Hawaii Volcanoes National Park on the Big Island also offer cabin accommodations for visitors, as does Kokee State Park on Kauai, all three with spectacular scenery.

Oahu

- **Division of State Parks, Oahu District** P.O. Box 621, Punchbowl Street, Honolulu, HI 96809 (tel: 808/587-0300).
- **Honolulu City and County Department of Parks and Recreation** 650 S. King Street, Honolulu, HI 96813 (tel: 808/523-4525).

Kauai

- **Division of State Parks, Kauai District** 3060 Eiwa Street, Lihue, HI 96766 (tel: 808/241-3444).
- **Kauai County Department of Parks and Recreation** 4280A Rice Street, Lihue, HI 96766 (tel: 808/241-6660).

Molokai

- **State Parks** (see Maui below).
- **Maui County Department of Parks and Recreation** P.O. Box 1055, Kaunakakai, HI 96748 (tel: 808/553-3204).

Maui

- **Division of State Parks, Maui District** P.O. Box 1049, Wailuku, HI 96793 (tel: 808/243-5354).

Haleakala National Park P.O. Box 369, Makawao, HI 96768 (tel: 808/572-9306).

Hawaii

- **Division of State Parks, Hawaii District** P.O. Box 936, 75 Aupuni Street, Hilo, HI 96721-0936 (tel: 808/961-7200).

Warning signs

Beaches
Ask people why they vacation in Hawaii and most of them will tell you they go for the beaches. The 50th state has some of the most beautiful stretches of sand and surf in the world. Facilities, however, will vary greatly from place to place. Most areas have fresh running water, bath and changing rooms, and outside showers. Picnic tables are less common. Some areas offer equipment rental for windsurfing, snorkeling, sailing, and parasailing. Hawaii's beaches are clean compared to many coastal areas and visitors are asked to help keep them that way. All beaches are open to the public. Some beaches have undertow or riptides, you should enquire locally before swimming or swim only at guarded beache.s

On **Oahu**, Waikiki beach is nearly synonymous with Hawaii. Stretching from the Hilton Hawaiian Village to the foot of Diamond Head, it still ranks as the premier place to soak up the sun. Oahu's other beaches include the north shore's Sunset Beach, famous in the surfing world; Kailua Beach Park, home to international windsurfing competitions; and Makapuu Beach near Sea Life Park, with some of the best bodysurfing in the state.

On **Hawaii Island**, Hapuna Beach has sparkling white sand, while near the southern tip, there are green- and black-sand beaches. Newest beaches in the state are stretches of black sand formed by the lava from the active Kilauea volcano flowing into the sea.

On **Maui,** Kaanapali Beach is close to a number of luxury hotels anda fine place to stroll at sunset. Hookipa Beach Park, near Paia, is a windsurfing mecca.

Molokai has the sensational 3-mile long Papohaku Beach, the largest white-sand beach in the state. On **Lanai**, Hulopoe Beach offers excellent snorkeling.

Poipu Beach Park on the south shore of **Kauai** is popular with bodysurfers and sunbathers. On the other side of the island is Lumahai, a small beach rimmed with black lava and vegetation that proved the perfect setting for the movie *South Pacific.*

Keep off the reefs

- **Hawaii County Department of Parks and Recreation** 25 Aupuni Street, Hilo, HI 96720 (tel: 808/961-8311).
- **Hawaii Volcanoes National Park** Volcano, HI 96718 (tel: 808/967-7311).

Lanai
- **Lanai Company** P.O. Box 2, Lanai City, HI 96763 (tel: 808/565-7233).

Health
The Hawaiian sun is hot, hot, hot, so be sure to take it easy, spending only a short time on the beach in the first few days. Use a high-factor sun-protection lotion, and make especially sure that children are well protected.

Mosquitoes are a nuisance, and although less active in the cooler winter months, they can still prove a major irritant in rain forests. This is a warning not just for hikers, but also for anyone visiting rain forest gardens, waterfalls, and other warm, damp beauty spots. Keep a supply of mosquito repellent handy, and remember to use it before you set out.

In the water, beware of the coral; cuts can become infected. Also, you can easily damage coral by walking on it or kicking it with fins.

Occasionally, Portuguese man-of-war or box-jellyfish drift into the shallows. They can deliver a nasty sting. Remove tentacles and flush with lots of water. More serious stings and reactions should be treated by a doctor.

Pharmacies Drugstores are normally open 9–9.

Stock up on film to capture the moment

Hiking
Hawaii offers marvelous hiking in some of the most spectacular landscapes in the world. Trails (many of which are demanding and strenuous) are usually well maintained and marked, but it is important to be prepared for weather conditions and to give the park rangers an itinerary if you are trekking into back-country.

Maps and hiking information are available from the **Department of Land and Natural Resources, Division of Forestry and Wildlife,** 1151 Punchbowl Street, Honolulu, HI 96813 (tel: 808/587-0166; fax: 808/587-0160), or from the state parks information centers (see Camping, page 188).

Always carry sunscreen, drinking water, and mosquito repellent. Wet

Treat the Hawaiian sun with respect

weather gear is a must for overnight campers, and take warm clothing for the high altitudes of the Hawaii Volcanoes National Park, Mauna Kea, and Haleakala, where it may snow.

Opening times

- **Banks** Mon–Thur 10–3, Fri 10–5:30.
- **Pharmacies** Daily 9–9 (some 24 hours).
- **Offices** Mon–Fri 8 or 8:30–5:30 or 6.
- **Post offices** Mon–Fri 8:30–5, Sat 8–noon.
- **Shops** Supermarkets, Mon–Sat 8 or 9–9, Sun 9–7 (some 24 hours); shopping malls and tourist areas, Mon–Sat 10–9, Sun 10–6; country areas, Mon–Sat 8 or 8:30–6, Sun closed.

Places of worship

Hawaii's multicultural society means that most local communities are served by churches of several denominations including Protestant, Catholic, and Buddhist places of worship.

Visitors with disabilities

The **Hawaii State Commission on Persons with Disabilities** distributes a guide to accommodations and facilities for travelers who use wheelchairs. The guide also lists beaches and shopping malls offering reasonable access and restrooms for people with disabilities. The guide is available free (small charge if sent by mail) from the commission at 919 Ala Moana Boulevard, Suite 101, Honolulu, HI 96813 (tel: 808/586-8121).

Books on Hawaii

Hawaii by James A. Michener gives a historical perspective of the islands as the background to a novel. *Hawaii: An Uncommon History*, by Edward Joesting looks at the factual side of some of the same events in *Hawaii*. Captain James Cook's *A Voyage to the Pacific Ocean* could be considered the first guidebook to the islands. Robert Louis Stevenson's *Travels in Hawaii* brings history to life, while *A Residency of Twenty-one Years in the Sandwich Islands* by Hiram Bingham records missionary life in the early years. *Chanting the Universe*, by John Charlot, examines Hawaiian culture through its poetry and chants. The ancient Hawaiians' gods and goddesses are discussed in *Hawaiian Mythology* by Martha Warren Beckwith. *Hawaii's Birds* by the Hawaii Audubon Society is perfect for the bird watcher.

Pro Bowl pagentry at Oahu's Aloha stadium

Tourist offices

The head office of the Hawaii Visitors and Convention Bureau in Waikiki is open Mon–Fri 8–4:30. It also maintains offices on most of the main islands, as well as regional offices on the U.S. mainland and many countries overseas.

The bureau publishes an official state travel guide, *The Islands of Aloha*, as well as various brochures, a comprehensive calendar of events, an accommodations guide (which includes everything from the distance of a property from the beach to its amenities), and a restaurant listing containing one-line descriptions.

There are more than 3,000 members of the bureau, including hotels, car-rental companies, restaurants, cafés, and many tourist attractions.

Members can easily be identified by the distinctive Hawaii Visitor and Convention Bureau logo, a Hawaiian warrior wearing the traditional red and yellow feather cape and helmet.

• **Oahu** Hawaii Visitors and Convention Bureau Main Office, 2270 Kalakaua Avenue, 8th Floor, Honolulu, HI 96815, tel: 808/923-1811 or 1-800-GO-HAWAII; web: www.gohawaii.com; fax: 808/ 922-8991.

• **Kauai** Visitors Bureau, Lihue Plaza Building, Suite 207, 3016 Umi Street, Lihue, HI 96766, tel: 808/245-3971; fax: 808/246-9235.

• **Molokai** Molokai Visitors Association, P.O. Box 960, Kaunakakai, HI 96748, tel: 808/553-3876; fax: 808/553-5288.

• **Maui** Maui Visitors Bureau, P.O. Box 580, 1727 Wili Pa Loop, Wailuku, HI 96793, tel: 808/244-3530; fax 808/ 244-1337.

• **Hawaii**
Hilo: Big Island Visitors Bureau, 250 Keawe Street, Hilo, HI 96720, tel: 808/961-5797; fax: 808/ 961-2126.
Kona: Big Island Visitors Bureau, 75-5719 West Alii Drive, Kailua-Kona, HI 96740, tel: 808/329-7787; fax: 808/326-7563.

Hawaii Visitors and Convention Bureau on the Mainland

• **Washington D.C.**, 1100 Glebe Road, Suite 760, Arlington, VA 22201, tel: 703/525-7770; fax: 703/525-7771
For information about other Hawaii Visitors and Convention Bureau offices on the mainland, contact the Washington office or try the Internet: www.gohawaii.com

Ancient hula *traditions are kept alive at the Aloha Week Royal Court*

Accommodations & Restaurants

ACCOMMODATIONS

From beachfront condominiums,to golf-course resorts, and chic boutique hotels to upcountry bed and breakfasts, Hawaii has a range of accommodations. Room rates are seasonally adjusted, hitting a peak from mid-December to March (high season), and dropping 50 percent at other times. Check for discounted rates (particularly on weekends) and packages that include car rental, discounts on meals, entertainment, and sightseeing tours. Some hotels offer reduced room rates for senior citizens.

Many hotels have rooms in several price ranges. Accommodations listed are classified according to price categories based on a daily double occupancy rate for a standard room:

$ = under $85
$$ = $85–160
$$$ = over $160

Double rooms often sleep more than two people, so children can be accommodated at no extra cost. State excise tax amounting to about 4.17 percent, plus a room tax of 6 percent, is added to hotel bills. Bed and breakfast accommodations are increasingly popular in the islands. Several agencies provide booking facilities for bed and breakfast statewide:

- **Bed & Breakfast—Hawaii**
P.O. Box 449, Kapaa, HI 96746
tel: 808/822-7771 or 1-800/733-1632;
fax: 808/822-2723
- **Hawaii's Best Bed & Breakfasts**
P.O. Box 563, Kamuela, HI 96743
tel: 808/885-4550 or 1-800/262-9912;
fax: 808/885-0559

OAHU

Honolulu and Waikiki

Aston at the Waikiki Banyan ($$)
201 Ohua Avenue, Honolulu, HI 96815
tel: 808/922-0555 or 1-800/922-7866;
web: www.aston-hotels.com
This condominium with 870 rooms in a complex is just five minutes' walk from the beach, with pool, tennis, barbecue facilities, and a playground.

Aston Waikiki Beach Tower ($$$)
2470 Kalakaua Avenue, Honolulu, HI 96815
tel: 808/926-6400 or 1-800/922-7866;
web: www.aston-hotels.com
A luxurious condominium resort with 140 suites; full kitchens and *lanai;* pool, jet spa, and sauna.

Aston Waikiki Beachside ($$$)
2452 Kalakaua Avenue, Honolulu, HI 96815
tel: 808/931-2100 or 1-800/922-7866;
web: www.aston-hotels.com
An inviting and attractive boutique hotel with 79 rooms across the street from the beach.

Aston Waikiki Circle ($$)
2464 Kalakaua Avenue, Honolulu, HI 96815
tel: 808/923-1571 or 1-800/922-7866;
web: www.aston-hotels.com
At the heart of Waikiki, with 104 compact but comfortable rooms across from the beach. An inexpensive alternative.

Doubletree Alana Waikiki Hotel ($$$)
1956 Ala Moana Blvd, Honolulu, HI 96815
tel: 808/941-7275 or 1-800 367-6070
One of Waikiki's newest luxury properties, this 312-room business hotel is not on the beach but has all amenities including pool, fitness and business centers, meeting rooms and one of Hawaii's best restaurants, Padovani's Bistro and Wine Bar.

Halekulani ($$$)
2199 Kalia Road, Honolulu, HI 96815-1988 tel: 808/923-2311
One of the original Waikiki beach hotels founded at the turn of the century, rebuilt in the 1930s, and massively expanded to 456 deluxe rooms and suites in the 1980s. Elegant and much sought-after. Fabulous restaurants, pool, tennis, spa.

Hawaii Prince Hotel Waikiki ($$$)
100 Holomoana Street, Honolulu, HI 96815 tel: 808/956-1111
Ultramodern hotel at the city end of Waikiki, next to the Ala Wai marina; 521 rooms with ocean views. Pool, tennis, spa, shuttle to hotel golf course.

Hilton Hawaiian Village ($$$)
2005 Kalia Road, Honolulu, HI 96815
tel: 808/949-4321 or 1-800/445-8667;
web: www.hilton.com
An oceanfront resort within a resort, the 20-acre Village complex has 3,000 rooms in five high-rise towers, 10 restaurants, pools, shopping complex, children's programs, and nightly entertainment.

Hyatt Regency Waikiki ($$$)
2424 Kalakaua Avenue, Honolulu, HI 96815
tel: 808/923-1234 or 1-800/233-1234;
web: www.hyatt.com
Twin towers containing 1,230 well-appointed rooms and suites flank a 10-story atrium. Four restaurants, pool, shopping, spa.

Ilikai Hotel Nikko Waikiki ($$-$$$)
1777 Ala Moana Boulevard, Honolulu, HI 96815 tel: 808/949-3811 or 1-800/2-ILIKAI
Spacious rooms and condominium units overlooking the Ala Wai marina and Waikiki Beach. Restaurant, pool, terrace, tennis, spa.

Manoa Valley Inn ($$)
2001 Vancouver Drive, Honolulu, HI 96822
tel: 808/947-6019
Lovely old inn, with eight rooms, in the Manoa Valley near the university. Antique furnishings and ceiling fans. Continental breakfast; wine and snacks in the evening.

New Otani Kaimana Beach Hotel ($$$)
2863 Kalakaua Avenue, Honolulu, HI 96815
tel: 808/923-1555
On the beach, small (for Waikiki) but well priced, with 124 rooms between Sans Souci Beach and Kapiolani Park. Good restaurant and services.

Outrigger Reef on the Beach ($$$)
2169 Kalia Road, Honolulu, HI 96815
tel: 1-800/688-7444; web: www.outrigger.com
One of the Outrigger chain's "Royal" properties, with 885 rooms, restaurants, shops, pool and beach access. *Lanai* facing Diamond Head are worth the extra cost.

Royal Hawaiian ($$$)
2259 Kalakaua Avenue, Honolulu, HI 96815
tel: 808/923-7311;
web: www.royal-hawaiian.com
Waikiki's famous "Pink Palace" (see pages 76–77) is right on the beach, with 526 luxurious rooms in the elegant old-style main building or modern tower. Dining options, a pool, and nightly entertainment.

Sheraton Moana Surfrider ($$$)
2365 Kalakaua Avenue, Honolulu, HI 96815-2943 tel: 808/922-3111;
web: www.moana-surfrider.com
Gracious colonial-style beachfront hotel dating from the turn of the century. Do not miss tea or sunset cocktails in the Banyan Court.

W Hotel ($$$)
2885 Kalakaua Avenue, Honolulu, HI 96815
tel: 808/924-3111
Beachfront condominium of 90 units with Diamond Head views, and home to the excellent Diamond Head Grill restaurant.

Waikiki Joy Hotel ($$)
320 Lewers Street, Honolulu, HI 96815
tel: 808/923-2300
Waikiki's leading boutique hotel. Every room boasts a superb stereo and Jacuzzi tub; options include kitchenettes and bars. Restaurant, pool, and a karaoke studio.

Waikiki Parc Hotel ($$$)
2233 Helumoa Road, Honolulu, HI 96815
tel: 808/921-7272; web: www.parchotel.com
A more affordable offshoot of the Halekulani across the street, with 298 attractive rooms. Attentive service; good restaurant.

Waikiki Reef Tower and Ohana Hotel ($$)
227 Lewers Street, Honolulu, HI 96815
tel: 808/924-8844 or 1-800/688-7444
Budget accommodations in downtown Waikiki; 479 rooms/studios, some with kitchenettes. Restaurant, pool, showroom.

The South

Kahala Mandarin Oriental ($$$)
5000 Kahala Avenue, Honolulu, HI 96816
tel: 808/739-8888;
web: www.mandarin-oriental.com
Ultimate luxury on the south coast beyond Waikiki, popular with celebrities. Completely renovated in 1996; 371 plush rooms, attractive land-scaped grounds, restaurants, pool, beach, spa.

North Shore

Backpacker's Inn and Vacation Rentals ($)
59-788 Kamehameha Highway, Haleiwa, HI 96712 tel: 808/638-7838
Budget accommodations near the coast's surfing beaches with a choice of dormitories, private rooms, and cottages for groups.

Turtle Bay Hilton & Country Club ($$–$$$)
P.O. Box 187, 57–091 Kamehameha Highway, Kahuku HI 96731 tel: 808/293-8811;
web: www.turtlebaycondos.com
Dramatically sited on the northeast coast at Kuilima Point, the 800-acre resort has great sports facilities including world-class golf and tennis, 485 rooms with ocean views, and children's activities.

West: Waianae Coast

J. W. Marriott Ihilani Resort & Spa at Ko Olina ($$$)
92-1001 Olani Street, Kapolei, HI 96707
tel: 808/679-0079 or 1-800/626-4446;
web: www.ihilani.com
Forty minutes west of Honolulu, yet light-years away from the hustle and bustle, with 387 deluxe rooms and suites operated at the touch of an electronic bedside button. Equipped with restaurants, pools, Thalasso spa, golf, tennis.

KAUAI

East Coast

Aston Kauai Beach Villas ($$$)
4330 Kauai Beach Drive, Lihue, HI 96766
tel: 808/245-7711 or 1-800/922-7866;
web: www.aston-hotels.com
Oceanfront condominium resort next door to the excellent Wailua Golf Course; 150 units with full kitchens, washer/driers, and private *lanai*. Pool, tennis, barbecues.

Aston Kauai Beachboy Hotel ($–$$)
4-484 Kuhio Highway, Kapaa, HI 96766
tel: 808/822-3441 or 1-800/922-7866;
web: www.aston-hotels.com
Affordable beachfront property next to Coconut Market Place; 243 rooms, a pool, tennis, and an activities desk.

Garden Island Inn ($)
3445 Wilcox Road, Lihue, HI 96766
tel: 808/245-7227 or 1-800/648-0154;
web: www.gardenislandinn.com
A handy budget option near the airport and across the street from Kalapaki Beach; 21 rooms.

Kauai Coconut Beach Resort ($$)
56 Kuhio Highway, Kapaa, HI 96746
tel: 808/822-3455 or 1-800/222-5642
An attractive full-service resort with 300 rooms set in a coconut grove alongside Waipouli Beach. Pools, tennis, children's summer programs, Hawaiian activities, and a *luau* six nights a week.

Kauai Marriott on Kalapaki Beach ($$$)
3610 Rice Street, Kalapaki Beach, Lihue, HI 96766 tel: 808/245-5050 or 1-800/845-5279; web: http://marriotthotels.com
Kauai's largest and only true high-rise hotel resort has undergone a complete facelift. Elegant and refurbished, with 355 rooms, it sits on a pretty beach, with shops, pool, tennis, and golf nearby.

North Shore

Hanalei Bay Resort ($$–$$$)
5380 Honoiki Road, Princeville, HI 96722
tel: 808/826-6522
A choice of one- to three-bed condominium units in a chic resort set among the Princeville golf courses. Fine hillside location overlooking Hanalei Bay.

Hanalei Colony Resort ($$–$$$)
5-7130 Kuhio Highway, Haena, HI 96714
tel: 808/826-6253 or 1-800/628-3004;
web: www.hcr.com
Condominium with 52 light and airy two-bed units with huge picture windows and *lanai*. Quiet location on the shore between Hanalei and Kee Beach. Friendly staff; adjacent restaurant.

Pali Ke Kua ($$)
Bali Hai Treasures, 5300 Ka Haku Road, Princeville, HI 96714 tel: 808/ 826-9066
Well-equipped, affordable condominium, 62 new units in the Princeville resort. Ocean views, *lanai*.
Princeville Hotel ($$$)
5520 Kahaku Road, Princeville, HI 96722 tel: 808/826-9644; web: www.princeville.com
The palatial, marbled, gilded, and plumply upholstered lap of luxury; 252 rooms, beach, pool, spa, stores, fine dining, and golf.

The South

Garden Isle Cottages ($–$$)
2666 Puuholo Road, Koloa, HI 96756 tel: 808/742-6717; web: www.oceancottages.com
Eleven pretty studios and cottages, some with kitchenettes, close to Poipu Beach. Pool. Shopping, tennis, and golf nearby.
Hyatt Regency Kauai Resort & Spa ($$$)
1571 Poipu Road, Koloa, HI 96756 tel: 808/742-1234; web: www.hyatt.com
Relaxing Hawaiian surroundings and superb service. Some 598 well-appointed rooms placed in landscaped gardens. Excellent dining, fresh- and salt-water pools, spa and Jacuzzis, tennis, golf, Hawaiian cultural programs, and entertainment.
Kiahuna Plantation ($$–$$$)
2253 Poipu Road, Koloa, HI 96756 tel: 808/742-6411 or 1-800/688-7444
Attractive low-rise condominium complex partly on the beach; 333 one- and two-bed units with full kitchens. Restaurant, pool, tennis, children's programs; shopping, dining, and golf nearby.
Kokee Lodge ($)
3600 Kokee Road, P.O. Box 819, Waimea, HI 96796 tel: 808/335-6061
Twelve basic cabins in Kokee State Park, the largest of which sleeps seven. Hot showers, stoves, linen and towels provided. Bring warm clothes for the evening.
Poipu Kai Resort ($$)
1941 Poipu Road, Koloa, HI 96756 tel: 808/742-7400 or 1-800/367-8020
A 350-unit condominium complex reaching down to the ocean. Comfortable and well-equipped, with pools, spa, tennis courts.
Sheraton Kauai Resort ($$$)
2440 Hoonani Road, Koloa, HI 96756 tel: 808/742-1661; web: www.sheraton.com
A 20-acre resort fronting onto Poipu Beach; newly renovated with a spa and activity program.
Waimea Plantation Cottages ($$$)
9400 Kaumualii Highway, Waimea, HI 96796 tel: 808/338-1625; web: www.royalhawaii.com
Forty-seven enchanting one- to five-bedroom cottages set in a coconut grove by the beach. Kitchens, claw-foot baths, tin roofs and wooden *lanai*. Pool, restaurant.
Whaler's Cove ($$$)
2640 Puuholo Road, Koloa, HI 96756 tel: 808/742-7571
These luxury oceanfront condominium units have terrific sea views and plenty of space. Shopping, restaurants, golf, and tennis are all nearby. Good snorkeling.

MOLOKAI

Kaluakoi Hotel & Golf Club ($$–$$$)
P.O. Box 1977, Kepuhi Beach, HI 96770 tel: 808/ 552-2555 or 1-888/552-2550; web: www.kaluakoi.com
Surrounded by fairways on the ocean's edge, this hotel comprises 138 spacious rooms and suites (some of which have kitchenettes) with *lanai* in low-rise Polynesian-style buildings. Restaurant, shops, lovely beaches, pool, watersports, golf, and activities.
Molokai Ranch ($$$) *See page 119.*
Paniolo Hale ($$-$$$)
P.O. Box 190, Maunaloa, HI 96770 tel: 808/552-2731 or 1-800 367-2984, www.lava.net/paniolo
Arguably Molokai's best value and probably its most accommodating place to stay. There are a total of 77 spacious studio, one- and two-bedroom apartments which overlook the Kaluakoi Golf Course and Kepuhi Beach. Pool, paddle tennis and barbecue facilities.
Wavecrest Resort ($$–$$$)
P.O. Box 1037, Kaunakakai, HI 96748 tel: 808/558-8103 or 1-800/535-0085
A small number of units in a secluded condominium on the road out to the East End. Pool, tennis, shuffleboard; swimming nearby.

MAUI

West Maui

Best Western Pioneer Inn ($–$$)
658 Wharf Street, Lahaina, HI 96761 tel: 808/661-3636; web: www.maui.net/~pioneer
Historic inn that is part-attraction and part-bed and breakfast; 48 simple rooms with *lanai*. Bar and restaurant.
Hyatt Regency Maui ($$$)
200 Nohea Kai Drive, Lahaina, HI 96761 tel: 808/661-1234; web: www.hyatt.com
A superb property on the beach at Kaanapali, with 815 luxurious rooms, grounds landscaped to resemble a South Seas amusement park, and every facility.
Kaanapali Beach Hotel ($$–$$$)
2525 Kaanapali Parkway, Lahaina, HI 96761 tel: 808/661-0011
Old-fashioned, friendly beachfront hotel, with 430 rooms, restaurant, pool, golf. Emphasis on things Hawaiian.
Kapalua Bay Hotel & Villas ($$$)
1 Bay Drive, Lahaina, HI 96761 tel: 808/669-5656
Sensitively designed and beautifully executed resort 30 minutes north of Lahaina; 294 spacious and attractive rooms and suites; excellent facilities including three championship golf courses; lovely beach; excellent restaurant.
Maui Park ($$)
3626 Lower Honoapiilani Highway, Lahaina, HI 96761 tel: 808/669-6622
Across from the beach between Kaanapali and Kapalua, 288 condominium units with kitchens and barbecues. Stores and dining nearby.

Plantation Inn ($$)
174 Lahainaluna Road, Lahaina, HI 96761
tel: 808/667-9225;
web: www.plantationinn.com
Bed and breakfast just steps away from bustling Front Street, with 18 individually decorated rooms furnished with antiques; pool, superb restaurant.

Ritz Carlton Kapalua ($$$)
1 Ritz Carlton Drive, Kapalua, HI
tel: 808/669-6200; web: www.ritzcarlton.com
Ultradeluxe resort of 10 acres with impressive ocean views; 548 rooms and suites, huge pool, 10 tennis courts, beach, golf.

Sheraton Maui ($$$)
2605 Kaanapali Parkway, Lahaina, HI 96761
tel: 808/661-0031; web: www.sheraton.com
Recently reopened after an impressive renovation program, the highly regarded Sheraton occupies a prime position on Kaanapali Beach.

The Whaler at Kaanapali Beach ($$–$$$)
2481 Kaanapali Parkway, Lahaina, HI 96761
tel: 808/661-3484; web: www.the-whaler.com
Oceanfront condominium with 340 attractive units in separate buildings. Stores, pool, tennis, spa.

Westin Maui ($$$)
2365 Kaanapali Parkway, Lahaina, HI 96761
tel: 808/667-2525 or 1-800/228-3000;
web: www.westinmaui.com
Sleek beachfront hotel with swimming pool, water gardens, children's camp, ocean activities, even a "director of romance" for wedding arrangements; 761 elegant rooms and suites; fabulous dining.

East Maui

Aston Maui Lu Resort ($–$$)
575 S. Kihei Road, Kihei, HI 96753
tel: 808/879-5881; web: www.aston.com
Aging resort complex with 120 rooms on a beachfront site. Pool, tennis, activities desk, barbecues.

Destination Resorts Wailea ($$)
3750 Wailea Alanui Drive, Kihei, HI 96753
tel: 808/879-1595;
web: www.destinationresortshi.com
Central reservations service for over 900 condominium units and golf course villas ($$$).

Ekena ($$-$$$)
P.O. Box 728, Hana, HI 96713
tel: 808/248-7047; web: www.maui.net/~ekena
Spacious accommodations with complete privacy and a commanding view of East Maui, in a manicured 8.5 acre tropical setting, set this vacation rental apart from all the rest in Hana.

Four Seasons Resort Maui at Wailea ($$$)
3900 Wailea Alanui, Wailea, HI 96753
tel: 808/874-8000 or 1-800/342-3442
Maui's best, most luxurious resort. All guest rooms open onto *lanai*, most with ocean views. The extensive amenities include a children's activity program. Enjoy the views and the superb cuisine.

Grand Wailea Resort & Spa ($$$)
3850 Wailea Alanui Drive, Wailea, HI 96753 tel: 808/875-1234 or 1-800/888-6100;
web: www.grandwailea.com
Grand by name and grand by nature. Impressive reception areas; 761 lovely rooms and suites; golf, tennis, spa, program of children's activities.

Hotel Hana-Maui ($$$)
P.O. Box 9, Hana-Maui, HI 96713
tel: 808/248-8211 or 1-800/321-HANA
Once luxurious country resort with 97 rooms and suites in cottages dotted around beautiful gardens. Ceiling fans and pretty tropical décor; Tennis, horseback-riding, spa, beach shuttle to Hamoa.

The Huelo Point Flower Farm ($$)
Huelo, HI 96779 tel: 808/572-1850
Stay in the gazebo or the carriage house of this spectacular bed and breakfast perched atop a north-shore cliff. There is an adjoining orchard and a private trail down to the beach.

Kea Lani Hotel ($$$)
4100 Wailea Alanui Wailea, HI 96753
tel: 808/875-4100 or 1-800/659-4100;
web: www.kealani.com
Moorish-style hotel with 450 luxurious suites and villas containing full kitchens and patios. Full catering services in rooms if you want privacy.

Maui Prince Hotel ($$$)
5400 Makena Alanui, Kihei, HI 96753
tel: 808/874-1111
Set in marvelous landscaped grounds, 310 rooms and suites with *lanai* and views of the Neighbor Islands. Restaurants, swimming, tennis, golf.

Olinda Country Cottages & Inn ($$)
2660 Olinda Road, Makawao, HI 96786
tel: 808/572-1453 or 1-800/932-3435;
web: www.mauibnbcottages.com
This truly "up-country" bed and breakfast on an 8.5 acre protea farm above Makawao has five delightful, spacious suites and cottages, and is surrounded by 35,000 acres of open range offering a panoramic view down over central Maui.

Silver Cloud Ranch ($–$$)
RR2 Box 201, Old Thompson Road, Kula, HI 96790 tel: 808/878-6101
A peaceful bed and breakfast; nine comfortable rooms or studios plus a cottage with glorious views.

Wailea Beach Outrigger ($$$)
3700 Wailea Alanui Drive, Wailea, HI 96753 tel: 808/879-1922; web: www.outrigger.com
Recently renovated 516 spacious and airy rooms and suites lead down to the ocean. Restaurants, pool, children's activities, excellent Hawaiian culture program, and fine *luau*.

LANAI

Hotel Lanai ($–$$)
P.O. Box A-199, Lanai City, HI 96763
tel: 808/565-4700
Affordable, small, pretty rooms in an attractive, restored 1920s plantation guesthouse. Bleached pine furniture, patchwork quilts, and Hawaiian prints. Good restaurant.

The Lodge at Koele ($$$)
P.O. Box 310, 1 Keamo Ku Drive, Lanai City, HI 96763 tel: 808/565-7300 or 1-800/321-4666; web: www.lanai-resorts.com
Upcountry hotel with 102 charming rooms. Roaring fires, huge sofas; superb dining and service; golf, pool, hiking, sporting clays, spa, and beach shuttle.

Manele Bay Hotel ($$$)
P.O. Box 310, 1 Manele Bay Drive, Lanai City, HI 96763 tel: 808/565-7700 or 1-800/321-4666; web: www.lanai-resorts.com
Oceanfront hedonism with 250 rooms and suites laid out around tropical gardens. Excellent restaurant; golf course designed by Jack Nicklaus; hot-spring spa, pool, snorkeling in the bay.

HAWAII

Hilo

Arnott's Lodge and Hiking Adventures ($)
98 Apapane Road, Hilo, HI 96720
tel: 808/969-7097
Ideal for backpackers on a budget; 58 rooms and bunks in dormitories; kitchen, laundry, and barbecues. The hiking/4WD adventures around the island are great value.

Hawaii Naniloa Hotel ($–$$)
93 Banyan Drive, Hilo, HI 96720
tel: 808/969-3333
Great position on the bay, and 325 rooms. Restaurant, pool, spa, stores, and golf course.

Volcano

Chateau Kilauea: The Inn at Volcano ($$-$$$)
P.O. Box 998, Volcano, HI 96785
tel: 808/967-7786 or 1-800/937-7786;
web: www.volcano-hawaii.com
Nestled in the forest a mile from Hawaii Volcanoes National Park, the personal service and attention to detail found at this luxury six unit bed and breakfast is similar to that of a five-star resort. Most units have hot tubs; one unit sleeps six.

Kilauea Lodge ($$)
P.O. Box 116, Volcano, HI 96785 tel: 808/967-7366; web: www.kilauea-lodge.com
A welcoming upcountry inn popular with Volcano visitors; 12 rooms, some in a modern annex, others in the original building with lots of polished wood and fireplaces. Good food.

The Kona Coast

Aston Royal Sea Cliff Resort ($$–$$)
75-6040 Alii Drive, Kailua-Kona, HI 96740
tel: 808/329-8021; web: www.aston-hotels.com
A terraced oceanfront condominium resort with 154 large units. Full kitchens and *lanais*. No beach, but fresh- and salt-water pools; tennis courts.

Four Seasons Resort Hualalai at Historic Ka'upulehu ($$$)
100 Ka'upulehu Drive, Ka'upulehu-Kona, HI 96740 tel: 808/325-8000
The utmost in understated luxury; 243 rooms with private entrances, *lanai*, and ocean views, in charming bungalows. Jack Nicklaus-designed golf course, spa services, snorkeling, scuba-diving, and the excellent beachfront restaurant Pahu i'a.

Holualoa Inn ($$-$$$)
P.O. Box 222, Holualoa, HI 96725
tel: 808/324-1121 or 1-800/392-1812;
web: www.konaweb.comm/HINN
This delightful six unit bed and breakfast sits on 40 acres about 1,300 feet above Kailua-Kona. Spectacular views, library, jacuzzi, and pool—and a sumptuous breakfast (with locally grown coffee).

King Kamehameha's Kona Beach Hotel ($$)
75-5660 Palani Road, Kailua-Kona, HI 96740
tel: 808/329-2911
Large hotel bordering a small beach close to Kailua Pier, with 460 rooms, restaurants, pool, tennis, and a guest activities desk.

Kona Tiki Hotel ($)
75-5968 Alii Drive, Kailua-Kona, HI 96740
tel: 808/329-1425
A budget bargain with breakfast included. An oceanfront position just out of town; 15 rooms, some with kitchens; pool.

Manago Hotel ($)
P.O. Box 145, Captain Cook, HI 96704
tel: 808/323-2642
Low prices near Kealakekua Bay in Kona coffee country; 64 rooms in an old-style, family-owned hotel. Restaurant serves local food. No children.

Outriggers Kanaloa at Kona Resort ($$)
78-261 Manukai Street, Kailua-Kona, HI 96740
tel: 808/322-9625; web: www.outrigger.com
Resort with 166 one-, two-, and three-bed deluxe condominium units with ocean or golf-course views. Beach and snorkeling, pools, tennis, and an activities desk. One of the Island's best deals.

Kohala

Hapuna Beach Prince Hotel ($$$)
62-100 Kaunaoa Beach Drive, Kamuela, HI 96743 tel: 808/880-1111
A large, luxurious 1994 hotel overlooking Hapuna Beach; all 350 rooms have ocean views and every convenience. Restaurants, watersports, pool, tennis, golf; horseback-riding nearby.

Hilton Waikoloa Village ($$$)
425 Waikoloa Beach Resort, Waikoloa, HI 96743 tel: 808/885-1234;
web: www.hilton.com
A 62-acre oceanfront fantasy carved out of lava fields, with a lagoon, tropical gardens, waterways, golf courses, and a 1-mile Museum Walkway with Polynesian and Asian artworks; 1,241 rooms with every facility. Dolphin encounter program.

Kona Village Resort ($$$)
P.O. Box 1299, Kailua-Kona, HI 96745
tel: 808/325-5555 or 1-800/367-5290;
web: www.konavillage.com
Voted "Best Tropical Resort in the World" by Condé Nast "Traveler" readers, There are 125 luxurious Robinson Crusoe/Polynesian-style thatched *hale* (cottages) around an oceanfront grove and lagoon. Restaurants, watersports, tennis, children's programs, Friday night *luau*. No phone in room, or TV.

Mauna Kea Beach Hotel ($$$)
62–100 Mauna Kea Beach Drive, Kamuela, HI 96743-9706 tel: 808/882-7222;
web: www.maunakearesort.com
A grand dame of Hawaii's luxury resorts, decorated with antiques and artifacts; 310 deluxe rooms, restaurants, beach, pools, championship golf.

Mauna Lani Bay Hotel and Bungalows ($$$)
68-1400 Mauna Lani Drive, Kohala Coast, HI 96743 tel: 808/885-6622;
web: www.maunalani.com
Lovely beachfront resort with 372 rooms, bungalows, and villas. Golf courses fashioned out of lava fields, spa, tennis, watersports.

Orchid at Mauna Lani ($$$)
1 North Kaniku Drive, Kohala Coast, HI 96743
tel: 808/885-2000;
web: www.orchid-maunalani.com
Home to the renowned Francis H I'i Brown golf course, this full-service resort has Hawaiian-themed bungalows, spa services, and a children's program. Dining options include a torchlit beach luau, and moon-lit canoe rides.

Outrigger Waikoloa Resort ($$$)
69-275 Waikoloa Beach Drive, Waikola, HI 96738 tel: 808/885-6789;
web: www.outrigger.com
Recently renovated, and beautifully situated right on Anaehoomalu Beach; 547 comfortable rooms, restaurants, pool, spa, tennis, golf, island activities.

RESTAURANTS

Hawaii's dining options come in a wide range of culinary styles and price brackets. While the all-American hamburger is everywhere and the Japanese influence is strong, the choices do not end there. The latest gastronomic craze is Hawaiian regional cuisine, a sometimes inspired (at its best) combination of the freshest local ingredients with Asian and a hint of Mediterranean cooking styles, and it is well worth seeking out. (See also pages 74–75.)

Price categories are per person and do not include taxes, tips or drinks:

$	= under $15
$$	= $15–30
$$$	= over $30

OAHU

Honolulu and Waikiki

Alan Wong's Restaurant ($$$)
1857 S. King Street, 5th Floor, Honolulu
tel: 808/949-2526
One of the best new restaurants in Hawaii, featuring Hawaiian regional cuisine from star chef Alan Wong. Clean, modern space and innovative dishes such as macadamia and coconut-crusted lamb, and ginger *onaga*. (Dinner only.)

Bali by the Sea ($$$)
Hilton Hawaiian Village, 2005 Kalia Road, Honolulu tel: 808/941-2254
An elegant oceanside dining-room providing excellent continental cuisine with Hawaiian regional accents: try shrimp and scallops with ginger or seared *ahi* (tuna) with hot *wasabi* sauce.

California Pizza Kitchen ($)
1910 Ala Moana Boulevard, Honolulu
tel: 808/955-5161
Designer pizzas cooked over wood fires and served with enormous salads big enough for two.

Chef Mavro Restaurant ($$$)
1969 South King Street, Kaimuki
tel: 808/944-4714
Chef George Mavrothalassitis brought the style of his native Provence and mixed it with the fresh ingredients and cuisines found in Hawaii, delivering memorable meals, first at La Mer, then at the Four Seasons Resort Wailea, now at his own restaurant. His *prix fixe* dinners are a paean to the delightful marriage of two different culinary worlds.

Duke's Restaurant and Barefoot Bar ($$)
Outrigger Waikiki Hotel, 2335 Kalakaua Avenue, Honolulu, tel: 808/922-2268
Casual beachfront eatery full of surfing memorabilia. Steaks and fresh seafood in the dining room; burgers and pizzas at the outdoor bar.

The Garden Café (Honolulu Academy of Arts) ($)
900 South Beretania Street, Honolulu
tel: 808/532-8734
In a breezy *lanai*, the café serves some of the area's tastiest lunch fare. Well worth a visit, even if you're not visiting the museum.

Hau Tree Lanai ($$$)
New Otani Kaimana Beach Hotel, 2863 Kalakaua Avenue, Honolulu tel: 808/923-1555
Fresh seafood and Pacific Rim-influenced dishes served under a giant *hau* tree by the beach. Waikiki's best breakfast venue.

Hoku's Kahala Mandarin Oriental ($$$)
Mandarin Oriental Hotel, 5000 Kahala Avenue, Honolulu tel: 808/739-8779
This superb newcomer offers a pan-Asian menu with European touches. Try the chef's unique daily specials for optimum gustatory satisfaction. Save room for dessert, especially if you love chocolate.

Indigo Eurasian Cuisine ($$)
1121 Nuuanu Avenue, Downtown Honolulu
tel: 808/521-2900
This historic building opens onto the incongruous garden setting of a downtown Honolulu mini-park. Chef Glenn Chu masterfully blends European and Asian influences using fresh Hawaiian produce, meats, and fish with his unique culinary styling.

Keo's Thai Cuisine ($$)
Ward Center, 1200 Ala Moana Boulevard, Honolulu tel: 808/596-0020
Good curries, spicy fish, barbecued chicken, and other dishes using freshly grown herbs and vegetables from North Shore farms. Also a branch in Waikiki (2028 Kuhio Avenue; tel: 808/951-9355).

La Mer ($$$)
Halekulani Hotel, 2199 Kalia Road, Honolulu tel: 808/923-2311
A beautiful dining room with ocean views. Hawaiian regional cuisine, with a Provençal accent: *bouillabaisse* of local fish or *onaga* (red snapper) baked with a rosemary-salt crust. Try the killer desserts.

Ono Hawaiian Foods ($)
726 Kapahulu Avenue, Honolulu
tel: 808/737-2275
No-frills neighborhood restaurant in Waikiki serving plate lunches piled high with Hawaiian favorites.

Padovani's Bistro & Wine Bar ($$$)
1956 Ala Moana Boulevard, Waikiki
tel: 808/946-3456
The best restaurants of several top Hawaii hotels have won rave reviews under the fine hand of Philippe Padovani who now has his own place from which to share his creative Hawaiian/European fusion, enhanced by Hawaii's best wine selection.

Palomino ($$)
66 Queen Street in the Harbor Court Building, Downtown, Honolulu tel: 808/528-2400
Overlooking Honolulu Harbor in the heart of downtown is a trendy new hot spot with a vivacious bar scene, impressive architecture and service, and cuisine replete with *kiawe*-grilled and spit-roasted menu items, savory gourmet pizzas and scrumptious breads, as well as exquisite pastas and salads, and a deliciously decadent dessert menu.

Parc Café ($$)
Waikiki Parc Hotel, 2233 Helumoa Road, Honolulu tel: 808/921-7272
Renowned for its elaborate and generous theme buffets. A favorite is the excellent Hawaiian buffet. Call to check schedules in advance.

Roy's Restaurant ($$$)
Hawaii Kai Corporate Plaza, 6600 Kalanianaole Highway, Maunalua Bay tel: 808/396-7697
Roy Yamaguchi is a renowned master of Hawaiian regional and Pacific Rim cuisine. The menu changes nightly, and is always memorable.

Singha Thai Cuisine ($$)
1910 Ala Moana Boulevard, Honolulu tel: 808/941-2898
Thai dancers accompany dinner here. Specialties include spicy beef salad, curries, enormous hot chicken and cashew stir-fry.

Windward Coast

Ahi's Restaurant ($)
53-146 Kamehameha Avenue, Punaluu tel: 808/293-5650
A great place to eat on any trip around Oahu, this throw-back to an earlier era of Hawaiian hospitality and airy, tropical ambience serves fresh shrimp four ways, fresh fish simply, and charms you throughout your dining experience. Saturday is Hawaiian plate day—real Hawaiian food!

North Shore

Jameson's by the Sea ($$)
62-540 Kamehameha Highway, Haleiwa tel: 808/637-4336
Renowned for its harbor and sunset views. Fresh fish and seafood are specialties.

Kua Aina Sandwich ($)
66-214 Kamehameha Highway, Haleiwa tel: 808/637-6067
Sandwiches a mile high and burgers to match. Casual and fun with a couple of outside tables, great for people-watching.

KAUAI

East Coast

Café Portofino ($$)
Pacific Ocean Plaza, 3501 Rice Street (HI-51), Lihue tel: 808/245-2121
Modern Italian restaurant close to Kalapaki Beach. All the classics from pasta to prosciutto, plus local-style *ahi* (yellowfin tuna) carpaccio.

Caffé Coco ($)
4-369 Kuhio Highway, Wailua tel: 808/822-7990
This gourmet bistro fronts a forest of fruit trees that deliver tantalizing juices and the fillings for tropical desserts. Fresh and creative fare, everything from turkey-sausage omelettes for breakfast, spiced *ahi* sandwiches on focaccia for lunch, to Tuscan chicken on the torchlit back courtyard.

Hamura Saimin ($)
2956 Kress Street, Lihue tel: 808/245-3271
Serving traditional and authentic *saimin* noodle soup, this famous, out-of-the-way lunch counter is frequented mostly by Hawaiians. Open all day for eat-in or take-out meals.

Hanamaulu Restaurant and Teahouse ($–$$)
3-4291 Kuhio Highway, Hanamaulu-Kauai tel: 808/245-2511
Japanese and Chinese selections. Reserve one of the traditional teahouses that flank the serene Japanese garden.

Hanapepe Café and Espresso Bar ($)
3830 Hanapepe Road, Hanapepe tel: 808/335-5011
Healthiest eats on the island, gourmet vegetarian for breakfast, lunch, and dinner—and that doesn't mean boring food. Try the homemade sourdough bread French toast with espresso in the morning, a choice of seven kinds of garden burger at lunch and gourmet pastas and puff pastries at dinner.

Kapaa Fish & Chowder House ($$)
4-1639 Kuhio Highway, Kapaa tel: 808/822-7488
Casual, outdoor dining in a nautical setting. Fish is served every which way from coconut shrimp to seafood pasta, with a choice of sautéed or grilled local catches. (Dinner only.)

King and I Thai Cuisine ($)
Waipouli Plaza, 4-901 Kuhio Highway, Kapaa tel: 808/822-1642
A great restaurant inside a mall. Delicious salads with green papaya or beef and mint. Good vegetarian dishes, three styles of curry. (Dinner only.)

A Pacific Café Kauai ($$$)
Kauai Village, 831 Kuhio Highway, Kapaa tel: 808/822-0013
One of the state's most renowned restaurants; Jean-Marie Josselin's Hawaiian regional cuisine is a revelation. Signature dishes include sautéed crab cakes with a mango and ginger sauce, and stir-fried lobster with eggplant and cashews. Attractive Asian-Hawaiian décor; open kitchen. Reservations are a must. (Dinner only.)

North Coast

Hanalei Dolphin Restaurant ($$)
Hanalei Trader Building, 5-5016 Kuhio Highway, Hanalei tel: 808/826-6113
Busy restaurant right beside the Hanalei River. The menu includes local scallops, shrimp, crabs, and fresh fish, plus steak and chicken. (Dinner only.)

Hanalei Gourmet ($)
Hanalei Center, 5-5161 Kuhio Highway, Hanalei tel: 808/826-2524
Laid-back café and delicatessen/bar. Homemade pastries and bagels for breakfast; plus salads, sandwiches, seafood. Nightly entertainment.

Hanalei Wake-Up Café ($)
Kuhio Highway at Aku Road, Hanalei
tel: 808/826-5551
Open daily at the crack of dawn (5:30) for serious breakfasts—omelettes, French toast, pancakes, hash browns. Lunch and dinner are also served.

La Cascata ($$$)
Princeville Hotel, 5520 Ka Haku Road, Princeville tel: 808/826-2761
Excellent Italian food in an elegant room decorated with murals. Specialties include salmon with pesto, potato salad, and green beans; cannelloni of roasted duck; warm mango tart, and Kona coffee custard. (Dinner only.)

Roadrunner Bakery and Café ($)
2430 Oka Street, Kilauea tel: 808/828-8226
The café, decorated with an epic mural of Mexico's history, offers authentic Mexican fare with local accents. Try the *chili relleno* and the Hawaiian taco with pineapple salsa. The bakery offers treats such as taro baguettes and Kauai sweet bread.

Tahiti Nui ($)
55-134 Kuhio Highway, Hanalei
tel: 808/826-6277
Good food and a friendly atmosphere in a plantation-era building. Pacific Rim/local menu; outdoor seating on the veranda. Weekend entertainment.

The South

The Beach House ($$)
5022 Lawai Road, Poipu tel: 808/742-1424
Enjoy beautiful sunsets and occasional whale sightings at this beachfront restaurant. Managed by one of Hawaii's famous chefs, Jean-Marie Josselin, the menu features a traditional *kiawe* grill.

Gaylord's at Kilohana ($$–$$$)
Kilohana Plantation, 3-2087 Kaumualii Highway (HI-50), Lihue tel: 808/245-9593
Dining room and outdoor tables around a grassy courtyard of this 1930s plantation house turned craft gallery. Omelettes, salads, and burgers at lunch, steaks, pasta, and seafood in the evening.

Keoki's Paradise ($-$$)
Poipu Shopping Village tel: 808/742-75634
A dependable steak and seafood house, Keoki's does a great job, especially with fresh fish that you can have in tacos for lunch or exotically finished in lemon-grass and breadcrumbs in the evening. Then it is "oh, my" Hula Pie for dessert!

Roy's Poipu Bar & Grill ($$)
Poipu Shopping Center, 2360 Kiahuna Plantation Drive, Poipu tel: 808/742-5000
Master chef Roy Yamaguchi's Kauai outpost. Inspired Hawaiian regional cuisine: Thai stuffed chicken and oven pot roast with apple-ginger-pineapple sauce. Reservations advised.

MOLOKAI

Kanemitsu Bakery ($)
Ala Malama Street, Kaunakakai
tel: 808/553-5855
Downtown bakery famous for Molokai sweet bread, also loaves flavored with apple and cinnamon, guava, pineapple, and more. Salads, sandwiches, plate lunches to eat in or take out. (Closed Tue.)

Maunaloa Room ($$-$$$)
The Molokai Ranch Lodge, Maunaloa
tel: 808/552-2741 or 1-800/254-8871
Like an up-country ranch lodge from a far earlier era in Hawaii, a brand new 22-room luxury facility overlooking the west end of Molokai and, at night, the lights of Honolulu across the channel. In this unique setting Molokai's finest food, service, and ambiance are found, with real Hawaiian music.

The Village Grill ($-$$)
Maunaloa tel: 808/552-0122
The restored pineapple plantation building and nouveau *paniolo* (cowboy) architecture of the facility reveals one of the island's better restaurants, a Molokai-style American steakhouse. Where else could you find ox-tail stew, fresh *mahimahi* and "Stallion" T-bone steaks sharing the menu?

MAUI

West Maui

Anuenue, Ritz Carlton Kapalua ($$$)
Kapalua tel: 808/669-6200
The most elegant dining room of Maui's Ritz Carlton Kapalua delivers memorable fare that changes nightly. Created from the freshest produce, meat, and fish available in the islands that day, served with charm and warm hospitality, in a walnut paneled drawing room that opens into the tropical night. *Anuenue* is the Hawaiian word for rainbow and the cuisine here sparkles like the vibrant colors of an afternoon Kapalua *anuenue*.

David Paul's Lahaina Grill ($$$)
127 Lahainaluna Road, Lahaina
tel: 808/667-5117
Probably the best food in Lahaina. Pacific Rim and southwestern influences yield dishes like tequila shrimp seasoned with chilli, coriander, tequila, and brown sugar. Great desserts. (Dinner only.)

Gerard's ($$$)
174 Lahainaluna Road, Lahaina
tel: 808/661-8939; web: www.gerardsmaui.com
Chef Gerard Reversade has been delighting guests with his contemporary island French cuisine for over 20 years. Kona lobster and avocado salad, and medallions of peppered venison with jelly of Ohelo berries are sure to please. Excellent wine list.

Hula Grill ($–$$)
2435 Kaanapali Parkway, Lahaina
tel: 808/667-6636
Hawaiian-themed, beachfront restaurant with barefoot bar and full dining-room. Peter Merriman's menu features fresh seafood and local specialties.

Kimo's ($$–$$$)
845 Front Street, Lahaina tel: 808/661-4811
Catch a gorgeous sunset at this popular restaurant with basic food at moderate prices. Steak or lobster-tails are reliable choices and the breads are wonderful. For a snack, try the *pupu.*

Lahaina Coolers ($)
180 Dickenson Street, Lahaina
tel: 808/661-7082
Laid-back bistro with pizzas, pastas, salads, tortillas, *pupu*, fresh fish, and steaks.

Old Lahaina Luau ($$)
Mala Wharf, across from Lahaina Cannery
tel: 808/667-1998
With its new 1-acre waterfront site, Maui's best *luau* is now even better. Hawaiian artisans display quality crafts as the sun sets behind the island of Lanai, just across the channel, and the *hula pahu* (drums) and conch shell trumpets sound. Superb traditional and modern Hawaiian dishes are served in the comfortable open air setting, and the entertainment is the real thing.

Roy's Kahana Bar & Grill ($$–$$$)
Kahana Gateway Shopping Center,
4405 Honapiilani Highway, Kahana
tel: 808/669-6999
Roy Yamaguchi's Hawaiian regional and Euro-Asian cooking titillates the palate with imaginative specialties such as spinach with ricotta, ravioli of *shiitake* mushrooms, smoked and peppered duck with gingered sweet potatoes, and spicy rimfire shrimp.

Roy's Nicolina ($$–$$$)
4405 Honoapiilani, Kahana tel: 808/669-5000
Next door to Roy's Kahana, and quieter than Yamaguchi's other restaurants (no open kitchen). It serves the same wonderful Hawaiian cuisine with specials changing nightly. (Dinner only.)

Sansei Seafood Restaurant and Sushi Bar ($$)
Kapalua Shops tel: 808/669-6286
This newcomer to the Maui restaurant scene has caught the attention of every foodie on the island, and soon the trendy fusion of traditional eastern and western cuisines got rave reviews across the industry. Sushi, yes, but not like you've ever had it before—tastier, prettier, and more creative. Traditional tempura, pasta and wok-warmed, up-country veggies, and exotic crème brulee like no other.

East Maui

Casanova ($–$$)
1188 Makawao Avenue, Makawao
tel: 808/572-0220
Upcountry Italian restaurant with its own delicatessen. Pizzas from the *kiawe* wood grill, homemade pasta, salads, fish, chicken, and steaks. In the deli: *paniolo*-sized sandwiches, espressos, and pastries. Entertainment Wed–Sat nights.

Haliimaile General Store ($$)
900 Haliimaile Road, Haliimaile
tel: 808/572-2666
An art gallery-cum-restaurant that's casual and funky. Delicious Asian-influenced cuisine, most notably Hunan rack of lamb and wonderful desserts.

Joe's Bar & Grill ($$)
Wailea Tennis Club tel: 808/875-7767
As the name suggests, American-style cooking, but with a Hawaiian regional twist, often using rarely found local commodities like sweet-succulent slipper lobster and Molokai (mashed) potatoes. Bev Gannon (of the acclaimed Haliimaile General Store) is involved in hubby Joe's unpretentiously warm, Wailea outpost, and his daughter Cheech's extraordinary pastries and desserts are dreamy.

Mama's Fish House ($$-$$$)
799 Poho Place, Kuau tel: 808/579-8488
Mama's was born into excellence 25 years ago and has blossomed into one of Hawaii's finest purveyors of fresh fish. If location is everything, Mama's has it in spades. Windsurfers fly by during lunch, and at night the crashing surf in Kuau cove, the eerie sound of the wind crying in the ironwoods and the warm Polynesian ambience of the setting makes for a perfect dining experience. Then there are the daily choices of local fish and modes of preparation...the choices can be mind boggling.

Milagros Food Company ($)
Corner Hana Highway and Baldwin Avenue, Paia
tel: 808/579-8755
In the heart of Paia lies a little quasi-Mexican bistro that marries southwestern cuisine and fresh Hawaiian produce and fish, to deliver a delightful fusion of tastes and textures, bountifully served alongside Maui's best margaritas. Sit at the sidewalk tables for uniquely colorful Paia people watching, especially around Sunday brunch.

A Pacific Café ($$$)
Azeka Place II, 1279 S. Kihei Road, Kihei
tel: 808/879-0069; web: www.pacific.cafe.com
This Valley Island outpost is presided over by that maestro of Hawaiian regional cuisine Jean-Marie Josselin. Try grilled *opah* with banana salsa and Thai coconut curry sauce, or herby goat cheese-encrusted salmon. (Dinner only.)

Pic-nics ($)
30 Baldwin Avenue, Paia tel: 808/579-8021
Stop on your way to Hana for sandwiches to eat at the many picturesque spots nearby. The delicious spinach-nut burger is their specialty.

Prince Court ($$$)
Maui Prince Hotel, 5400 Makena Alanui Drive, Kihei tel: 808/875-5888
Elegant restaurant with Pacific views and innovative Hawaiian regional cuisine. Excellent fresh fish and seafood. Legendary Sunday brunches. (Dinner only except Sun.)

Seasons ($$$)
Four Seasons, Wailea tel: 808/874-8000
This restaurant is easily the best in any major hotel on Maui and one of the top five in any of the major hotels of the State. Superlatives only begin to describe the ambiance, view, service, and the extraordinary Euro/Pacific Rim cuisine that changes nightly but has included succulent delicacies like deep-fried goats' cheese stuffed zucchini flowers, and salt and herb crusted *onaga* (red snapper) fillets. Pricey, but never fails to deliver.

The Waterfront at Maalaea ($$)
Maalaea Harbor tel: 808/244-9028
Word of mouth has sustained this well-hidden seafood house on the ground floor of a characterless condominium in the east corner of Maalaea Harbor. The early French whorehouse ambiance opens onto an extraordinary view (especially at sunset), and the seafood, service and culinary dependability keep loyal patrons returning for more. Fresh fish is served nine ways—try the steamed whole *opakapaka* (pink snapper) for two, a wholesome Caesar salad and the scrumptious desserts.

LANAI

Henry Clay's Rotisserie ($$)
828 Lanai Avenue, Lanai City
tel: 808/565-4700
Creole cooking in cozy surroundings. Fresh fish, venison, pasta, salads, and cajun delights.

Ihilani Room ($$$)
Manele Bay Hotel, Hulopoe Bay
tel: 808/565-2290
Overstated elegance that opens out onto one of Hawaii's most exquisite views. Gracious, knowledgeable service rarely equaled in Hawaii and a chef who oversees the vegetable and herb garden, knows the fishermen personally, and builds on a tradition of excellence in the art of Euro-Pacific fusion and fine dining. Hawaii's best cheese cart, extraordinary desserts, and a wine-lover's dream.

The Lodge at Koele Dining Room ($$$)
P.O. Box L, Lanai City tel: 808/565-4580
Stylish and delicious Hawaiian regional cooking. Wild game sausage, venison carpaccio, pine nut-encrusted rack of lamb, and a knock-out vintage chocolate soufflé. Jackets required. Scaled-down menu in the less formal **Terrace Room**.

HAWAII

Hilo

Café Pesto ($$)
308 Kamehameha Avenue, Hilo
tel: 808/969-6640
Pastas, wood-fired oven pizzas, salads, and fresh seafood served with Pacific Rim flair.

Volcano

Kilauea Lodge ($$)
Old Volcano Road, Volcano tel: 808/967-7366
Welcoming lodge with good, fresh seafood, *ahi* (yellowfin tuna) with macadamia nuts and mango, and rich stuffed prime rib.

The Kona Coast

Aloha Café ($$)
Highway 11, Kainaliu tel: 808/322 3383
Hippy-dippy and wholesome, this well-proven café makes healthy food taste great, with hearty servings to boot. Daily specials include fresh fish, gargantuan burgers, veggie delights, thick smoothies and bakery goods that'll leave you salivating. Breakfast, lunch and dinner. Try to get a table at the *makai* (seaward) end of the veranda.

Huggo's ($$)
On the waterfront just off Alii Drive in Kailua-Kona tel: 808/329-1493
This long-time Kona institution has the kind of over-the-water (literally) location many restauranteurs would kill for—with the best sunset views on the Big Island. It built its reputation on quality steaks, prime rib, and seafood, but in keeping with the times, there is also a Pacific Rim influence on the menu. Don't miss the colossal mud pie for dessert. Bar scene is entertaining and first rate.

Keei Café ($$)
Highway 11, Honaunau tel: 808/328-8451
This is one of those off the beaten path, unlikely looking, culinary wonderlands that is worthy of a long sunset drive. Only nine tables, those ubiquitous plastic chairs and eclectic table settings, but everything is made from scratch, most of it using produce from just down the road, and fish caught that day from just offshore. Menu items span the globe from the Mediterranean to the Pacific Rim. Hospitable, affordable and so *ono* (delicious).

Quinn's Almost By the Sea ($-$$)
75-5655 A Palani Road, Kailua-Kona
tel: 808/329-3822
What looks at first glimpse like a dreary bar, opens out onto an airy garden courtyard, and delivers some of the most dependable beef and seafood anywhere in the vicinity of the once sleepy fishing village of Kailua. Affordable, comfortable, accessible, heartily-portioned and surprisingly tasty.

Sam Choy's ($$)
73-5576 Kauhola Pl. Bay 1, Kailua-Kona
tel: 808/326-1545
The crucible of "Kona cooking," this fun restaurant serves local cuisine at its finest. Try Japanese *saimin* noodle soup, three-fish *laulau* parcels wrapped in *ti* leaves, or honey duck with orange sauce.

Kohala

Coast Grille ($$–$$$)
Hapuna Beach Prince Hotel, 62-100 Kaunaoa Drive, Kamuela tel: 808/880-1111
The circular dining room with sea views is the ideal setting for sunset cocktails. Seafood specialties and an oyster bar, fresh pastas, and innovative appetizers. (Dinner only.)

Francis Brown Beach House ($$$)
The Orchid, Mauna Lani, 1 North Kaniku Drive, Kohala tel: 808/885-2000
Hawaiian regional cuisine with tables under the stars. Try the lamb carpaccio, Lanai venison with *ohelo*-berry sauce, and marvelous seafood and fish. (Dinner only.)

Kona Village *Luau* ($$–$$$)
Kona Village Resort, Kaupulehu
tel: 808/325-5555
One of the best and most authentic *luau*, every Friday night. Pork and *laulau* from the *imu* (see page 16), *poi*, salads, fresh mangoes and much, much more. Live entertainment.

Maha's Café ($)
Highway 19, Spencer House, Waimea
tel: 808/885-0693
The hearty, tasty breakfasts and lunches from the tiny kitchen in Waimea's first wood-framed house, are amazing. Meals will set you up for an island drive, using the bounty of the big island's farms and fishermen, at prices that won't break the bank.

Merriman's ($$$)
Opelo Plaza, HI-19 at Opelo Road, Waimea-Kamuela tel: 808/885-6822
Creative Hawaiian regional cooking by Peter Merriman, seen at work in the open kitchen. Roasted bell peppers with Puna goat's cheese, seafood paella, Big Island beef, and game in season.

Pahu i'a ($$$)
Four Seasons Hualalai, Kaupulehu, North Kona
tel: 808/325-8000
This oceanfront masterpiece is one of the best resort restaurants in the State. *Pahu i'a* roughly translates as aquarium. This is an elegantly marine eatery, with anchialine pond, massive saltwater aquarium, open-to-the-ocean-breezes, and right-on-the-beach ambiance. An ever-changing menu with Euro-American-Asian touches to Hawaii's freshest produce. Impeccable service goes without saying, but a chef who visits your table is an uncommon touch. And then there are those desserts!

Index

Bold figures denote the main entry of a subject

B

C

D

E

F

G

M

N

O

Author's Acknowledgments

The author, Emma Stanford, would like to thank the following for their help in the production of this book: Hawaiian Airlines; the U.K. office of the Hawaiian Tourist Board; Nicole Vosshall Dugan at Sheila Donnelly & Associates; Connie Wright at Avatar; Jan Loose and Lyn Utsugi.

Publisher's Acknowledgments

The Automobile Association would like to thank the following photographers, libraries and associations for their assistance in the preparation of this book.

BISHOP MUSEUM 84b (Tai Sing Loo) used with the permission of the Outrigger Duke Kahanomoku Foundation;
BRUCE COLEMAN COLLECTION 115
CORBIS/DOUGLAS PEEBLES 120
RONALD GRANT ARCHIVE 65a;
JACK HOLLINGSWORTH F/Cover silhouette;
HAWAII STATE ARCHIVES 34b, 38b, 43, 44b, 44c, 46b, 48c;
G HOFHEIMER 74b;
THE HULTON GETTY PICTURE COLLECTION LTD 49;
THE MANSELL COLLECTION LTD 36a, 36b, 37a, 37b;
NATURE PHOTOGRAPHERS LTD 22b (J Hancock);
NEW BEDFORD WHALING MUSEUM 40b, 41;
SPECTRUM COLOUR LIBRARY 17a, 30a, 59, 63b, 67a, 70, 71b, 144b, 145a, 176b, 179a, 181a, 187b;
E STANFORD 16b, 33, 69, 113b, 119b, 163b;
WAIMAEA VALLEY 29b;

The remaining pictures were taken by **KIRK LEE AEDER** with the exception of those listed below and are held in the Association's own library **(AA PHOTO LIBRARY)**
2, 3, 6/7, 6, 10b, 11a, 11b, 13, 14b, 18a, 19a, 21b, 23a, 25b, 28a, 28b, 35b, 39, 46a, 51, 54, 55, 56a, 57b, 60, 61, 62, 63a, 64, 66, 67b, 68b, 71a, 76a, 78, 79a, 79b, 83, 86, 87, 94a, 94b, 95, 96, 97c, 101, 103b, 105, 108, 109, 111, 114, 121, 129a, 136, 137b, 138, 139, 149, 159a, 165b, 168, 170b, 179b, 180, 186a, 186b, 187a, 189, 193b **(R HOLMES).**

Contributors

Revision copy editor: Adele Linderholm Original copy editor: Susan Whimster
Revision verifier: Rick Gaffney